Rural Life in Victorian England

'The Country Squire'. Published in 1841.

Rural Life in Victorian England

by G. E. Mingay
Professor of Agrarian History
at the University of Kent at Canterbury

HEINEMANN · LONDON

William Heinemann Limited
15 Queen Street, Mayfair, London WIX 8BE
LONDON MELBOURNE TORONTO
JOHANNESBURG AUCKLAND
First published 1977
© 1976 Lund Humphries Publishers Ltd

434 46750 2

Designed and produced by
Lund Humphries Publishers Ltd
26 Litchfield Street London WC2

Made and printed in Great Britain

Contents

A reaper in the 1890s.

Foreword

An eminent scholar, Herbert Finberg, has argued that in the writing of agrarian history 'the English countryman should never be far from the centre of the stage.' History, he held, should not be engrossed with processes, trends or problems but with human beings, in this instance English countrymen of all ranks. This book tries to follow his precept, as a glance at the list of contents will show. The chapters deal in turn with the various social groups, landowners, farmers, labourers, industrial workers and professional people, who constituted the main strands of the complex pattern of rural society. Who they were, what they did, and how they lived, are the subjects which mainly engage our attention.

But it has to be recognized that we are not dealing here with a static society. There is a tendency for us to think of country life as essentially stable, conservative and unchanging. In fact, this is far from the truth, and especially so in the hundred years after 1815 with which we are concerned. This was a hundred years which saw fundamental and dramatic changes in the nature of the country, and many of these changes had an indelible impact on life in the countryside. There occurred at this time the rapid growth of a new industrial system based on steam power, machinery, railways and steam shipping. As one result of these developments the typical Englishman ceased to be a countryman and became a town-dweller. A large part of the food he ate now came in from overseas, and the clothes he wore, and the articles he used in his home and work, were mass-produced in factories and workshops. It was an age of movement: the attractions of town life drew many of the poorly-paid and under-employed from the countryside, and numerous villages saw their growth level off and their numbers stagnate or decline as the nineteenth century advanced.

Some important changes originated in the countryside itself, particularly those connected with the enclosure and disappearance of common fields, commons and waste lands, and the gradual mechanization of some farm operations. But agriculture was also much influenced by external forces, as it was forced to adapt itself to changes in the demand for food and the growth of

7

competition from abroad. Changes in technology, in markets, and in overseas supplies also led to the decline of rural crafts, though some survived as factory trades in the countryside. Government legislation, too, affected agricultural employment and country workers' education.

In the welter of change many country people found their lives altered, some for better, some for worse. Periods of prosperity gave way to years of depression, with farmers bankrupted, landlords plagued by falling rentals, and farmworkers unemployed. In the long term landlords lost some degree of their old pre-eminence, farmers achieved more independence, and the labourers, very slowly, emerged with a higher standard of life. The country professions of the clergy, lawyers, doctors, land agents and others also had to try and meet new circumstances and different standards. And when the times were most adverse for the labouring population unrest was rife, rioters pillaged food stores and broke machinery, and the work of incendiarists illuminated the night sky.

Country people of this era have to be seen, therefore, in the context of far-reaching economic, social and technological change. In the opening chapter we attempt to sketch in this background to their lives and their work, and in the last chapter we try to assess the effects of the changes which the century wrought in the countryside. But all this is only the essential backcloth to the action. The reader will find that we are concerned primarily with the actors themselves, and the countryman, indeed, is never far from the centre of the stage.

The Bridgewater Canal from Dr White's Bridge, looking towards Manchester. Painting by S.C.Parlby, 1857.

1 Introduction

In the nineteenth century the English countryside saw more rapid and remarkable changes than had been wrought in perhaps all the preceding centuries. The national population was growing rapidly, and at the outset of the new century it was not only the brash industrial towns which were expanding, adding every year to the ranks of factory chimneys and dreary rows of red-brick streets, but also, though less markedly, many of the villages and country towns. True, those rural communities which were still purely agricultural, still based solely on a farming economy, grew only slowly, and in some instances not at all. But a number were being rapidly transformed by the influence of industry, becoming offshoots or isolated eruptions of the revolution in cotton, coal and iron which increasingly fevered the country's anatomy. Quiet little country places, which once were disturbed only by the blacksmith's hammerings or the rumble of waggons, now resounded with the clamour of dozens of little nailers' forges or the thud and click of cottage handlooms and stocking frames. Sometimes a cotton master or woollen manufacturer had decided to build a factory by the village's swift-flowing stream. Then, almost overnight, the village's character was changed, and those who knew nothing but farming found themselves outnumbered by factory hands, whose own rural origins rapidly disappeared without trace, if they had ever existed. Coal mines, quarries, brick works sprang up, their communities seemingly independent, isolated, and even hostile to the nature of traditional country life.

These newly-expanding industrial communities in the countryside were fairly widely scattered, and examples might be found in almost every county in the kingdom. But they were more common in the midlands and the north, and in the valleys of Glamorgan and parts of the West Country. The majority of country communities remained essentially agricultural and more unchanging in their character. Even here, however, some remarkable mutations were in train. The early decades of the century were the heyday of the canal age, and long sinuous fingers of narrow waterway snaked across the countryside, linking Trent with Mersey, Mersey with Severn, and Severn with Thames. The cottages of the lock-keepers, and the new inns frequented by the canal people – the *Boatman's Rest*, the *Navigation* – dotted the long lines of canal. The inhabitants of the narrow boats, the boatmen themselves, also formed a separate independent kind of community, comparable somewhat to those of the miners and quarrymen. They still had connections with the countryside, however, for many had families in cottages along the canal banks, and they bought their provisions in the country towns and hay for their horses. Numbers of canal boatmen had once been carters and small farmers, and perhaps still combined the driving of a horse and cart with the manning of a horse-drawn narrow boat. The canals created some new permanent communities too, at places where the different lines of canal joined, cargoes were transferred and manufacture was stimulated, places like Stourport and Runcorn in Cheshire, and Tamworth on the complex of canals emanating from Birmingham. The canals had relatively little impact on village life. The farmers made use of them, of course, for sending produce to market, as did manufacturers of bricks and pottery, and indeed some farmers had helped to promote them, but in general the barges which moved slowly through the countryside were not part of it. Their primary cargo was coal, and their destinations the rising centres of industry. Mostly the canal banks were a favourite spot for the village lads and their girls, and on a fine Sunday in summer many a young country boy got his first experience of fishing and bathing in the murky water.

The railways, beginning in earnest in the 1830s, had a more permanent and far-reaching influence. Railways could reach where the canals could never penetrate; and the life-giving injection of cheap and rapid transport revived old, decayed fishing harbours like Grimsby, turned seaside villages into shipbuilding centres and resorts, like Barrow-in-Furness and Southend, converted tiny inland route centres into railway towns, the home of engine works, like Crewe, Swindon, Wolverton, Norwich, Worcester and Ashford. The scenery itself was changed. To secure the easy gradients demanded by railway engineers great embankments and high viaducts were thrown across wide valleys, soaring bridges made light of deep river barriers, and tunnels, their portals massively decorated with turrets and battlements, penetrated steep hillsides. Little hamlets of railwaymen grew up around the stations, which were generally a mile or two from the centre of the villages they served. These new communities were related to existing villages, because railways served as major outlets for farm commodities and as a means of obtaining supplies of fertilizer and farm equipment.

Slow passenger trains, stopping at country halts, provided a new, and eventually cheap, way of getting to market towns, and there was the occasional excursion trip to the seaside or beauty spot. The poorest class of villagers, however, the farm labourers, began to enjoy the advantages of railway travel only towards the end of the century, when wages had risen and the fares had come down. But long before this the railways had offered village lads a new and more attractive means of employment, and country men made up a fair proportion of the quarter of a million employed by the railways in the 1870s, and the 600,000 employed before 1914.

Though railways offered a new field of employment, they also destroyed an old one. The advent of cheap, fast railway travel spelled the early demise of the coaches. The era of the flying coaches parallelled the great days of the canals. Both suffered at the hands of the railways, but while the canals fell into a protracted decline the end of the coaching business was more dramatic. Within a few years it was no longer possible for the roadside cottager to set his clock by the passing of the mail, or for country children to wait excitedly for the great event of the stage's appearance, emerging suddenly over the brow of the hill with whip cracking and steam rising from the horses. Allan Jobson, in his book on *Victorian Suffolk*, tells us of an old resident of the eastern part of the county who could remember how the coaches brought the breath of life to the little town of Woodbridge:

> A more restful, sleepy, uneventful town of its size than the Woodbridge of to-day it would be difficult to find in all England. In the earlier decades of the Nineteenth century, from dawn to dusk the town was alive with stage-coaches driven by skilful whips, the private carriages of the great quality, and the post chaises of the rich traveller that passed through narrow Cumberland Street and the still narrower Thoroughfare of the quaint old town. Drawn by foaming four-in-hand teams, the stage coaches were attended by the rude but stirring music of the guard's horn. Drawn by the best posters of the road and guided by smartly equipt postillions, the chariots of the great were sometime preceded by outriders, wearing brave liveries.

With the passing of the coaches an element of colour went out of country life, and a living proof of connection with great cities and distant events was broken. The old coaching inns fell into quiet decay, their kitchens and dining rooms once bright with fires and dishes now disused, the stables tumbled down into ruins, and weeds grown unchecked in the yards. The army of drivers, guards, ostlers, postboys, cooks, waiters and serving-maids dispersed, though where they all went was a mystery. Fortunately for those engaged in breeding the thousands of horses used every year in the coaching business, the railways helped provide an alternative market. Railway passengers and goods had to be brought to the stations and delivered home again, and within the towns movement depended almost entirely on the horse, until the coming of electric tramways, and later the arrival of motor buses and lorries. Perhaps it was as carters, waggon drivers, cabbies and private grooms that many of the old coaching hands found a living, while new city hotels and inns helped absorb the displaced domestic staff of the coaching inns.

About the time that the coaches were disappearing from the roads another change had nearly been completed. This was the enclosure of open fields, commons, and waste lands, a development which, after centuries of sporadic activity, had culminated in a final upsurge about the end of the eighteenth century. The surviving open fields, largely concentrated in the midlands, formed an obstacle to more efficient and more profitable farming. The big rise in agricultural prices which marked the fifty years between the early 1760s and the early 1810s made it attractive to landowners to invest substantial sums in converting scattered open-field holdings into compact farms, and in bringing overstocked commons and unproductive waste land into the cultivated acreage. Between 1793 and 1815, the era of exceptionally high wartime prices, there were some 2000 private Acts of Parliament authorizing the enclosure of a rather greater number of parishes, and in the hundred years after 1750 about six million acres, perhaps a quarter of the farm acreage, was affected. After 1815 the number of enclosures dropped away, mainly because there were by then relatively few parishes left to enclose, and most of the subsequent enclosures affected remote and little-used hill pastures and rough grazing.

The social effects of enclosure on the village community have long been controversial. In general, the landowners and the larger farmers certainly gained from it, and many smaller farmers probably did so also. For a relatively small investment, ranging from under 20s to a few pounds per acre, they obtained a more compact, more easily-worked holding, one no longer subject to the restrictive rules of communal husbandry but entirely under individual control. In many cases enclosure also resulted in the land becoming tithe-free, with improved means of drainage, and new and more convenient roads within the parish – all advantages of importance. And enclosure could be very profitable, leading often to a doubling, even a trebling, of the value of the land. It was the great form of land development of its day.

Some very small farmers and the cottagers, however, may often have been worse off. The smallholder's land was somewhat diminished in acreage where it was necessary for all the owners to give up part of their acreage to compensate the titheholder for abolition of his tithes, and also to find land for the building of new roads. The new, reduced holding, while now compact and tithe-free, might be too small to be viable, except for some form of specialized farming, such as dairying or market-gardening. In a costly enclosure the financial burden of administrative, legal and fencing costs, and the further expense of changing to some different kind of farming, might prove to be beyond the small man's resources. These costs, however, were spread over a lengthy period of years, and farmers had long been in the habit of borrowing informally from friends and neighbours. When the common was enclosed the cottager might lose, without com-pensation, the ancient right to graze a cow upon the common and gather fuel there. This arose either because in some instances the so-called 'right' was in fact permissive and extra-legal, or because the cottager enjoyed the common-right only as the tenant of his cottage and not as its owner. All *owners* of common rights were compensated by an allocation of land, but again the size of the plot allocated to them might be too small for the keeping of a cow, and in other ways it might prove no adequate substitute for the common.

It is difficult to generalize, for conditions varied so greatly from parish to parish. Over much of the midlands the commons had long been inadequate even before enclosure, and their use had been carefully 'stinted' or regulated. Elsewhere, as in parts of Norfolk, for instance, large areas of common still remained after enclosure. In any case, only those cottagers who had land sufficient to keep a cow in winter were strictly entitled to graze the commons in summer, and it is doubtful how many cottagers could afford to buy a cow in the first place or replace it when it died. In some instances the enclosure commissioners allocated land for cow pastures to be let to the poor. In some, again, rights of gathering fuel were at least partially compensated when the commissioners set aside an area of land to be let, its rent specifically reserved for the purpose of buying fuel for the poor. In many areas the very small farms had long been in decline, and in some parishes had totally disappeared before the enclosure came about. Where small farms survived, the growth of towns and improved means of transport widened the scope for those types of farming in which the small man could do best. In large areas of ill-drained clayland the changes in the farming which followed enclosure were necessarily small because of the natural limitations imposed by such factors as the inflexible nature of the soil, the backwardness of drainage techniques, and the restricted capital of the farmers. Sometimes the cost of enclosure was kept down by leaving the private fencing of the new holdings undone, and in areas of marginal land, like the North York Moors, the conversion of rough pasture to cultivated land was deliberately kept at a slow and gradual pace. Finally, it was frequently the case that only a portion of the parish was affected by parliamentary enclosure, the open fields and commons having been subject to a long drawn-out process of piecemeal conversion to closes over the preceding centuries.

It is not surprising, then, that while the growth of under-employment and poverty in the English countryside paralleled the years of active parliamentary enclosure, the two were generally not connected. Much of the worst rural poverty was found in the southernmost districts of the country, in a belt stretching from east Kent westwards to Hampshire, Dorset, southern Wiltshire and parts of Devon. This was a region of little activity in the age of parliamentary enclosure; on the other hand, it was also an area where little industrial development was taking place to provide surplus labourers with alternative employment, and where the labourers themselves were firmly anchored in their parishes by the operation of the settlement law, and even more effectively, perhaps, by their own poverty and ignorance. In the heavily-enclosed regions of the midlands any surplus labour created by the growth of rural population was more readily taken up by the expansion of towns and industry. On balance, rural employment benefitted from enclosure because it meant more land under cultivation, more advanced and labour-intensive methods of cultivation, and a greater yield of farm produce to be harvested, transported, and processed. The enclosure itself also had an effect on the demand for labour: there were fences to be built, new farmhouses to be erected, drains to be dug, water-courses diverted, and roads laid out, constructed, and main-tained. Land newly enclosed from the common and waste had to be cleared of turf, weeds and stones, and it had to be drained, and then brought to a tilth by a laborious programme of ploughing and harrowing. Only where old open-field arable was converted to permanent pasture was the demand for labour actually reduced, and in fact much of the increased acreage of pasture was

The London and Birmingham Railway: construction of the Boxmoor Cutting. Lithograph by John C.Bourne, 1837.

rotation grass that was alternated with arable crops, and required a considerable labour force for cultivation.

The social and economic consequences of enclosure, therefore, varied widely from place to place in a largely random and unpredictable manner. On the whole the effects were much less pervasive and less damaging, and much more beneficial to employment and incomes than used to be supposed. The physical effects on the countryside were in many cases the more obvious and permanent. In the lowlands the familiar post and rail fences and quickset hedges, in the uplands dry stone walls, broke up the former great expanses of open fields. A patchwork quilt, mixed of crops and grass, replaced unbroken stretches of wheat and barley. Trees and bushes planted along the hedgerows grew to maturity to provide shade and shelter from the wind. New isolated farmhouses appeared among the fields, remote from the ancient matrix of the village. Numbers of the old, narrow, meandering lanes disappeared, stopped up by order of the enclosure commissioners. Their newly-built roads provided shorter, more convenient routes to neighbouring villages or turnpikes, and they were strikingly straight and broad, the forty feet width laid down by Parliament. The carriageway itself, correctly constructed of small packed stone and surfaced by gravel, took up only part of the road's width, and was bordered by strips of grass useful for driving cattle and sheep. When awkward boundaries of farms broke up the straight line, the commissioners' roads made sharp ninety-degree turns, then resumed their inflexible straightness.

The post-enclosure landscape delighted some, horrified others. Those who welcomed it took pleasure in the flowers and birds of the hedgerows and the beauty of the trees which broke up the former great open fields, a void which had little of the picturesque but rather 'strained and tortured the sight'. Tennyson, too, made his *Northern Farmer (Old Style)* point out that improvement had converted the wild, bracken-covered waste, which would not support even one poor cow, into a rich pasture bearing eight beasts and a quantity of clover. But John Clare, the poor demented village poet of Helpston, Northamptonshire, saw the change in a different light. He preferred the wild, natural countryside to the newly-imposed pattern of regular fields and orderly hedgerows:

Inclosure, thou'rt a curse upon the land,
And tasteless was the wretch who thy existence plann'd.

On the other side of the fence was John Dyer, the Carmarthenshire painter-poet. Like Tennyson he was impressed by the material benefits of the change, and urged it on his fellow countrymen:

Inclose, inclose, ye swains!
Why will you joy in common field, where pitch,
Noxious to wool must stain your motley flock
To mark your property? . . . Besides, in fields
Promiscuous held all culture languishes;
The glebe, exhausted, thin supplies receives;
Dull waters rest upon the rushy flats
And barren furrows; none the rising grove
There plants for late posterity, nor hedge
To shield the flock, nor copse for cheering fire;
And in the distant village every hearth
Devours the grassy sward, the verdant food
Of injur'd herds and flocks, or what the plough
Should turn and moulder for the bearded grain . . .
Add too, the idle pilf'rer easier there
Eludes detection, when a lamb or ewe
From intermingled flocks he steals; or when,
With loosen'd tether of his horse or cow,
The milky stalk of the tall green-ear'd corn,
The year's slow rip'ning fruit, the anxious hope
Of his laborious neighbour, he destroys.

Those villages of the midland plain affected by enclosure were mainly of the nucleated type, i.e. with farmhouses and cottages clustered close together round the nucleus provided by the church and vicarage or perhaps the manor house or ruins of an ancient castle, the whole nestling at the bottom of a hill or by a river crossing or road junction. Before the age of enclosure outlying farmhouses and detached hamlets were few. Physical features determined location. Thus, in the chalk downlands of southern England the villages lie in the fertile and sheltered valleys, where also run the streams. In forested areas, or those districts which once were heavily forested, it is more common to find villages which consist of scattered hamlets, each a mile or two from its neighbour. This hamlet-type development sprang originally from the early clearings in the forest, the smallness of the population, and the limited amount of good land which was available. Again, in upland areas, on the Pennines, the Yorkshire moors and the Welsh hills, the little villages in the vales are complemented by isolated farmsteads on the hills, remote, and often cut off in winter.

Generally, in forested and upland areas the farms were small, often no more than part-time holdings, where the cultivator spent much of his time at some forest craft, cutting wood, and making charcoal or such things as barrels, posts, rails, and hop-poles. Frequently the small cultivators were engaged in some industrial occupation, like the farmer-cutlers around Sheffield, and might eventually give up their land to become full-time industrial workers. By-employments of this kind arose because of the smallness of the holdings or the poverty of the soil. Migrants were attracted to such districts by the possibility of getting a little land and taking up a trade. In lowland England the farms, especially the large arable farms, required many hands. A farm of 1000 acres might employ as many as forty men and boys, as well as dairymaids and women employed part-time in the fields. As a consequence industrial by-employments were less common, for most of the available hands were already employed in farming. The villages grew less fast because land was often not available for smallholdings, permission to build a cottage might be withheld, and the lack of by-employments discouraged migrants.

Within these broad regional distinctions there were many variations. The presence of a resident squire was important. In some instances the village grew up by the gates of the big house and stretched along the walls of the park, like humble dependants who hoped that close proximity would bring favour and protection. Occasionally the village had at some time been moved by the squire away from its original site, perhaps down the hill out of view of the mansion, or to make room for a park and pleasure grounds. Where this happened, as at Nuneham Courtenay in Oxfordshire, the village was often uniform in style, the houses all having been built of the same materials at the same period. Squires' villages were usually small, mainly because nearly all the land was in the hands of the great family and there was little or no possibility of small proprietors buying farms to settle themselves and multiply. It was not uncommon for the squire, in conjunction with the large farmers, to follow a policy of deliberately restricting the expansion of the village. Few new cottages were built, and old ones were pulled down as soon as they became empty, and were not replaced. The object was to limit the number of poor cottagers who might conceivably become paupers and fall upon the parish for relief. The 'close' parishes, as they were called, tried to keep the poor rates low at the expense of population. When the farmers required more hands they had to be hired from nearby villages which were more populous.

The converse of the 'close' parish was the 'open' one. This was a village where the land was dispersed among many owners and there was no squire who held a near monopoly of the parish. Sometimes open villages were the consequence of an increased demand for labour created by enclosures of waste; sometimes they were situated on the edge of towns and resulted from a growth in local trade and population; sometimes they were communities of craftsmen or petty dairymen who settled on the numerous surviving commons and heath lands. Open parishes were marked by a numerous class of small freeholders and small tenants, and they often held a large non-agricultural population employed in some local works or village craft. The villages tended to be large, straggling, ill-planned, and poorly-built. The leading inhabitants were frequently tradesmen and small builders whose liberal policy towards new residents sprang in part from good business sense. They acquired small pieces of land and ran up little rows of cheap cottages, often miserably constructed of the cheapest materials, and without any attempt to provide proper foundations, drainage, or water supply. Such new cottages supplemented the limited housing resources of the countryside but inevitably added to public health hazards. Estate villages, where the houses were all owned by the principal landowner, who might sometimes be a manufacturer, were usually, though not always, better. Generally the cottages were larger and better built, and equally important, were properly maintained and modernized as innovations like gas lighting, and later electricity, became available. What troubled some residents of estate villages was the extent of the estate's supervision and its all-embracing

The grounds of Nuneham Courtenay, shown in this 1819 engraving, were laid out by Capability Brown. The village was moved to make room for the park.

character. The landlord often frowned on drunkenness and might evict tenants who proved not to be 'respectable'. Sometimes no alehouses were permitted, and there was a long walk to the next village for a drink. In other instances the one inn allowed was required to serve tea and coffee as well as beer, and not to open on Sundays. Inhabitants of the free and easy open villages, though less well housed, scoffed at the residents of estate villages who, they said, dare not blow their noses without the squire's permission.

There were, then, many kinds and sizes of village, and of course the moulds in which they were cast were not fixed for all time. In squires' villages families changed or sold up, and the property might then be divided. Estate offices sometimes sold houses off to the inhabitants, and the estate ceased its paternal watch over the villagers' morality. Open villages straggled into small towns, losing much of their original connection with the land. Growth and decline were influenced by markets and changes in transport, by the coming in or passing away of sources of employment. Once important places in Sussex, like Robertsbridge, decayed with the passing of the old wealden iron industry; while Eastwood, on the Nottinghamshire-Derbyshire border, D.H.Lawrence's childhood home, grew and lost its rural character as the coal mines expanded and ugly rows of new cottages and shops appeared.

Migration from the countryside continued throughout the nineteenth century. The towns, with their better-paid and more varied range of occupations were a powerful attraction to many country-dwellers. The towns, too, offered the possibility of housing which might be substantially better than that in the country, as well as more amenities and a more exciting social life – schools, libraries and Mechanics' Institutes, shops, parks, newspapers, more public houses, clubs, theatres, music halls. In the early decades of the century the attractive force rarely penetrated the deep countryside. Studies of migration indicate that most new towndwellers came from within a radius of some twenty or thirty miles from the town. It was only gradually, in the second half of the century, that such factors as railway travel, the competition of town-made goods, the slow spread of newspapers and other urban influences among rural labourers, and the activities of shipping companies and emigration agents, began to have much influence on more distant parts of the country, such as central and western Wales, the Devon and Cornish peninsula, and the moorland country of Northumberland, Durham and Westmorland. There was, however, a certain amount of seasonal movement, of Irish and English harvesting gangs, for example, and some Welsh hill farmers left their remote homes to find winter work in the coal and iron centres of Glamorgan or the industrial towns of west midlands, returning home each spring for the summer work on the farms.

Such seasonal movement could lead eventually to a permanent change of habitat, but in general migration rarely went far enough or fast enough to cause more than occasional local falls in the rural population. There was little depopulation, in the strict sense of the term. Partly this was because the rural population was itself growing quite rapidly, and it was merely the surplus growth which was creamed off by migration, leaving the numbers remaining at about the same level. The insularity and conservatism of country people also retarded the pace of migration. They had no experience and but little conception of life in a large city, or of any kind of work but farming and country crafts. Early marriage, large families, poverty, the fear of losing their settlement or right to relief, were all discouragements. Eventually, a lessening of ignorance, education and a widening horizon, a growing discontent with low wages and low living standards, increasingly stimulated movement. Bolder spirits were inspired by newspaper advertisements telling of the high wages, plentiful employment, and cheap land available across the oceans. Once a few made the attempt, others were encouraged to follow suit. Emigration societies, and individuals promoting new settlements in land already selected and marked out, also played their part. By the end of the century the numbers leaving the land had fallen off, largely because those capable of migrating had already gone, leaving behind the unskilled and unambitious, the men with large families, and the old. By this time, too, the disappearance of the labour surplus had contributed to better wages and living standards in the countryside.

English agriculture in the nineteenth century was in general highly commercial, as compared with much of the farming on the continent. Observers from France, for example, commented on the contrast, and saw the reason for it in the great expanding markets offered by Britain's industrial towns and seaports. By continental standards the scale of the farming was large and technically advanced. In the middle decades of the century 'high farming' was the religion of the progressive agriculturists, and James Caird, the Scottish farmer-journalist, its high priest. High farming meant intensive farming, using the best available seed and livestock, and putting large quantities of fertilizer into the soil in order to produce the greatest quantity of produce. It was a policy which paid so long as markets kept expanding, prices were profitable, and labour remained cheap. And, until the great depression of the 1870s, all these factors were highly favourable. The urban population, already fifty per cent of the whole by mid-century, continued to grow rapidly. By 1881 it was double the rural. Moreover, living standards were rising, so that as Caird himself remarked,

> in the manufacturing districts where wages are good, the use of butcher's meat and cheese is enormously on the increase; and even in the agricultural districts the labourer does now occasionally indulge himself in a meat dinner, or seasons his dry bread with a morsel of cheese . . . the great mass of the consumers, as their circumstances improve, will follow the same rule . . . Every intelligent farmer ought to keep this steadily in view. Let him produce as much as he can of the articles which show a gradual tendency to increase in value . . .

The result was that while wheat, until the 1870s, remained fairly stable in price, the value of other farm commodities, beef, lamb, cheese, rose steadily. The wages of farm labourers began a slow rise about mid-century, but the cost of labour remained very low. Average weekly wages for men on farms rose only from 9s 7d in 1850–51 to 13s 9d in 1879–81, though there were wide variations between north and south and from one district to another. The great cheapness of labour in southern England was a factor retarding the introduction of farm machinery, a novelty which made more rapid progress in the north where labour was scarcer and dearer. The threshing machine, a source of grievance among labourers in southern England because it reduced winter employment, only became very widely used there about 1830, when its appearance was a factor in the famous Swing riots. The horse-drawn reaper was not much used anywhere until after 1850, and after that was long in displacing the customary scythe, sickle or hook. Other improved implements, mainly appearing in the early decades of the century, such as drills, horse-hoes, cultivators, harrows, clodcrushers, scarifiers, probably added to the total amount of farm work because they usually represented additional operations or more intensive methods of cultivation rather than a saving of labour. On the whole, machinery made little impact on labour demands in farming, and indeed the total numbers employed on the land continued to rise up to the 1850s, and then began to decline only slowly.

High farming, involving the use of superior livestock, new implements, and from the 1840s, costly 'artificial' chemical fertilizers, hardly made sense unless the land was adequately drained. Only a well-drained, fertile soil would enable the heavy investment of material and labour to yield profitable results. Consequently, under-drainage was regarded as the great prerequisite for high farming, without which all else was wasted. Advice was given by drainage experts like Joseph Elkington, James Smith of Deanston and Josiah Parkes, conqueror of the infamous morass of Chat Moss, and by the early 1840s new mobile machines for manufacturing pipes and tiles right on the farm had been invented. There followed a spate of activity. Landowners and farmers invested heavily, at between £4 and £8 per acre, in draining large acreages, often borrowing heavily to do so. Drainage operations created a great deal of work, and even more when landowners thought it only prudent to match the newly-drained fields with new barns, well-designed bullock yards, dairies, cowpens and pigsties.

Most of this activity came to an abrupt halt after the middle 1870s. The market for farm produce, it is true, continued to grow rapidly. The numbers living in towns expanded at a faster pace than did the national population. The inhabitants of the six major conurbations of Greater London, south-eastern Lancashire, the West Midlands, West Yorkshire, Merseyside and Tyneside rose from 8,345,000 in 1871 to 14,726,000 in 1911, an increase of more than 75 per cent. In the thirty years after 1860, moreover, real wages, the people's purchasing power, is estimated to have risen

WE the undersigned Magistrates acting in and for the Hundred of Gallow, in the County of Norfolk, do promise to use our utmost Endeavours and Influence we may possess, to prevail upon the Occupiers of Land in the said Hundred,

To discontinue the use of Thrashing Machines, and to take them to pieces.

Dated this 29th. day of November, 1830.

CHAS. TOWNSHEND.
ROBERT NORRIS.
EDW. MARSHAM.

Local magistrates lent their support to those who opposed threshing machines in Norfolk in 1830.

by some 60 per cent, though there was subsequently a slight decline in the years between the end of the century and the First World War. At all events, there is no doubt that the towns of Britain came to contain many more people, and that many more of these urban residents were able to spend more on food. There was in fact a substantial rise in the consumption of meat and dairy produce, while less was spent on bread, and this was the trend even among the poorest paid, such as the farm labourers. Unfortunately for Britain's farmers, a large share of the expanding market was taken up by imports of food from abroad. American and Russian grain poured in to bring the price of wheat down to levels unknown for more than 150 years. The price of a four-lb loaf in London fell from 10d in the dear year of 1867 to 5d in 1901. Danish butter and bacon captured the middle-class market, beef and mutton shipped from the Americas and Australasia filled the counters of butchers' shops in working-class districts, and Covent Garden was invaded by fruit and vegetables from the continent. The British consumer enjoyed a range of food cheaper than it had been for at least a century, but the farmers and landlords did not prosper in the new age of plenty. Some farmers went bankrupt, others gave up, and a great many who survived experienced hard times. Their landlords cut down on outgoings, closed up or sold ancestral mansions, and put tenant-less farms in the hands of the auctioneers.

The 'great depression' in agriculture from the late 1870s was really the delayed impact of a decision taken thirty years earlier – the Repeal of the Corn Laws. Agricultural protection was of ancient origin: in the past it was natural enough that when the country's important industrial and trading activities were sheltered from foreign competition, protection should be extended equally to agriculture, by far the largest source of employment. But in 1815, when the most highly protective Corn Law of all was enacted, there were protests, some of them violent, from an expanding urban population who wanted cheap bread – and from, too, a growing group of manufacturers and political radicals who believed in the advantages of free trade. The agitation died down, and it was seen that high protection did not necessarily mean dear bread: for prices were still mainly determined by the size of the home harvest, not by the level of imports. The unpopular Act of 1815 was replaced by more flexible measures. Farming, despite the Corn Laws, ceased to thrive as wartime prosperity collapsed into depression, and the long runs of poor harvests and exceptionally high prices of the years before 1815 came to an end. Protection could not ensure good prices for the farmers when harvests were excessively benevolent, and especially now that all the land brought into cultivation by wartime enclosure contributed its quota to the market. Banks failed, landlords found their leases thrown up, and farmhouses were full of sheriff's officers.

In the 1820s and 1830s farming gradually recovered – in some areas, indeed, there had been few signs of distress – and again the Corn Laws came under attack. The occasion was the terrible industrial depression of 1839–42 – the 'hungry forties' – and the instrument was a new and highly organized political pressure group, the Anti-Corn Law League. The League's power base was in the heart of the cotton manufacturing district, in Manchester, for it was financed by the cotton interests and, in a sense, served as their mouthpiece. Using newspapers, pamphlets, itinerant lecturers, and even the impassioned voice of the nonconformist pulpit, the League attacked the Corn Laws as unjust, wicked, even blasphemous. Soon the Commons itself resounded to the thunder of free trade's leading exponents, Cobden and Bright. Scorn and abuse were poured on the landed interest. The landlords were characterized as 'a bread-taxing oligarchy', 'titled felons', and 'blood-sucking vampires'; their dupes, the farmers, as 'bullfrogs', 'chawbacons' and 'clodpoles'. Though the League's motives were ostensibly humanitarian – cheap bread, industrial prosperity, international harmony – their real objects were political. The parliamentary reform of 1832 – that 'most aristocratic measure' as Lord Grey called it – had made hardly a dent in the landed interest's control of Parliament. The infamous rotten boroughs had been abolished, but the slightly expanded electorate was still minuscule, and the counties and country towns even now were over-represented in the Commons; the landowners still maintained a powerful hold over their traditional constituencies, and continued to do so until the coming of the Secret Ballot in 1872; and in Parliament the landowners yet filled the majority of seats on both sides of the House.

The ultimate objective of the League's propaganda was the ending of the landowners' continuing political domination. The new attack on the Corn Laws was launched at an opportune moment, when the industrialists were pinched by bad trade, and urban discontent was inflamed by dearer bread from poor harvests, severe unemployment, and by the strident cries of the

By the 1860s threshing by machinery was well established. This illustration is taken from Copeland's *Agriculture Ancient & Modern* published in 1866.

Chartists and other working-class radicals. To Peel, the Prime Minister, the Corn Law issue resolved itself into one of giving way on agricultural protection or risking a shift of the agitation towards demands for further reform of Parliament. He chose the first alternative, partly because, as an improving landlord himself, he knew that the Corn Laws were not essential for the well-being of efficiently-managed estates and up-to-date farms. Significantly, he coupled Repeal with measures designed to help landowners undertake farm improvements, especially under-drainage of clay soils. Furthermore, the demand for cheap bread was fraudulent. In 1846, when the Corn Laws were repealed, there was no very great surplus of foreign grain ready to enter our unbarred ports. In America the railway had not yet reached Chicago, let alone the great plains of the West, and the cost of shipping corn from the Baltic still gave British farmers a natural protection worth some 10s a quarter. The great majority of the population was still fed on British grain, and the predominating influence on the prices paid in the market remained the size of the home harvest. Moreover, the landed interest itself was not solidly behind the Corn Laws. It was generally the smaller Tory squires and farmers who were avid protectionists, while some of the great aristocratic owners, like Earl Fitzwilliam, saw the Corn Laws as unnecessary and inequitable. 'It was unjust and unchristian to raise the price of bread for the benefit of a few landowners', he said.

The Earl's remark, however, was more than a little exaggerated. In 1846 English agriculture supported, in addition to several thousand landowners, some 200,000 farmers and nearly $1\frac{1}{2}$ million labourers, both male and female. Over a quarter of all the men aged over 20 were directly engaged in agriculture. Not all of these, by any means, relied on corn production for a living, but those who did represented a large proportion of what was still by far the country's largest occupational group. Could the farmers, even those who farmed 'high', survive without protection? T.T.Clarke, an Essex landowner, thought not:

Notwithstanding muck manuals, scarifiers, tiles, Mechi's and Liebig's, I despair of being able to compete with the foreigner, and if such is the case, down goes Rent, down goes the Landocracy and up the Cottonocracy, and the present social position of this country extraordinarily altered.

However his agent, John Oxley Parker of Woodham Mortimer, was more optimistic:

I am not one who clings to a high price of wheat as the only hope of the Farmer. I may say that I have given up all idea of it since the very first passing of the Repeal of the Duty. I fully believe that other things will in time accommodate themselves to the price of corn, and that, under a new state of circumstances, the energetic and skilful farmer may prosper again as he has done.

In terms of national wealth and employment agricultural protection had made sense, but the claims of industrialists and merchants, and the interest in cheap bread of the nine million inhabitants of towns, could not be denied. And for a generation Peel's gamble paid off. Under free trade imports of grain, meat and dairy produce gradually rose, but the general effect on the prices paid to farmers was not adverse until the 1870s; parliamentary reform was postponed to 1867, and even then, had little influence on the rural electorate. Only in 1884 was the franchise extended beyond the ranks of skilled workers, and it was another generation after that before all males had the right to vote.

The slow march of democracy did, however, put paid to hopes of tariff reform, and restoration of agricultural protection was never really on the cards before 1914. Extension of the electorate and redistributions of seats, together with the Secret Ballot and the introduction of County Councils in 1888, meant a gradual deterioration in the political power of the landed interest. Decline in Parliament, and in the gentry's ancient bastion of the county, were parallelled by the diminished importance of agriculture itself. At the same time as country houses were ceasing to be vital centres of influence, the farms were losing their place in the country's economy. In 1851 agriculture had employed more than a fifth of the occupied population and produced about the same proportion of the national income; fifty years later it employed less than a tenth of the labour force and its share of national income had fallen even more, to less than a fifteenth. So far from being at the centre of the national life and mainstay of a great proportion of the people, farming had fallen to the status of only one among a number of major industries, and a problem industry at that – one whose problems were neglected in the interest of foreign trade and cheap food.

Agriculture, therefore, had to adjust to its reduced role in a hostile economic climate. Increasingly, long-established estates came under the hammer and were broken up. Farming itself became a more harshly commercial business as its practitioners struggled to survive. The least profitable arable farming was abandoned, and the labour force cut back. The most able farmworkers deserted the land, even fled the country altogether. These changes left their mark on the village, and those contemporaries who bothered to put their observations into print recorded a perceptible shift in village life and attitudes. Old ideas were passing away, even the country folk-lore, the old songs and stories, were discarded and forgotten. To regret the change was perhaps sentimental, and certainly futile. The past, if looked at truthfully, held much that was beyond regretting, and those who deplored the fading of an old way of life revealed an ignorance, perhaps a deliberate ignorance, of the poverty and misery, the unrest and violence, which had been so often the reality of the years since Waterloo. The future represented at least some promise of progress: better wages, shorter hours, improved housing, more education, a wider and more hopeful environment. The countryside that was invaded by foreign competition, by party politics, by the motor-car, was not one that could look back on unbroken prosperity or long years of undisturbed solitude. Its people had seen many vicissitudes, many times of trouble as well as of happiness. But in one sense the idea that an epoch was ending was justified, for a certain kind of rural society, one that had its advantages as well as its weaknesses, was fast disappearing at the beginning of this century. The politically powerful but often paternal landlord, the old-fashioned gentleman farmer who respected the land which he tilled and the men he employed, and the old-style labourer, ponderously ignorant and conservative, but steeped in his country skills, were all passing away. It is with these vanished figures, and those other villagers who contributed so much to the life of the country – with parson, land agent, schoolteacher, with tradesman, carpenter and blacksmith – that this book is concerned.

2   The Landowners

Landowners dominated the nineteenth-century countryside, as they had done for many, many generations. As much as three-quarters or more of all the land was in the hands of affluent proprietors, landowners who in the main lived on their rents and left the farming to their tenants. The remaining quarter was divided between yeoman farmers or owner-occupiers, who ranged from petty smallholders to substantial gentleman farmers, and institutional owners, principally the Crown and the Church, and hospitals, colleges, and various charities which had received land as benefactions. But the great bulk of the land was in the hands of private owners. And land gave power. Land was still a major economic resource. Agriculture, even as late as the middle nineteenth century, was still the largest single source of employment. In 1851 more than a fifth of the labour force depended on farming for a living. And even as agriculture declined in importance relative to industry and commerce, the value of land was enhanced because it so often had non-agricultural uses. Land was the source of valuable minerals, coal, iron, copper, and lead. It produced timber, building stone and brick clays, slate for roofing, sand and gravel for roads. Numerous if narrow tranches of soil were essential for the canals, and then for the railway tracks which from the 1820s began to criss-cross the country. Moreover, while population grew, towns expanded, factories multiplied, only land remained fixed in quantity. Greater demand for it meant increased scarcity value, and as an American land investor once remarked, 'I hear they're not making it any more'. Those owners who were fortunate enough to have land wanted for mines, quarries, housing, industrial works, canals or railways were in a position to exploit that scarcity, and so it was that the non-agricultural value of land often came to the rescue of proprietors whose farm incomes were static or declining.

But landownership conferred political as well as economic power. Before the reform of Parliament in 1832, and for several decades thereafter, ownership of land combined economic strength and political influence with the highest social status. True, the growing wealth of merchants, financiers, and industrialists presented a rising threat to the supremacy of land; but, for the time being, land managed to retain much of its old influence. Fighting a series of rearguard actions, retreating slowly from the first defeat of 1832 to the tactical withdrawal of 1846 and the subsequent concessions, landowners still contrived to hold on to a major voice in Parliament and government for as long as the nineteenth century lasted.

The most obvious symbol of landed power was the great country house. This had long since ceased to be a provincial stronghold, a baronial castle, bristling with armed retainers behind a moat and drawbridge. Though sometimes still a castle in name, and even castle-like in its ancient structure, the country house had adapted to the needs of a more peaceful and settled civilization. It had become instead a place of aristocratic resort for purposes of leisure and sport, and a centre of political discussion and influence. Alnwick, Belvoir, Chatsworth, Cliveden, Hatfield, Raby – these were names to conjure with. In these country mansions, as also their London residences, the great proprietors, and a number of the less great too, continued to play a part in shaping the country's destiny. Disraeli, resting from his Parliamentary labours, entertained extensively at Hughenden, his home on a spur of the Chilterns. Much as he liked his home life, as statesman and leader of a party it was incumbent on him to stay occasionally with eminent members of the nobility and gentry, though for Disraeli – no sportsman – life in the great country houses seemed tedious and time-wasting.

If alien to a *parvenu* like Disraeli, a country-house life – the days spent in riding, shooting, paying calls or receiving them, the evenings in cards after a lengthy formal dinner – was a natural enough existence to that majority of politicians who had been brought up to it. It was, after all, the traditional way of life of the English ruling class. Occasionally, men of affairs, used to husbanding their time in order to cope with a heavy round of business – men like Disraeli – found it boring and unsatisfying, especially in the long English winter. The great Duke of Wellington, whom no-one could describe as prone to idleness, was highly critical. Visiting Belvoir on the occasion of the Duke of Rutland's birthday, Wellington deplored 'the immense waste of time in the manner of passing the day, and the inconvenience of it to a man like him who when he was either out or receiving company at home could scarcely find time to answer his letters. "I who have been engaged in business, commanding armies, or something of that sort, can scarcely conceive how people contrive to pass their time so totally without occupation."'

Sir Robert Peel, the Tory statesman and Prime Minister, was

in January 1833 another guest who made up a distinguished gathering at Belvoir Castle. The dinner, he wrote to his wife,

> was magnificent. I have seen nothing like it, or indeed like the whole establishment, since we were at Windsor Castle when George 4th. was there. The dining room is very splendid, lighted in parts by four chandeliers each having several wax candles, and by lamps singly on the walls and candles on the table. The plate (with the exception of the candle-sticks) beautiful, of frosted silver . . .
> We sat late, rather, after dinner, the Duke of Gloucester not making a move, and afterwards the Duke of Gloucester, Duke of Portland, Lord Rokeby, and I played at whist till bedtime about 12 . . . The rest of the party were in another room, not, I should conceive, in the new drawing-room. At least, when I went to see it this morning it had not the appearance or the feel of a room constantly inhabited. I never saw anything approaching to it in splendour or beauty . . . On the walls are panels of a very light blue damask, not occupying nearly the whole of the wall, with white and gold between and round each panel. The gold is the most beautiful carving that can be imagined, very light, brought from Marie Antoinette's apartment at the Trianon at Versailles. The carpet is a Tournay carpet made for the room . . .

Apthorpe, however, which Sir Robert visited about the same time, made a less flattering impression:

> There is no shooting today, for it is the most wretched day here I ever saw. Eyes never beheld a place so little calculated as this for confinement to the house . . . The house is exactly like a small college in Oxford. It is a building about 200 years old, built round a tolerably sized quadrangle which is large enough to be entirely of grass, a little field. Its equal in discomfort cannot be produced. Lord Westmorland told me that I had an excellent apartment full of comforts for my bedroom. To go to it to bed last night from the drawing-room I had to pass first through an old room of tapestry which was fitted up as a bedroom for King James 1st, and remains just as it was . . . The second was a sort of morning room, with nothing particular in it. The window shutters and other parts of the room repaired with wood which has never been painted since it was put up, common deal. The third room was a long gallery, 115 feet long, that is just about twice the length of

ours. Low, but rather a handsome room, without a single fire in it, and with windows certainly not excluding the air of heaven.

Having paced through the whole of this, I came to another room, on opening the door of which my candle was blown out, and I felt my way back as well as I could through the gallery, in which there was no light whatever, to procure one. Having returned with my light, I came to the fourth room, a large deserted library, with all the books in confusion, something like the library at Lulworth, but a larger room. No fire in this. Then came a long passage. Then came my bedroom, a room with family portraits, very dark by day, looking into the quadrangle. There are four doors open into the room, two of them into passages and staircases that lead I know not where. Another into a long sort of closet that has been cut out of the thickness of the wall, and seems occupied at present by nothing but spiders and rats.

Only the wealthiest of landed proprietors could afford to maintain a great country house with all it entailed in upkeep, servants, entertaining and sport, in addition, often enough, to keeping a costly house in the capital for regular use in the London season. The majority of landowners, possessing more modest estates and lacking perhaps a useful income from coal, urban property, railway investments and other non-agricultural resources, had necessarily to make do with smaller mansions and a more restricted style of life. In fact, the range of landowners' incomes was extremely wide, stretching down from the great proprietor with his tens of thousands a year through the ranks of the greater and lesser gentry to the modest country gentleman who lived quietly on a few hundreds. Despite, however, the wide disparity of incomes there were unifying forces which tended to link the greatest aristocrat with the most humble village squire. They shared, in the first place, a common background in the classical education, a general love of sport, and indeed a feeling for country matters at large. Frequently their families were interrelated, the families of the daughters and younger sons of the aristocracy proliferating among the ranks of the gentry. And though they might be divided by a controversial political question, such as the problem of the Corn Laws, they joined in a broad point of view, a general attitude towards politics and the outside world, which derived basically from their great common interest, the land, and what it meant in terms of political and personal power.

Fly fishing, an engraving by R.G.Reeve after James Pollard, 1833.

Though usually coming well below the nobility in point of wealth, political influence, and prestige, the gentry were nevertheless figures of significance in their own districts. Their estates did not embrace whole strings of villages, even most of a county, as did for instance those of the Sutherlands or Northumberlands, nor were their houses of the size which could entirely overawe a country town or village, as did Petworth or Rockingham Castle. In the absence of great proprietors – and in some areas they were distinctly sparse – the gentry dominated country affairs and carried the views of their fellow-proprietors into Parliament. Some few leading families of wealthy gentry stood high in the landowning hierarchy, occupying for long periods the county seats in the Commons and mixing on equal terms with the nobility and great magnates.

But for the most part the gentry's true sphere of interest was the county, particularly that part of the county in which lay their estates. Here they commanded the influence and respect properly due to a family long connected with the district and eminent for their superiority in wealth. Respect arose not merely because as landowners such families controlled and supported in some degree the local farming industry, but also because they were frequently patrons of the church, benefactors of schools and charities, and leaders in village sport and feasts. Moreover, as Justices of the Peace the more eminent gentry, together with leading parsons, some few retired military officers, bankers, and the like, maintained the law and dispensed justice. They punished petty crime, licensed alehouses, and regulated fairs and markets, weights and measures. True, from the 1830s some of their old administrative functions were transferred to other, more representative, hands, such as those of the Poor Law Guardians and the Police Watch Committees, though the Justices were still members of these new bodies. In time, too, the Justices began to lose some of their old independence and freedom of action. Civil servants in Whitehall began to intervene in local matters, with the object of introducing more uniform, more professional standards of administration. Eventually, in 1888, the new elected County Councils usurped most of their remaining powers, although it was often the fact that those gentry families from which the Justices were drawn reappeared to sit on the committees of the County Councils. The thread of tradition was not entirely broken, and the process of transferring power from the paternal if uncontrolled individual to the more impersonal if accountable public committee and its salaried administrators was a protracted one.

Before 1888, however, the Justices continued to assert themselves and ran county business much as ever. They went on supervising the jails, visiting houses of correction and lunatic asylums, and arranging repairs to roads and bridges. They were *ex officio* members of the Boards of Guardians which now dispensed relief to the poor and administered the workhouses. It had always been possible for a pair of Justices, or even one sitting on his own, to deal with petty crime and routine matters between Quarter Sessions. A single Justice could commit a wrongdoer to the house of correction, or more mildly, accept a recognizance to be of good behaviour. Many country houses had a special room, the 'Justice room', set aside for the purpose. Serious charges were referred to the full Bench at Quarter Sessions, but the single Justice sitting in Petty Sessions could deal with common assaults and minor thefts, drunkenness, offences concerning false weights and measures, misbehaviour on the roads and – new categories these – offences concerning railways and factory regulations.

The active Justice, one who took up his duties in full seriousness, had much to do. He spent long days in the saddle or in his carriage, even on foot, attending meetings at a distant venue, conferring with fellow-magistrates, discussing the conduct of the workhouse with a Poor Law Inspector, listening to prisoners' complaints in the county jail, and ensuring that public works went on as they should. He shouldered an onerous and unremunerative burden of widely varying duties. Surviving diaries show that on average as many as two days a week throughout the year might be taken up by Petty and Quarter Sessions, visits of supervision, conferences and correspondence. Much of this involved extensive travelling and absence from home. And it was all done for nothing but the satisfaction gained from being useful to the community and from securing at considerable cost a little additional prestige and influence – indeed, the traditional rate of expenses allowed the Justices hardly began to meet their outlay.

Only a tiny minority of gentry, however, were chosen to fill the limited number of places on the Justices' Bench. Many landowners, no doubt, were never much interested in undertaking such arduous public responsibilities. They were content to spend their time in running their homes and estates, improving the property as opportunity offered and helping their tenants out of difficulties. A number engaged in a little farming or indulged an interest in agricultural societies and gardens. A select few experimented avidly with new rotations and improved breeds of livestock, or with plant nutrition and fertilizers, playing a key role in agricultural advances. Such were Philip Pusey, farming squire of Pusey in Berkshire and editor of the Royal Agricultural Society's *Journal*, and Sir John Bennet Lawes of Rothamsted, originator of superphosphate. Others took more than a *rentier's* interest in their industrial concerns, and like the fourth Earl Fitzwilliam became conversant with mining and its problems, and spent leisure hours in studying texts on steam engines and industrial management. Some took an active part in supporting the village church and school, and went as far as providing a village hall, reading room or playing field. Their wives visited the sick, dispensed old-fashioned remedies in their kitchens, prepared soup for the poor, and distributed coal and blankets to needy families at Christmas. Some squires buried themselves in their libraries, and occasionally emerged as distinguished antiquarians and authorities on esoteric subjects ranging from astronomy to zoology. Others took up some good cause, a missionary society perhaps, or nearer home, cottage improvement or temperance. Sir Thomas Fowell Buxton, for instance, appeared as a leading figure in the anti-slavery campaign, spending much of his time in earnest consultation with other leaders of the movement and preparing his Parliamentary speeches on the subject. Lord Wantage, later in the century, provided his villagers at Ardington and Lockinge with schools, well built roomy cottages, a co-operative retail store, a savings bank and friendly society, and made the tenant of the *Bull* offer soup, tea and coffee as well as the customary refreshments.

Richard Jefferies shows us a picture of the typical squire directing his affairs from his study. This was a bare room with

nothing in it but a large table, a bookcase, and two or three of the commonest horsehair chairs; the carpet was worn bare. He had selected this room because there was a door close by opening on the paved passage. Thus the bailiff of the Home Farm, the steward, the gamekeeper, the policeman, or any one who wished to see him on business, could come to the side door from the back and be shown in to him without passing through the mansion. This certainly was a convenient arrangement; yet one would have thought that he would have had a second and more private study in which to follow his own natural bent of mind. But the squire received the gardener and gave him directions about the cucumbers – for he descended even to such minutiae as that – sitting at the same table on which he had just written to an Italian art collector respecting a picture, or to some great friend begging him to come and inspect a fresh acquisition. The bookcase contained a few law books, a manual for the direction of justices – the squire was on the commission – a copy of Burke, and in one corner of a shelf a few musty papers referring to family history . . .

In this study he spent many hours when at home – he rose late, and after breakfast repaired thither. The steward was usually in attendance . . . One morning perhaps he would come in to talk with the squire about the ash wood they were going to cut in the ensuing winter, or about the oak bark which had not been paid for. Or it might be the Alderney cow or the poultry at the Home Farm, or a few fresh tiles on the roof of the pigsty, which was decaying. A cart wanted a new pair of wheels or a shaft. One of the tenants wanted a new shed put up, but it did not seem necessary; the old one would do very well if people were not so fidgety. The wife or daughter of one of the cottage people was taking to drink and getting into bad ways. This or that farmer had had some sheep die. Another farmer had bought some new silver-mounted harness, and so on through all the village gossip.

36

Sport was an all-embracing enthusiasm for many landowners. They rode to hounds while still children, kept horses and rode two or three days a week while at Oxford, and devoted the greater part of their later life to racing, hunts, shoots, cricket and similar interests. Active participation in racing was very costly, and could be indulged in only by proprietors of large incomes. The £1500–£3000 a year spent early in the century by Lord Fitzwilliam on his racing stables at Wentworth was modest by later standards. Hunting was also expensive, especially if one were the Master of Foxhounds, and because of the cost – Lord Fitzwilliam spent £500 a year on his kennels – most hunts came to be run on the subscription principle. Both hunting and cricket were sports which brought the squire into contact with other members of the community. Subscription hunts were attended by professional men and business figures from the towns, and many Masters expected to find their wealthier tenants among the company as a matter of course. The farmers, together with the squire's own domestic servants and gardeners, helped make up his cricket eleven. Shooting was much more exclusive, since it was restricted by law to landowners, though after 1831 tenants could shoot game on their farms with the landlord's permission. But to join an organized shoot depended on receiving an invitation from the

Pheasant shooting (from the *Illustrated London News*, 4 February 1843).

owner of private preserves, and such invitations were usually restricted to the higher ranks of society. Yet it could be an arduous sport, as a letter from Sir Robert Peel shows. Writing from Longshawe House, Bakewell, in August 1838 he told Lady Peel:

> We had a very good bag yesterday. The Duke of Rutland and I shot together and Sir Richard Sutton and Lord Southampton were the other party.
>
> | I shot | 24 brace of grouse |
> |---|---|
> | The Duke | $13\frac{1}{2}$ brace |
> | Sir R.Sutton | $18\frac{1}{2}$ brace |
> | Lord Southampton | 16 brace |
> | | 72 brace |
>
> I walked the whole day fagging through the thick heather and up the steep hills, and I really can walk better than I ever could in my life.
>
> I have nothing to tell you but the shooting adventures, for we are up pretty early and retire very early – there is not much variety in our proceedings.
>
> The Duke of Devonshire has left Chatsworth and our party has received the addition of Lord George Manners, one of the Duke's younger sons, and a Mr. Cooke, an agent to the Duke's Derbyshire estates. They sleep at the public-house where our horses and servants are, there not being room for them in the house here. I am very glad indeed to hear that the horse is likely to suit my dear child. I hope she looks well on horseback, and holds herself upright and shows confidence in her seat . . .

Sport certainly enlivened the countryside but it had its darker side. Game preservation annoyed the farmers and caused friction between landlord and tenant. This was a recurring problem, though, in fact, the farmers had some compensation for the ravages made by birds and foxes in the form of rent reductions and the cash payments made for particular heavy losses. More serious, the deliberate preservation of game birds in enclosed woods encouraged poaching, especially as the well-to-do house-wife was prepared to pay good prices for grouse or pheasants for her table. Before 1831 the sale of game was illegal, though an extensive illicit trade flourished in the major cities and watering places, sometimes, indeed, with birds provided by the preservers themselves. Organized poaching gangs invaded the preserves, and the stolen birds passed through a chain of middlemen –

innkeepers, coachmen and ostlers – to reach the shops of the fashionable poulterers. A succession of Game Laws, each harsher than the last, made little impact on the trade, but to fill the jails and houses of correction. Landlords sought to protect their property by employing armed gamekeepers, and at one point resorted to dangerous spring-guns and brutal mantraps, some models armed with sharp teeth which tore the flesh, and another, the 'Bruiser', which crushed the leg and left the victim crippled for life. A running war broke out between poachers and gamekeepers, with casualties on both sides. In 1821 two very prominent landowners, Lord Palmerston and Thomas Assheton Smith, were involved in Game Law trials. Two men were sentenced to death, and subsequently executed, one for killing a gamekeeper, and the other for shooting at a keeper. After 1831, with the changes in the law, these bucolic battles, fought silently in the woods at dead of night, diminished in ferocity.

Poaching continued, but it was now more largely the risky sport of village lads and a useful means for the labourer to supplement the meagre cottage cookpot. It continued because shooting became a fashionable sport, taken up by wealthy townsmen who bought or rented shooting land, as well as the country aristocracy. The *grande battue*, when parties of distinguished gentlemen gathered for days at a time, was established as a high point in the social calendar. Great pride was taken in the numbers of braces shot, the figures carefully recorded for posterity in game books. And when eventually, for reasons of economy, some landowners gave up their shoots, there were numerous *nouveaux-riches* who could afford the luxury of a shooting box in the country.

Foxhunting at least had the justification that it destroyed a farmers' pest, though this was counterbalanced by the damage done by protected foxes, kept in being for the hunt's pleasure. The huntsmen, too, were apt to be careless of damage. They knocked down fences, left gates open, and blithely trampled over growing crops. In their excitement they sometimes broke through private pleasure grounds and smashed their way across market gardens, 'up to their hocks in glass'. On estates owned by keen huntsmen, however, the farmers were often closely associated with the business of the hunt. They often joined in the chase, and sometimes were required by their leases to board and exercise foxhound puppies on their farms. Hugo Meynell of Quorndon Hall was one of the first to breed hounds especially for foxhunting, and his part of the midland counties, with its ideal terrain of rolling fields and scattered pockets of woodland, became famous as the Quorn country. Other hunts rapidly sprang up and the traditions of the sport were quickly established. However, it was a costly business to keep hounds, employ a professional huntsman, breed and maintain suitable mounts, and protect fox coverts. Anthony Trollope, the novelist, who knew a lot about the subject, claimed that at least £2000 a year was needed for a hunt which went out as many as four days a week. Hence the need for subscriptions and the opening of the sport to distant, urban as well as rural, enthusiasts. Famous Masters of Foxhounds, such as Ralph Lambton, Thomas Assheton Smith, the Duke of Beaufort, spent a great deal of their own money on their packs, horses, and huntsmen. It was the huntsman of a Cumberland enthusiast, Sir Frederick Fletcher Vane, who was the famous John Peel, celebrated in song. In his coat made of the local gray wool, Peel frequently covered fifty miles in a single day's riding.

Too often the love of sport was accompanied by a mania for gambling. The landed aristocracy spawned a breed of wealthy young men, made up largely of heirs to estates, known in the parlance of the day as 'bloods', 'bucks' and 'plungers'. In the country they thought of nothing but horses, hounds and guns; in town they gathered at their clubs, dined, drank, and spent expensive and noisy evenings over cards, interspersed with amorous adventures of a disreputable character and occasional forays to Newmarket, Goodwood or Ascot. These were the dissolute young noblemen pictured by Trollope in his biting novel, *The Way We Live Now*, and by Dickens in *Nicholas Nickleby* – feckless, unscrupulous individuals who, like Sir Mulberry Hawk, looked out for the main chance in money and marriage, associated with dubious financiers, such as the fraudulent Melmotte, or the grasping Ralph Nickleby, and gambled away their patrimony at the Beargarden. They were the young men, too, who used their wealth to buy commissions in fashionable regiments, spending most of their time in London on half-pay but managing, nevertheless, to advance rapidly to high rank through the pernicious system of purchase.

Some of them were, however, sportsmen of great natural talent whose feats won national renown. There was the celebrated Sir Tatton Sykes, the squire of Sledmere in Yorkshire, a legend among sportsmen and a tyrant among his family. In a long life he attended the St Leger no fewer than 74 times, and once rode 740 miles from Yorkshire to Aberdeen in five days, merely to win a race for Lord Huntly. Grantley Berkeley, younger son of an Earl of Berkeley, travelled as far afield as the Great Plains of North

Hunting in 1870 (from the *Graphic*, 19 March 1870).

America in order to hunt buffalo, in the days when that vast region was still the undisputed territory of fierce tribes of Indians, the Sioux, Cheyennes, Kiowas, and Comanches. Berkeley was a champion of the cause of game preservation but an otherwise undistinguished Member of the House of Commons, and he also had aspirations of a literary kind. He once horsewhipped the editor of *Frazer's Magazine*, who had the temerity to publish a critical review of his book on Berkeley Castle. Henry Chaplin was another famous hunting squire, renowned for his lavish hospitality and munificent gifts – when he won the 1867 Derby with an outsider he gave his trainer £5000 and his jockey another £1000. Before extravagance brought about his ruin he kept as many as four packs of hounds and went hunting six days a week.

Most famous of all the great sporting eccentrics was Squire Osbaldeston, known to all as 'Squire of all England'. The Squire had been known to bring down 100 pheasants with 100 shots, and to put ten bullets from a duelling pistol through the ace of diamonds at 30 feet. He was brilliant at rowing, tennis and cricket, and a celebrated horseman. For a wager he once rode 200 miles across country in nine hours, and at the age of 68 he rode his own horse at Goodwood and lost by a neck. He was a man who could never resist a wager, and this, together with the thousands he lavished on racehorses, was his downfall. He piled up huge debts until the income of his very considerable estate – eventually sold for £190,000 – was almost entirely absorbed in meeting the charges of his creditors.

There were, of course, numerous other causes of impoverishment among landowners. Some spent too heavily on replacing an old-fashioned mansion by one in the new approved Gothic style, or on developing and adding to a park. Others, carried away perhaps by the current enthusiasm for subsoil drainage and influenced by a persuasive agent, involved themselves in heavy estate expenditures. Large sums were sunk in drainage, new farm buildings, and cottages, in some cases just before the fall in agricultural prices from the middle 1870s pricked that particular balloon. Others yet had a gift for making bad investments, were taken in by plausible promoters and lost heavily on speculative companies, like Melmotte's South Central Pacific and Mexican Railway. Not a few inherited property already dangerously encumbered by debts and onerous family settlements, and never had the spare resources needed for cutting away the deadweight and bringing the estate properly afloat again.

Urban property, steadily increasing in value as the cities grew, was the salvation of some families and the making of others. The Grosvenors, for instance, once modest Cheshire squires, inherited through marriage land which became immensely valuable, lying as it did between Oxford Street and Pimlico, and embracing Grosvenor Square and much of the fashionable West End. By the nineteenth century their London income had raised them to be counted among the very wealthiest families in the land, and conferred on them the prestigious title of Dukes of Westminster. The possession of coal, lead and copper mines, ironworks, quarries, canals, harbours, and similar assets raised the fortunes of many families, especially in the midlands and the north. The Earls of Dudley earned very little from their limited agricultural property as compared with the impressive revenues which accrued from their coal mines, ironworks, quarries and transport undertakings in the Dudley area of the Black Country. The fortunes of many substantial northern gentry were entirely founded on coal. It was coal for which Squire Osbaldeston vainly searched his estate in the desperate hope of staving off financial ruin. In some instances a large non-agricultural income was used to subsidize the less profitable elements of an estate. The Sutherland family, for example, in the early decades of the century used their revenues from the Bridgewater Canal to finance the re-location and re-employment of the poor crofters displaced by sheep in the over-populated and infertile highlands of Sutherland. The Marquess of Bute, too, made use of his extensive income from the port of Cardiff and the South Wales coal industry to keep down the rents of his Glamorgan farm tenants.

It was those landowners with varied and buoyant sources of income who were best able to ride out the storms of the Great Depression of the last quarter of the century. Between the late 1830s and the later 1870s, and especially from the fifties, agriculture in general had been prosperous. Farmers recovered gradually from the depression which followed the Napoleonic Wars, survived the Repeal of the Corn Laws with no great difficulty, and went on to enjoy rising prices and a 'golden age' in the third quarter of the century. Free trade proved to be much less than a disaster as the urban population, gradually improving its dietary standards, rapidly expanded and took up the growing imports of grain, meat, and dairy produce. Many farmers had adopted higher standards of cultivation, with more varied crop rotations, higher yields, superior breeds of livestock, and newly-invented farm machinery. The landlords, or a proportion of them at least, played their part. They invested considerable sums in draining the wet claylands and in new farm buildings, sums which the modest rise in rents hardly justified. Indeed, those owners who started late upon the business of improvement lost heavily when rents slumped after 1879.

What happened was not entirely unforeseen – well-informed farming experts like Sir James Caird saw it coming – but was nonetheless damaging, both materially and psychologically. Since mid-century railways had penetrated the prairies of America, opening up vast new wheat lands of unparalleled fertility. The iron fingers, too, were probing into the hinterland of the Russian empire, the back country of Brazil and Argentina, the outback of Australia, the plains and valleys of New Zealand. At about the same time, in the closing decades of the century, the oceangoing vessel was transformed from what was fundamentally a sailing ship, supplemented by some inefficient steam power, to a much more economical coal-burning steamship that could cross oceans at increased and predictable speeds. The world's merchant fleets grew rapidly, and competition between steam and sail brought freight rates plummeting down. By 1902 a quarter of wheat could be brought by rail a thousand miles from Chicago to New York and then shipped another three thousand miles across the Atlantic to Liverpool for less than 3s. Thirty years earlier it had cost nearly four times as much. A pound of wool could be shipped from New Zealand halfway round the world for less than a penny. Then it was the turn of meat. Chilled beef came in from America and Argentina. In 1880 the first shipment of frozen mutton arrived from Australia, and before the First World War some 350,000 tons of beef and 250,000 tons of mutton were being imported annually.

At the same time as the railway and the steamship were causing the globe to shrink, less spectacular but significant changes in European farming were affecting the British food market. The Danes met the threat of a world flood of wheat by shifting to dairying. The cheap imported grain was fed to dairy cattle and pigs, and the produce, systematically processed and carefully standardized in up-to-date cooperative dairies and bacon factories, was exported to England, soon to capture a large share of the market. Danish exports to Britain were supplemented by dairy produce from Ireland, Holland, and France, and this traffic was accompanied by shipments of vegetables and fruit. The British dairyman gave up his home market without very much of a fight and turned instead to liquid milk. This was not subject to foreign competition, and moreover the railways had opened up expanding markets for milk in the towns.

Fortunately, the urban markets at home were expanding for other things too. Total population in Britain was rising nearly as fast in the half-century after 1850 as in the preceding fifty years. Between 1800 and 1910 it quadrupled, and the urban part of the population was growing at an even faster rate. Not only were more and more Englishmen town-dwellers, but as time went by a higher proportion of them could afford a little more luxury by way of diet. Living standards, steadily on the rise from at least the 1840s, climbed fast in the last quarter of the century. The cheapness of bread and other staple items of working-class consumption made it possible to eat meat more regularly, to acquire a taste for butter and eggs and bacon, and to fill out a dinner plate with a wider variety of vegetables.

The agricultural depression, consequently, was felt much more by the grain farmers, whose prices and profits fell off sharply, than by the livestock producers and dairymen who met a more buoyant and expanding market. The effects on the landlords, similarly, varied. If their estates were in the pastoral north and west then the fall in their rents might be no more, might even be less, than the fall in prices generally. If, however, their lands were in the arable south and east it might be a very different story. The less productive claylands – like much of Essex – which were costly to work and difficult to convert to grass saw rents sink to very low levels. When landlords had met their customary outgoings their net income might even be nil. The profits of the farmers, too, fell drastically. Tenants staggered on, hoping for the better times which eluded them, until they finally had to give up. Some bankrupted and left farming altogether; some went off to start again in Canada or New Zealand; some moved away to other districts, to more profitable kinds of farming. Their survival was not helped by catastrophic seasons which marked the period of the depression. In the terrible year of 1879 the rains lasted all summer long and the corn was carried in from the fields sopping wet. The more general wetness of the years 1879–82 caused widespread outbreaks of pleuro-pneumonia among the cattle and liver-rot in the sheep. Excessive wet was succeeded by damaging droughts and severe frosts. Many farmers had little to sell, their livestock was decimated, and what could be marketed brought reduced prices, not the higher figures which scarcity had ensured in previous experience.

The landlords were not accustomed to stand idly by in periods of adversity. Traditionally they had always come to the aid of their tenants when times were bad. They helped the farmers keep going by making rent abatements, provided assistance in meeting the local rates, and offered improvements to farm buildings and help with repairs. Partly this was *noblesse oblige*, partly good economic sense. No landlord wanted to see his farms without tenants, and when whole districts were hit by bad weather or low prices it was not easy to re-let farms, even at much reduced rents. Landlords accepted a temporary financial loss in the expectation of gaining long-term stability. But in the great agricultural depression of the late nineteenth century there was not much prospect of stability. It was difficult to see when, if ever, the flood of expanding world food supplies would abate, and there seemed little prospect of the resurrection of protection. France and Germany resorted to higher tariffs to check the influx. But their farming populations still accounted for some two-fifths of the whole, and still carried political weight. In England, by this time, the farm labour force was down to a tenth of the whole, greatly outnumbered by the urban millions who were doing well on cheap food; and the issue of protection had been settled a generation before, in the Corn Law Repeal of 1846.

So the landlords did what they could. Rents were widely abated, and some landlords helped in the conversion of arable land to pasture, paying for instance for the piping of water into fields now carrying cattle instead of corn. But the help they could afford to give was generally too limited to be of much use. They found themselves having to accept new tenants, strangers from the West Country or Scotland, economical men of thrifty habits who could make a living on land that had tumbled down to some apology for a pasture. A few were bold enough, or wealthy enough, to take their farms into hand, like Lord Wantage, who became the farmer of almost the whole of his Berkshire estate, and still managed to finance village improvements and introduce a profit-sharing scheme for his labourers. Marginal lands, it was found, could produce more as game preserves than as farmland. Partridges, it was said, were the major product of parts of Norfolk. Landlords there, as elsewhere, rented out their property, and sometimes the house too, to sporting businessmen, and retired to live in a London villa or perhaps in an upper-class seaside resort, such as Bournemouth or Folkestone. Some preferred to go abroad, claiming they could live more cheaply there than in England, and joined the communities of English *émigrés* who found a congenial existence in Brussels or spas like Baden-Baden and Marienbad.

Rider Haggard, himself the heir of a Norfolk estate in this difficult period, took up a professional career, and supplemented his income by the royalties on his novels. At the very beginning of the new century he embarked on a country-wide tour to see for himself how bad things really were and what had happened to the ancient ruling class. Complaints of the heavy fall in rents and land values were almost universal. In Wiltshire he inspected a farm of 700 acres which in 1812, at the height of wartime prices, had been sold for £27,000. In 1892 it was sold again for £7000. When Rider Haggard's host had hired it, just before the depression set in, he paid £600 a year rent and £196 tithes. In 1901 he was paying £250 rent and the landlord paid the tithes – and, said Rider Haggard, 'that gentleman must be fortunate if this property puts £100 a year into his pocket'. But, added the old farmer, 'those times was better for I than these is. I made more money when I paid £800 a year than now when I pay £250.' In Norfolk Mr George Beck, J.P., with 1500 acres the largest farmer of Ormesby St Margaret, said that

> farmers in this part of Norfolk were losing ground every day. Men who held their own three years before had been broken and their place taken by others; he did not know one who was doing well at legitimate farming, but he could recall many who had faded away. They did not go bankrupt, but they vanished, and some of them died broken-hearted.

Some complaints concerned the high charges made by the railway companies. Mr John Wade, of Broomehill Farm, near Watton, Norfolk, argued that it was 'difficult to see much light when a sack of wheat could be delivered from America for less than it cost to send it from Watton to London'. Everywhere farmers stated that good hands were scarce. Young men went off to the towns, to the building trades or the army, leaving only the old and the poorly-skilled and workshy. The men had become careless and independent, since they could easily find other work. The schools were blamed for failing to give lads an interest in farming. Mr Wade, again, thought that

> education did the mischief, as the lads did not get into the fields young enough. The wages were 13s a week, and 14s and a house for horsemen but some farmers had dropped them 1s. There were now plenty of very ordinary men of whom the more youthful only cared to do light work.

Impoverished owners, in circumstances such as those described by Rider Haggard, increasingly sought to sell land. Families who for generations had set their sights on keeping what they had and accumulating more were now forced at last to contemplate parting with it. The truth was that land no longer carried the same degree of political power and social prestige as in the past, and as an investment was now markedly inferior to mortgages or government stock. Moreover, the drift of economic thought and of government policy was towards heavier taxation of land. At first the would-be sellers were stymied by the lack of a market, for there were many sellers but few purchasers. It was not until the years just before the Great War, when agricultural prices had levelled out and even improved a little, that conditions were ripe for large-scale selling. Then, and also in the years immediately following the War, a great deal of land changed hands.

When landowners sold they normally offered the first refusal to their tenants, and many farmers thought this a good time to buy. In this way a large part of landed estates came into the hands of owner-occupiers, a process which has continued to the present. Owner-occupiers had sunk to a low level by the later nineteenth century, possessing only about a seventh of the total acreage. From this low point they rapidly recovered, reaching over a third by the 1920s. From then on they probably owned as high a proportion of the countryside as they had ever done in historic times. But the change was not entirely beneficial. They exchang-

The young squire – 'By smiling Fortune blessed/with large demesnes hereditary wealth', Sommerville.

ed a rent, which in bad times could be lowered, for a mortgage payment, which was much less flexible. Their mortgagor might not be a landowner, traditionally sympathetic towards tenants in bad times, but an impersonal bank or land company.

What of the landowners themselves? They were now in a new environment, in which land was less valuable, not merely in economic terms, but also in terms of the political and social advantages which it once conferred. Even landowners who had done well out of the growth of towns and industry often found themselves eclipsed by the *nouveaux-riches*, by new titles springing up among soap manufacturers like the Levers, grocers like the Liptons, armament tycoons like the Armstrongs, and cigarette makers like the Wills's. Henry Brassey, the great contractor, installed himself in Lord Westmorland's Apthorpe, and Jesse Boot, builder of a retail-chemist empire, acquired an eighteenth-century mansion outside Nottingham. In itself, of course, this irruption of industrial and commercial wealth was nothing new. Many families of the old nobility and gentry had sprung originally from similar sources, and in some instances not too far back either. But then it had been a matter of new men making their way into a superior ruling class; now it was more a question of a declining ruling class coming to terms with new and superior wealth. It could be done to some extent: old-established land-owners gave an aristocratic *cachet* to Boards of Directors, and their children married into industrial fortunes. But the prestige of land was not so great as it once had been, and its powers of absorption were much reduced.

Strong forces worked in the direction of disruption. The old ties of respect and self-interest which bound landlord and tenant were fatally weakened. The landowner's pre-eminence in the community was diminished as his political and economic strength declined. Even the country houses, the homes which had been associated with families for many generations, centuries, were changing hands. The cost of modernizing, the maintenance of the grounds, the very way of life which they embodied became insupportable. It was a way of life which was made possible only by cheap labour, and when servants became scarcer, more expensive, and more independent then the writing was on the wall. The less affluent gentry were the first to go as their inelastic incomes simply became inadequate. The wealthier had more strings to their bow, had more scope for making economies, but often they too felt the pinch. In the end estates were sold whole or piecemeal, sometimes with the house, sometimes not. New-comers with new money established themselves on ancient ancestral acres – some houses were converted into training establishments, schools, nursing homes – others, unsold, moul-dered into decay.

The closing of the house and removal of the family signalled the end of a rural society which went far back in English history. Its passing meant the final snuffing out of a communal re-lationship which had its origins in the feudal bonds between lord and serf, merged gradually into the semi-social, semi-contractual relationship between landlord and tenant, and arrived eventually at the independent, equalitarian society of modern England. The change was rational, and it was inevitable – the coming of democracy ensured that. The intimate paternalism of the old order gave way to the impersonal, remote control of the state. But the welfare state is the concept of a wealthy society, and in the far poorer England that preceded the twentieth century the land-owning class had done much – as was their responsibility – to provide some limited degree of benevolence, a measure of welfare.

In the nineteenth century, in a new industrial, commercial state, the old rural benevolence declined. The population grew too fast, poverty proliferated, and the resultant problems were too big and too many. Yet in some places the old traditions continued, often in the hands of newcomers with new wealth. Lord Wantage, for example, assumed the traditional role *par excellence* when he presided over the modernization of his villages of Ardington and Lockinge. Lord Overstone, banker turned squire, had his social obligations called to his attention when he became a landed proprietor in Bedfordshire. In January 1848 he received an appeal from the Rev.J.G.Joyce, the curate of Wing. The curate spoke of 'the excessive destitution of the poor', and went on

> So far as my own cramped means have suffered me I have done all in my power to alleviate their distresses, but between the almost entire failure of their common business the Straw Platting, and their general illness they are now quite at the worst: this day the Parish officer has not less than 50 applications from this place alone for tomorrow's Board, and of these a large proportion must be inevitably refused and the remainder but scantily relieved.
>
> A Distribution of flannel and other clothing takes place next week through the liberality of the Vicar partly, and partly through the beneficence of a private friend of my own, but there is not upon any, *so direct a claim as on yourself*, the owner of the soil; and therefore I trust you will aid me with some funds (and they need not be very large ones) to provide against such mere necessities as clothing and sustenance . . .

To Lord Overstone it seemed less than certain that the responsibility indicated was entirely his; his reply pointed out that for a long time the clerical duties of the parish had been sadly neglected:

> Hence you find on coming into the Parish, a Church altogether deserted, the Glebe land, as I am informed, in a shocking condition, the influence of the Clergyman over his parishioners wholly lost, and, as the inevitable consequence, the population ignorant, immoral, ill-conditioned, and distressed. Do you not then express yourself hastily and unadvisedly, when you state that, *under these circumstances* 'there is not upon any so direct a claim for the relief of this distress as on myself'? Permit me to observe that next to the unfortunate people themselves, the Owner of the Soil is the party most injured by the unfortunate state of things to which I have alluded; but for which, *I* am not responsible. But are you convinced that contributions to relieve the symptoms of

distress, which are not based upon any principle which is directed to the correction of the cause of the distress, will work effectual good ? Is there not great danger that they may do the very reverse ? that they may tend to perpetuate the existing distress, by preventing the painful but necessary resort to those w^h are the only efficient, and therefore only really beneficial correctives of the existing state of things ?

Casual charity, administered only under the influence of kind feeling, and not directed by any principle to an effectual correction of the evil causes at work, usually does but little of even apparent, nothing of real, good.

He went on to argue that statutory poor relief was 'charged principally upon the soil – which of course, indirectly reaches the Owner of the soil'. What was needed, he said, was to *cure* poverty, not merely treat it with unsystematic, casual, blind charity. This he had tried to do, first by taking measures to improve the standards of farming on his property, and second, by the encouragement of education, in which he hoped for help from the new resident clergy in the parish.

Rejection of charity was perhaps more the view of the new businesslike proprietors than of the old ones. But the extent and complexity of the social problems of the countryside were forcing all thinking owners into more objective, less sentimental attitudes. The result was a growing distance, a greater hostility between the wealthy and the poor. In the end the problems proved to be too deep-seated to be treated by better farming and more schools. And as the problems of poverty, unemployment, housing, became national rather than parochial, so the landowners were obliged to give way in the conduct of affairs to the urban middle classes. The great depression marked more than a realignment of agricultural resources: it announced the approaching end of parochial paternalism, the end of land's age-old supremacy, the passing of the traditional society.

3 The Farmers

The Anti-Corn Law League, driving home its great assault on the landed interest in the 1840s, characterized the farmers as 'brute drudges', 'clodpates', and 'bullfrogs'. The farmer was unflatteringly portrayed as a rustic dullard, an ignoramus, a servile retainer who unthinkingly followed the landowners' lead in politics and county affairs. If there were indeed many such farmers, their ignorance does not seem to have greatly coloured the picture which contemporaries convey of the farming class as a whole. True, many farmers, especially the smaller ones, were deeply conservative in both their farming and their politics, highly resistant to new ideas in either sphere. But it must be said that a degree of conservatism made sense when many widely-advocated crops were unsuited to particular soils, the advantages of new livestock breeds were uncertain, and the functioning and reliability of novel machinery were unproved. Equally, it was sensible to continue to vote with one's landlord when the farmer's well-being was bound up with the estate of which he was part, and when the farmers looked to the landlords to take up their grievances and represent their interests in Parliament.

The customary deference of the tenant farmer in political matters had a powerful traditional element, for its origins went back to the period when the lord offered physical protection as well as representation. Acceptance of a farm on the estate of a major owner involved acceptance of his political views, as it did also acceptance of his interest in game and sport, and the obligation to farm to the usual standards of the district. On the whole, the subordinate position of the tenant gave rise to little friction between farmers and owners. Partly this was because men of strong political views would avoid taking a farm under an owner who belonged to the other party. The relationship also succeeded, however, because it was rarely put to too much strain. Sensible proprietors refrained from putting excessive pressure on farmers for their votes. In Lincolnshire Lord Monson sent his tenants politely-worded letters regretting his inability to canvass them in person, owing to illness; Sir Montague Cholmeley asked his tenants to give their vote only if they could conscientiously do so – 'I should not *demand* it of them against their consciences':

and Sir John Thorold asked his tenants for only one of their votes, leaving them entirely free in their exercise of the other. Much depended on whether a particular estate had a strong tradition of tenant allegiance.

Also important was the landlord's personal popularity. When he was disliked by the farmers they might vote on the opposite side merely to spite him. Generally speaking, the farmers' votes were more uncertain when times were bad and farming issues were at the forefront of politics. But even then the farmers felt a sense of obligation to a landlord who had taken up local issues, had spoken up for lower taxes or tithe reform, and had done his best to deal with outbreaks of arson, machine-breaking, sheep-stealing and cattle maiming. And one major consideration was the low rents enjoyed by the tenants of large estates. Sometimes the 'good bargains' at which they held their land represented an acknowledgement of big sums laid out by tenants in improving poor land or restoring neglected farms; in many cases it was a *quid pro quo* for the depredations made by game and the hunting of the sporting owner; often it was the expensive means of securing the tenants' compliance at election times. Nevertheless, it was still true that low rents prevailed even where landlords had no interest in sport and took no active role in politics. Then a moderate attitude towards rents was the accepted obligation of the 'easy' landlord, the proprietor who was concerned to maintain his family's good name in the country, the magnanimous owner who thought it wrong to screw up his income by squeezing hardworking tenants of long standing.

It might be supposed that the informality of the landlord-tenant relationship would create a sense of insecurity among tenants. The most common form of tenure, in fact, was the annual agreement or a tenancy at will, i.e. six months' notice. Leases were standard practice only for the larger farms, and even there were not universal. There was a fairly general distrust of leases on the part of both landlords and tenants. The severe fluctuations in prices, markets and weather conditions which marked the nineteenth century made both parties wary of fixing a rent for a long period of time. Yet little insecurity resulted. Large farmers capable of stocking and managing extensive acreages were always fairly scarce, and landlords, knowing such men were difficult to replace, did their best to keep them happy in their tenancies. The large tenant had considerable bargaining power, and could insist on repairs to the farmhouse and buildings, or a low rent to compensate for his own outlays when he took a farm. Smaller tenants lacked the big man's financial independence and his scarcity value, but they were very rarely insecure. So long as they cultivated the land reasonably well, were not drunkards and a disgrace to the estate or disrespectful to the owner and his agent, and provided, too, they did not fall very far behind with their rents, they might expect to go on indefinitely. Responsible landlords felt an obligation to leave their tenants undisturbed, and allowed the farms to be passed on from father to son, even to widows or daughters. In fact farms held at will often remained in one family's hands for several generations and certainly for longer periods than was usual when farms were let on lease.

When farmers did not have the protection of a lease they could still count on 'tenant right' to protect their financial interest in the farm. This was a customary compensation given to occupiers who quitted their farms leaving fields freshly sown and fertilized. The value of 'unexhausted improvements' was assessed by some independent party and was paid by the incoming tenant. Tenant right, together with the unwillingness of landlords to have farms fall into hand, meant that the larger farmers, especially, hardly stood in fear of the landlord's agent. Where the farms ran to many hundreds, even some thousands of acres, the tenants were men of wealth and standing: those on the Lincolnshire wolds, for instance, having homes more like small mansions than farm-houses. Some of these farmers counted their profits in thousands of pounds a year, and retired worth very respectable sums. They were 'able to hunt in scarlet, riding the best of horses', and in 1832 a tenant of the Yarborough estate sold six hunters for a thousand pounds at the Horncastle horse fair. Much of their profit went back into more intensive stocking of their land or the taking on of additional acreage. A few Lindsey wold farmers bought land: Samuel Slater, for example, purchased the whole 1,795 acres of North Carlton on the Cliff from Lord Monson for £80,000 in 1838; and a generation later, William Wright, the sitting tenant of Wold Newton, paid the Earl of Yarborough over £100,000 for the whole parish. Two farmers joined with a surgeon to erect and operate Lincoln's first oil and cake mill, while wold farmers were on the Board of a firm of linseed cake manufacturers at Grimsby.

England's diversity of natural conditions, soil, relief, and climate, made for many different types of farming and a wide range of farm sizes. Statistics of the period record many holdings under five acres, though most of these were probably market gardens, orchards, hop grounds, and accommodation land held for convenience by carriers, butchers, and other village trades-men. Small farms of some 20–50 acres were quite viable in dairying, and even in some forms of mixed husbandry where local markets offered a ready sale for the products. However, most farms in England and Wales in 1851 fell into the 100–299 acres category, and the 'average farm' – something of a statistical abstraction – was 111 acres. There were, in fact, a substantial number of large farms: 4300 were of the 500–999 acres description, and 771 of more than 1000 acres. Most of the very large units were to be found in areas of sheep and corn husbandry, such as Northumberland, north-west Norfolk, the wolds of Lindsey in Lincolnshire, and the downlands of Wiltshire and Dorset.

Of course, the size of a farm was but an imperfect guide to the income of its occupier. Some large farmers held several farms at once, each having a substantial acreage. The object of this was not merely to extend the scale of operations and provide a good investment for surplus profits, but also to gain command of a variety of soils or secure ample grazing. Another purpose was to establish farms for their sons to take over once they had enough experience. The additional farmhouses were occupied by bailiffs and shepherds who undertook the superintendance of the various farms.

Big farmers and small alike were caught by sudden and steep falls in prices and panic among the country banks, as occurred at the end of the Napoleonic Wars. It was reported in some districts that numerous small farmers had failed and were coming to the parish for work, while even the wealthy large tenant farmers were forced to reduce the scale of their operations and retrench on personal expenditure. They were said to be drinking less wine, and 'their daughters come no longer to the milliners or dancing masters, etc. who have thus lost by far their best customers'. Some big men were more badly hit, as is evident from the complaints of John Boys, the author of the old Board of Agriculture's county *Report* on Kent, and a farmer on a large scale in the Sandwich district. When the Board made its enquiry into depression conditions in 1816, Boys was one of its many correspondents who wrote to report distress among the farmers and hardship on the part of the labourers. Boys himself was seriously affected by the restriction of credit and shortage of money. He was, he stated, 'an occupier of farms now about forty-five years, and my present concerns lying in thirteen parishes here, and in Romney Marsh and its vicinity . . .', but conditions had forced him to 'quit several farms at Lady Day and Michaelmas next, although I have two sons out of business (and in want of it), for whom these farms were intended, if I could have made them answer a good purpose'. He went on:

From the scarcity of money, and bad markets, I had not received from the sale of the last crop, up to the first of this month, (February,) sufficient to pay parish taxes, or labourers' weekly wages, by which, together with the non-payment of several sums that had been due to me, I had it not in my power to pay in proper time the last half year's property tax; so that I was obliged to transfer a bond of three hundred pounds I had of the Commissioner of Margate Pier, bearing interest of five per cent per annum, free from property-tax, at seventeen per cent discount, making a loss of above fifty pounds.

However, where big farmers did not over-extend themselves and managed to keep clear of bank failures, their profits were very ample, averaging perhaps 20 per cent on their capital, a level quite comparable with that obtained in industry. Farmers in a less extensive way of business probably earned profits nearer the 10 per cent which contemporaries judged to be about the average. (This figure, incidentally, is greater than it seems, for it was calculated after allowing for living expenses.) Capital was normally related to acreage, so that the smaller the farm the smaller the absolute amount of profit. Some types of farming, however, were capital-intensive, and a good income could be obtained from quite small areas of market gardens, orchards or hop gardens. The incomes of small farmers, too, were often eked out by other means. They might have time to spare for working on other men's land, or might follow some by-employment, perhaps as maltsters, millers or carriers, or as manufacturers of such useful things as hurdles, barrels or hop poles. Their wives and daughters might also be employed in some local industry, perhaps in lace or gloves. Generally though, the wife helped on the farm, looking after the dairy and the chickens – even the wealthy John Boys's good lady supervised the poultry side of his business. The 1851 Census showed that the 249,431 farmers and graziers of England and Wales had the help of 111,604 relatives, though many of these would have been sons employed on the farm full-time. The wife was a valuable asset to a farmer's business, and in the event of her early demise the loss gave rise to a serious labour problem as well as personal grief.

In the nineteenth century only a little over a tenth of the land was in the hands of owner-occupiers. Many of the small owners were in fact tradesmen and middle-class country residents who bought land as a convenience for their occupation, or as pleasure grounds for their family, paddocks for keeping ponies, private orchards, and the like. Where farmers owned some land it frequently accounted for only a part of their holding, for they often rented large acreages of additional land. It rarely paid farmers to put spare resources into buying land when the money could be used more profitably in extending the scale of their operations or buying new equipment. The purchase of one's farm represented a saving in rent of only three or four per cent of the capital required, while farming, as we have seen, could be reckoned to produce a good 10 per cent or more. The consequence was that most farmers were content to be tenants, seeing their capital produce a good return, and feeling perfectly secure under a good landlord. There was little or no tendency towards the purchase of land by farmers, therefore, and the English 'yeoman', the proud, independent owner-cultivator, was more a figure of fiction than of reality. Even the term 'yeoman' was itself dying out and had an archaic ring, and its disappearance from contemporary usage may be significant. In former times when its use had been more common its precise meaning was obscure. In Kent a yeoman might well be a substantial owner-occupier, but elsewhere he could be a smallish tenant. The term was more indicative of status, for it had passed into industry, where there were yeoman-colliers and yeoman-bakers, and into military usage – even the navy had its yeoman of signals.

The big farmers of the nineteenth century, then, were very largely tenants, but they were nonetheless men of wealth and enterprise. With the financial help and encouragement of the forward-looking owners and agents of great estates they created model farms, in which the land was systematically drained, fertilized by guano, bone manure, or the new superphosphate, and tilled by the latest iron implements. Pedigree stock of great value was carefully housed in specially-designed buildings. The farmyard itself was so arranged as to minimize the loss of profitable dung, and to make it possible to work barn machinery from a centrally-placed steam engine. As time went by farmers could hire steam ploughing tackle, and mole ploughs hauled by steam for drainage purposes. A few enthusiasts even went in for portable railway tracks or tramways, as Caird noticed when he was reporting on conditions in Lancashire for *The Times* in 1850:

> The farm of Mr Neilson, of Halewood, exhibits several points worthy of notice. A light tramway with waggons is made use of for taking the turnip crop off the ground in moist weather. The tramway is readily shifted, and the crop is thrown into the waggons, which are then each pushed along by a man, so

that the entire crop may be removed from the ground, which receives no injury from the feet of horses. The tramway can be constructed for 1s 4d per yard, and might be very advantageously introduced on all heavy farms where it is found difficult to take off the turnip crop in moist weather. A gang of men are at present employed on a considerable field of Mr Neilson's in taking off the turnip crop, which they draw from the ground, fill into the wagons, and convey outside of the gate at the rate of 6s an acre, shifting the tramway at their own cost. At this work they earn 2s 3d a day.

When Hippolyte Taine, the eminent French psychologist, art historian and critic, visited England in 1862, his wide-ranging tour included inspection of a number of farms. At the first, a small one of 100 acres, the cleanliness of the farmhouse 'was altogether Dutch; I have seen nothing better in the regions of Utrecht or Amsterdam. The farmer's wife told me that every year the inside walls are whitewashed, that the stone flags of the floor are scrubbed once a week: I felt quite ashamed to walk on them and soil them.' Another, larger, farm was graced by an ancient house, the principal room

furnished with antique pieces. The staircase of solid wood, and a sideboard both date from the 16th Century. The hearth was immense, capable of burning an entire tree-trunk, a real Yulelog; it is provided with a double, wooden screen which, in summer, closes the opening and, in winter, is a protection against draughts. Some quite good prints on the walls and a fair number of books in addition to the family Bible.

At a farm of 600 acres Taine was astounded to see

a cool and lofty drawing-room. Long curtains held back by gilt loops; two elegantly framed looking-glasses; chairs in good taste. In the middle a table with a number of handsomely bound books. In short, the country drawing-room of a Parisian with a private income of twenty-five thousand *livres* . . .

Taine's farming tour was rounded off by a visit to a model farm:

Twelve miles further on, we stopped at a model farm. No central farm-yard: the farm is a collection of fifteen or twenty low buildings, in brick, economically designed and built. Since the object was to put up a model, it would not have done to set

Trial of Lord Dunmore's new steam plough (probably about 1870–72).

the example of a costly edifice. Bullocks, pigs, sheep, each in a well-aired, well cleaned stall. We were shown a system of byres in which the floor is a grating; beasts being fattened remain there for six weeks without moving. Pedigree stock, all very valuable . . . Steam-engines for all the work of the arable land. A narrow gauge railway to carry their food to the animals; they eat chopped turnips, crushed beans, and 'oil cakes'. Farming in these terms is a complicated industry based on theory and experiment, constantly being perfected, and equipped with cleverly designed tools. But I am not a competent judge of such matters, and amused myself by watching the farmer's face: he had red hair, a clear complexion but marbled with scarlet like a vine leaf baked by the autumn sun; the expression was cold and thoughtful. He stood in the middle of a yard in a black hat and black frockcoat, issuing orders in a flat tone of voice and few words, without a single gesture or change of expression. The most remarkable thing is, the place *makes money*, and the nobleman who started it in the public interest now finds it profitable. I thought I could see, in the farmer's attitude, in his obviously positive, attentive, well-balanced and readily concentrated mind, the explanation of this miracle.

The farmhouses of the period showed enormous differences in style and character, as Taine's account makes clear. There were the substantial Georgian houses built during the heyday of new farm-making during the Napoleonic Wars, with names suitably redolent of the period – 'Waterloo Farm' or 'Trafalgar House'. These were followed by Victorian farmhouses of solid proportions, wide passages and spacious rooms. The front, with its grass and evergreens, and straight formal path from the iron gate to the stone doorstep and heavy front door, had a respectable but forlorn air, as if it were little used, which was often the case. Then there were the old rambling houses, whose origins probably went back to medieval times. Such was Emily Brontë's Wuthering Heights, where one step took the visitor straight into the sitting room or 'house' as it was called. There were 'ranks of immense pewter dishes, interspersed,with silver jugs and tankards, towering row after row on a vast oak dresser to the very roof', while above the chimney were 'sundry villainous old guns, and a couple of horse-pistols'; the floor 'of smooth, white stone; the chairs, high-backed, primitive structures, painted green: one or two heavy black ones lurking in the shade'.

The farm buildings of Victorian England also displayed remarkable differences of size, style and age. There were still great medieval barns and antiquated cowshelters of uncertain age, as well as recent brick-built bullock sheds and dairies. Northumberland was remarkable for its numerous wheelhouses, specially designed to house the horse gins, later the steam engines, which drove the threshing machines. A model dairy, built in 1870 by the Duke of Hamilton for his home farm in Suffolk, boasted marble shelves, walls tiled with bird and floral designs, and doors and windows filled with stained glass incorporating the family arms. Such extravagance was unusual, of course, but even the more utilitarian style of Victorian dairy or cowshed was a far cry from the old-fashioned sort of dairy yard found by Caird in Gloucestershire:

> An inconvenient road conducted us to the entrance gate of a dilapidated farm-yard, one side of which was occupied by a huge barn and waggon-shed, and the other by the farm-house, dairy, and piggeries. The farm-yard was divided by a wall, and two lots of milch cows were accommodated in the separate divisions. On one side of the first division was a temporary shed, covered with bushes and straw. Beneath this shed there was a comparatively dry lair for the stock; the yard itself was wet, dirty, and uncomfortable. The other yard was

exactly the counterpart of this, except that it wanted even the shelter shed. In these two yards are confined the dairy stock of the farm during the winter months; they are supplied with hay in antique square hay-racks, ingeniously capped over, to protect the hay, with a thatched roof, very much resembling the pictures of Robinson Crusoe's hat. In each yard two of these are placed, round which the shivering animals station themselves as soon as the feeder gives them their diurnal ration, and there they patiently ruminate the scanty contents. A dripping rain fell as we looked at them, from which their heads were sheltered by the thatched roof of the hay-rack, only to have it poured in a heavier stream on their necks and shoulders. In the other yard, the cows had finished their provender, and showed their dissatisfaction with its meagre character by butting each other round the rack. The largest and greediest having finished her own share, immediately dislodges her neighbour, while she in her turn repeats the blow on the next; and so the chase begins, the cows digging their horns into each other's sides, and discontentedly pursuing one another through the wet and miry yard.

Other examples of backwardness noted by Caird included the near-illiterate and ultra-conservative farmers of the Surrey clays, and the bullock teams drawing old wooden ploughs on the downs in Sussex. The teams, and perhaps the ploughs too, might still have been seen there in 1914, when a dozen or more bullock teams were at work in Sussex: the farmers hung on to them because they were cheaper to feed and less nervous than horses, making it possible to plough closer to hedges and in places where horses would not go.

Conservatism in farming methods owed a good deal to the unwillingness of some landowners to spend money on drainage or improved buildings. Some of it was due, however, to the tendency for estates to allow farms to be handed on from father to son. Continuity of this kind made for stability and constantly-occupied farms, but it encouraged also complacent acceptance of outdated techniques and low standards. Enthusiasm for new ideas sprang from gentleman farmers of capital, who were concerned to maximize their profits, and who, if tenants, could compel the landlords to modernize barns, dairies and stables. Some of these men were widely versed in the scientific discussions of the day, like Philip Pusey, the Berkshire squire and first editor of the Royal Agricultural Society's *Journal*, or Sir John Bennet Lawes, the pioneering agricultural chemist of

Rothamsted in Hertfordshire. Occasionally a total newcomer, a *nouveau riche*, made his mark. Such a one was John Joseph Mechi of Tiptree, Essex. Mechi, of Italian origin, set up as a cutler in Leadenhall Street and made a fortune from his patent Magic Razor Strop. He became an Alderman of the City of London and Sheriff of Middlesex, but in 1844 cut short his business career to take up farming. For £3400 he bought 130 acres of poor wet heath land at Tiptree Hall, and by dint of heavy outlays transformed it into a celebrated model farm. To drain the waterlogged soil Mechi laid some 80 or 90 miles of one-inch pipes, and the land was set out in square fields, served by surfaced roads. The ground was dug by hand at 2d per rod, and subsequently was stirred by a great subsoil plough. Stalls and covered yards were built for the stock, so contrived that the liquid manure drained into a huge tank, later to be pumped by steam into the fields. By 1847 Mechi was inviting visitors to see what money and steam power could do. He published his farming accounts, so that all could see that his methods were profitable, and the returns for 1865–8 indicate a return of about 18 per cent on his farming capital. He could get average yields of 20–24 bushels an acre of wheat, 28 of barley, and up to 40 tons of mangolds. Mechi was an admirer of the new mechanical aids for farming, and he was among the first to adopt an American reaper and to apply steam power to a wide variety of farming operations. His stationary engine threshed and dressed his corn, worked chaff cutters, cake crushers, root pulpers and millstones, and operated his manure and irrigating pumps. But even Mechi's enterprise and ingenuity could not cope with bad times. He lost money in a bank failure and some insurance company transactions; and illness, together with the disastrously wet seasons of the later 1870s, speeded the end. He died in 1880, 'broken in health and heart'.

Mechi's failure was symptomatic of the weakness of high farming, at least in its more extravagant forms: as a system it demanded costly inputs which could only be made to pay when prices were good and the seasons favourable. The urge of the enthusiasts to take up the latest advances in drainage, steam and machinery was to some extent one which blithely disregarded the harsh economics of farming. Nevertheless, in its heyday there were sufficient of such enthusiasts to give high farming an enormous impetus. The growth of the zeal for scientific improvement came to a head in the formation in 1838 of the Royal Agricultural Society. The occasion was the 9th May, the place the Freemason's Tavern. The room was crowded by enlightened landowners reflecting all shades of political opinion – Peel,

Graham, Shaw-Lefevre, Long, Pusey . . . A noted aristocratic innovator, Earl Spencer, was appointed President, and William Shaw, editor of the *Mark Lane Express*, Secretary. Earl Spencer's favourite saying, 'Practice with Science', was adopted as the Society's motto. In 1839 the Society's first show was held at Oxford. The railway age had only just dawned, and visitors and prize beasts had long and difficult journeys in order to reach the venue. Thomas Bates's celebrated stock had to be driven from Kirklevington to Hull, thence shipped by sea to London, conveyed by barge on the Grand Junction Canal to Aylesbury and finally driven on foot to Oxford – a journey of three weeks. It was said that 15,000 noblemen and gentlemen attended the first day, and 'immediately the gates were thrown open the rush was so tremendous that many gentlemen had their coats torn from their backs'. A dinner for 2450 guests was held in the quadrangle of Queen's College, specially roofed over at a cost of £800.

The next year was the turn of Cambridge, and Parker's Piece was chosen for the site, to the consternation of the cricketers. Long before the opening time of 6 a.m. on the first day the approaches to the city were blocked by coaches and gigs, and Sir Robert Peel made an oration to deafening acclamations. Subsequent shows were marked by a very rapid increase in the numbers of implements exhibited and put to the test on the trial grounds. The Society's shows did much to advance the use of machinery, as well as the adoption of improved livestock, new strains of seeds, fertilizers and tile drainage. The *Journal* became under Pusey's guidance a forum for the discussion of the latest scientific knowledge, and leading figures in the world of science, Buckland, Owen and Playfair, stumped the country addressing farmers' clubs and public meetings.

To a large extent, however, those who attended the Royal shows and read the *Journal* were the already converted. The gap between the large progressive farmer and the common run-of-the-mill muck farmer remained. very great, and indeed was perhaps greater at this time than ever before or since. On one side of the hedge, complained Caird, might be seen well-drained, well-fertilised soil tilled by modern equipment, while on the other persisted waterlogged, infertile clays, antiquated implements, and crops harvested by the sickle. One obstacle to change was the small farmer's intense suspicion of innovations, another his lack of capital. But the farm hands, too, had to be converted to new practices. Labourers who had tended the fields by methods unchanged for perhaps a century were extremely resistant to new ideas. They often had an almost proprietary attitude towards the land and its practices, and poured scorn on those who tried something new. Shepherds, in particular, tended to be autocratic, taking their own independent view of how fast the keep should be fed or how much hay should be kept in hand. A.G.Street relates how one shepherd of his acquaintance threatened to leave the farm because his master had not consulted him over selling a spare rick of hay. The unwillingness of the men to depart from old and tried ways was one reason for the long survival of traditional styles of implements, especially waggons and ploughs. Wooden ploughs of archaic designs were still being made well into the present century, and many regional varieties were to be found even in the 1930s: the Norfolk wheel plough, the various wooden swing ploughs found on the Essex clays and in the West Country, and the great turnwrest plough of Kent and Sussex. (The wrest was the mouldboard, which had to be moved on the completion of each furrow.) The factory manufacturers of iron ploughs provided a variety of shares and turn-furrows by which their implements could be made to meet local needs and prejudices.

On the large farm the labour force made up a considerable body of men, and did so up to 1914 at least. A.G.Street remembered that in the early years of this century his father's farm on the Wiltshire downs kept six plough teams and an odd horse, involving the employment of seven carters. There were 400 acres of arable, 90 of down, 40 of water-meadow, and 100 of pasture. The Hampshire Down flock of 400 ewes required two shepherds, and the 60 dairy cows six milkers. Six day-labourers, a foreman and a groom-gardener, brought the total year-round strength to 23, and many more hands were needed at haytime and harvest. Twenty-three men, not counting the farmer himself, looked after less than 650 acres, a proportion of one man to every 27 acres, about the average for farms with a fair proportion of arable. The biggest downland farms, like those in Norfolk and the Lincolnshire wolds, employed small armies of 40, 50, or even 70 or more hands. On a large concern of this kind the farmer was essentially an organizer and manager of labour, directing the men to the most urgent work. At the busy times he had to find additional help, and even went so far as to cajole the independent shepherd into leaving his flock for a few hours to help with some immediate task. Since the gentleman farmer was frequently away at market, or engaged in a local hunt or shooting party, there had to be an able foreman or bailiff to look after things in his absence. This was a numerous class of farmworker, numbering 22,662 in 1901, slightly over a tenth of all the farmers and graziers of that date.

Bailiffs were often the sons of small farmers, or might be men who had once held farms of their own. Some few of the younger bailiffs, a rising number, were graduates of the Royal Agricultural College at Cirencester or of one of the more recently established agricultural colleges.

The first men to arrive for work at the beginning of the day were the carters and milkers. They had to be up while the moon still cast a shadow, and at four or five made an early start on feeding the stock and preparing the teams for work before the day labourers came on the scene at six or seven. The carters generally ate their breakfast in the stable, while the milkers, having completed their first work of the day, might go back to their cottages for some hot tea by the fire. The milkers' advantage was offset by the conditions in which the milking was often done, squatting on a three-legged stool, in the middle of a puddle in a draughty yard, after having brought in the hay through the mud and wet of the fields. The carters often left off work before the day labourers in order to get the horses back and make a start on their feeding and grooming. On the other hand the carter might have to be up in the very early hours if there was an extra load to be taken to the mill or fertilizer to be fetched from a town some miles away. Then he was on the road by two, walking on the near side of the waggon, whip in hand, in his smock and his breeches tied up with whipcord, and a boy or under-carter with him to help fix the drag on the hills and to load and unload. In severe weather the teams might not go out for fear of poaching the soil, but the horses, like the cattle, had to be fed and attended to every day of the year, holidays not excepted. The extra shilling or two which the carter received at the end of the week hardly compensated for his extra hours and lack of holidays. The shepherds, too, had no regular hours but might be about their flocks at all times of day and night, especially in the lambing season. Perhaps the best-off of the farmworkers was the single day labourer. He enjoyed the shortest hours and the least responsibility, and had his money, little as it was, to himself.

Monotony was the main characteristic of the labourer's day in the fields, and of course he was always exposed to sun, wind, rain and snow. He might have to walk a mile or two from his cottage, and arrived at work in wet clothes which had to be kept on till he got home. The women engaged in field work were equally exposed to the elements, though their numbers were gradually falling off. Already by the 1880s it was becoming fairly rare to see women at field work in the winter, although some helped tend the threshing machine, spread manure in the meadows – hard, unpleasant work this – or sat long hours in a corner of the field trimming roots from a newly-opened clamp.

The farmer, too, was an early riser (though A.G.Street's father stayed in bed till nine). He had first to study the weather, and at 6.30 was ready to consult with his bailiff on the day's priorities. At six or as soon as it was light the day labourers were detailed off to their tasks, and the farmer departed to visit the sheepfold and see his teams moving before coming in to breakfast. The rest of his day varied with the seasons. In summer he had plenty to do supervising the haymaking and harvesting, but in winter he often went off for some shooting with the squire. There were frequent visits to the nearest market towns to attend markets, transact business at the bank, and perhaps attend a farmers' club. Although the large tenant farmer was not socially on a par with the gentry, and would hardly be welcome at the county ball, he was a person of standing in the local community, much superior to the tradesmen and shopkeepers. His custom was sought by the country bankers, seedsmen, and agents for farm machinery, and his position might be enhanced by his serving as a churchwarden or school manager, or as Guardian of the Poor, responsible for administering the workhouse.

Farmers were necessarily men of business, and where their personal records have survived they tell mainly of their transactions and day-to-day concerns. George Rope, of Grove Farm, Blaxhall, near the Suffolk coast, left this note of an agreement for the harvesting of his crops in the summer of 1861:

Agreed July 27th, 1861, with 6 men, viz. Joe Levitt, Jas. Hammond, Joe Row, Ben Keeble, Jas. Leggett & R.French for the harvest as last year. Viz. All the wheat @ 8/– pr acre & barley, peas & turnips @ 7/– pr acre, I finding drivers and to shock the sheeves. Allowances –
3 bls. malt given
1 coo. [mb] wheat @ 20/–
35lb mutton @ 4d pr lb
$\frac{1}{2}$ pint beer in the morning and
1 pint in the afternoon when after the corn
1 st. [one] mutton instead of dinners

The dreadful weather of 1879 caused severe flooding in George Rope's part of the country:

Aug. 23. Began cutting tolavera [wheat] – slightly sprouted as it stood – from continual rains for the last fortnight.

The wettest season since 1860 and similar, but not so cold – about two thirds of the hay & clover spoiled – and a large quantity carried away by floods – on the 22nd July we had the greatest flood I ever remember here . . .

At Framlingham boats & carts were used to take passengers to & from station.

Street & shops at Halesworth flooded and hay, where cut, carried away by the stream – after this we had a few fine days and then it came on wet with an occasional fine day till the 17th Sep. when in the evening about 9 a thunder storm came gradually on which was very severe. About 1 o'clock a cow was killed in the Dunningworth Hall meadows below John Hammonds – another cow was killed at Mr Chaplin's, Sudbourne.

At Ipswich it was said to be even more severe – and great floods followed – and here the rain was nearly as high as on the 22nd July – but at Leiston they had very little rain.

Sept. 24 Leiston marshes again flooded. Archer had given orders for some of his bullocks to come home on Monday but the rain came down in torrents on the 23rd & 24th Sept. and caused another great flood, so that he is completely flooded again. Langham is not safe to pass – the water runs over Mr Smith's wall, all the length of it – and foot planks are not visible.

The combination after 1874 of bad seasons, low prices, poor harvests and livestock losses led to many tenants giving up their farms. The years from 1875 to 1878 were notable for wet and cold summers, poor harvests, and shortages of hay for the stock. In 1879 the rain began in the early spring and persisted until the later part of September, accompanied, wrote S.G.Kendall, 'by a damp, dank cold atmosphere which struck a chill almost into one's bones, bringing ruined crops with widespread devastation in their train . . . We had no barley crops at all that season on heavy soil,' and the wheat 'turned blighty and black and seemed to shrink back in a different way yet not dissimilar to the barley two months earlier'. The following winter proved extremely cold: on 31st December of that terrible year the young Kendall wrote in his pocket book: 'This dismal, wet, dark, never-to-be-forgotten year is now at an end, may the coming eighties bring with it better luck and greater good fortune.' But the eighties produced little relief. The first half of 1880 saw very heavy losses of sheep due to the rot, and it is estimated that over five million sheep perished. January of 1881 brought with it a ferocious blizzard lasting over 48 hours, and again severe losses of sheep.

Above and opposite: Two early photographs of farm buildings and people
published in *Grundy's English Views*, 1857.

Kendall's sheep 'looked like small snow mounds', and great
coppers of boiling water were needed to get the farmhouse taps
going. The following summer was wet, and 1882 had a very wet
autumn, so that little wheat could be sown. The summers of 1885
and 1887, by contrast, were droughty, with shortages of roots for
the stock. Fortunately other seasons in the eighties were moderate, though the early nineties saw fresh disasters. The great
blizzard of 8–13 March 1891 brought twenty-foot snowdrifts to
parts of the West Country, and claimed over 200 lives on shore
and at sea. The farmers suffered great losses of livestock – some
sheep were blown over the cliffs into the sea – as well as
devastation in orchards and woodlands. The summer of 1891 also
produced a wet harvest, and 1892 and 1893 brought very severe
droughts. In Kendall's part of the country hardly any rain fell
between February and July 1893, and there was almost no grass
for haymaking. On the heavy land the harrow marks of April
could be seen right up to harvest. Then came a most bitter and
persistent frost in the winter of 1894–5, when drifts of snow from
6 to 14 feet deep covered the ground for weeks.

There can be little doubt but that the extraordinary succession of extreme weather conditions which marked the twenty years after 1874 combined with the upsurge of foreign competition and prevalence of low prices to create a sense of unending calamity among the farmers. One of the counties most badly affected by the wet of the later 1870s was Essex, and the heavy lands there were particularly difficult to let. John Oxley Parker, a local land agent, had repeated disappointments in trying to find a tenant for one of the farms in his care, Mosklyns, at Purleigh, near Maldon. One new tenant actually gave up even before installing himself in the farm:

> I thought that Mosklyns was off our hands, but luckily I did not write to tell you so. I waited till the thing should be settled. A man had agreed to take it and all seemed to be arranged. He had seen the farm once or twice – I think more during fine weather. The wet autumn came and when he made his move to Purleigh, with implements and horses and household goods, the farm was drenched by recent rain. It was

in such a state of mud that he was fairly frightened. He came to say that his things were on the road but on going to the fields he cried out to the man at the farm, 'I'm not going to stop here; I shall be ruined if I do!' and he stood in the road till the carts and wagons came up, turned them round and went straight off back to his own country on the borders of Cambridgeshire.

The owner of Mosklyns, Sir George Brooke-Pechell, met further problems when another of his properties, Hazeleigh Hall, fell into hand. It was advisable, he thought, to look further afield for prospective tenants, and he sent his agent some interesting information about the possibility of attracting farmers from Scotland, should a man called Payne fail to take up a lease of Hazeleigh:

> I have been lately in the North of England and Scotland . . . When in Scotland I heard that there are a great many young farmers wanting farms in England – they have a notion that they know a thing or two which we don't, and that if they could get cheaper labour and cheaper rents, which are to be had in the South, they could see their way to an eventual fortune. I propose therefore advertising in The Scotsman if this Payne(ful) nibble does not end in a bite.

Scotsmen, in fact did come to the rescue of landowners in Essex, as elsewhere, taking the farms on knock-down terms and converting them to dairying. In 1891 Primrose McConnell wrote in the Royal Agricultural Society's *Journal* of the 'Scotch Colony' which had grown up around Ongar, Brentwood, and Chelmsford. Many of these newcomers had come from the dairying district about Kilmarnock in Ayrshire, so it was natural that they should see dairying as the answer in Essex. Why did they come? Because, they said, of excessive rents at home, caused by the severe competition for small dairy farms in that part of Scotland.

> It is a gratifying feature of this Northern irruption that no English farmer has lost a home to make way for the in-comers, so far as I am aware. The farms were either quite unoccupied, worked by the landlord, or the old tenant was leaving in any case, and if the North-countryman had not arrived there would have been no tenant at all. As to the reasons why the latter succeeds where the former failed (or apparently does so – for ten years is perhaps too short a time in which to judge of

the success of a movement), I have my own opinion, but it is outside the scope of this paper to enter on this question.

The author's delicacy was perhaps needless, for the reasons for the Scots' success were embodied in the innovations described. Briefly, they brought in new ideas and new methods: they abolished bare fallows, and instead went in for heavier manuring and temporary pastures, and they replaced the old Essex wooden plough by modern implements requiring smaller teams. Hence their system economized in both men and horses, and that was their secret.

The failing English farmer who made way for the Scot was a familiar figure in the 1870s and 1880s. As Richard Jefferies remarked, the bankrupt farmer, unlike the bankrupt tradesman, could not just put up his shutters at once and retire from view.

So far as his neighbours are concerned he is in public view for years previously. He has to rise in the morning and meet them in the fields. He sees them in the road; he passes through groups of them in the market-place. As he goes by they look after him, and perhaps audibly wonder how long he will last. These people all knew him from a lad, and can trace every inch of his descent. The labourers in the field know it, and by their manner show that they know it.

His wife – his wife who worked so hard for so many, many years – is made to know it too. She is conspicuously omitted from the social gatherings that occur from time to time. The neighbours' wives do not call; their well-dressed daughters, as they rattle by to the town in basket-carriage or dog-cart, look askance at the shabby figure walking slowly on the path beside the road . . .

Many of those farmers who managed to survive the depression were nevertheless worn down by the long succession of adverse circumstances. At Ardleigh in Essex one man told Rider Haggard that if the landlord would let him out of his lease he would 'give up the following Michaelmas, as "he was tired of it" and ought to have left off twenty years before.' Another in Norfolk said he had not cleared £200 a year from his 332 acres for the past ten years, and had he not had private means 'could only have lived very roughly like a small farmer. Indeed he would have been better off if he had invested his capital and sat idle.' Many of those who did succeed in the depression years could draw on the income and capital of some other business. In the North Walsham district of

Norfolk nearly all the occupiers had some trade which they combined with farming. Often they managed because they lived very cheaply and farmed in the most economical way possible. In Dorset, Rider Haggard was told, the gentleman farmers had disappeared, having gone under one by one.

> Today there was a new type of farmer, who, as a rule, began life as a grocer, a village smith, or a shoemaker. This person lives on about 10s a week and goes to a sale to buy an old wagon for 50s. He has not a good horse on his farm, and no one would give 2s for the suit of clothes he wears. On an 800-acre holding he employs about four hands, and sometimes not so many, and is unprofitable to the landlord, the tradesman, and the labourer alike. But after a fashion, he makes farming pay.

With the depression came a breakdown of the old relationship between landlord and tenant. The landlord saw old tenants, whose families had occupied their land for generations, throw up leases and depart. Those landlords in the worst-hit areas, the arable districts of the east and south, were forced to find tenants among complete strangers, Scots, West-Country men, who not only had no connection with the estate but had no scruple in forcing the rent down to an unheard of level. The old tenants, for their part, saw that the landlords were powerless to halt the economic decline of farming, and were even unable to offer much in the way of new investment in buildings or help with the expense of converting arable land to grass.

The farmers' answer was to see what organization and self-help could do. Since the 1850s there had been a few farmer Members in Parliament, elected on current issues like the cattle plague or the malt tax, but they had been very few. For the most part, indeed, they had not been really representative of farmers in general, but rather they were well-to-do gentlemen, Conservative in their politics, men able to attract the support of the gentry as well as the farmers. The Chambers of Agriculture, too, like the various national and local agricultural societies, were joint affairs of landlords and farmers, but very much dominated by the former. The leading positions in the Chambers were held by men of title, and their spokesmen in Parliament were mainly Unionists, like Clare Sewell Read and Henry Chaplin, while the Chambers' attitude towards the farmers was traditionally paternal. As the forces of democracy and depression combined to erode the dominance of the landowners, the farmers turned more to new types of organization, ones specifically concerned with taking up the issues which most directly interested the farmers. One such issue was 'tenant right': there was a demand for legislation to make compulsory the compensation for unexhausted improvements customarily made to tenants leaving their farms.

The Farmers' Alliance was founded, significantly enough, in the fatal year of 1879. It had as its object the direct representation of farmers in Parliament, and played a part in obtaining the Agricultural Holdings Act of 1883, an Act which, in effect, made obligatory the permissive measure enacted in 1875. The Alliance was associated with the Liberals, who won the election of 1880, causing Disraeli to bemoan the 'insurrection of our old and natural friends, the farmers'. The role of the Alliance in the Liberal triumph was, however, a very limited one: only two independent tenant farmers were returned in 1880, and neither was connected with the Alliance. The Liberal victory did bring on some farming reforms: The Ground Game Act, which allowed tenants to destroy hares and rabbits on their own holdings, repeal of the unpopular Malt Tax, and the new Agricultural Holdings Act. Despite these concessions, the farmers' adherence to the Alliance proved shortlived. As rents fell after 1879 so the farmers tended to return to their old relationship with the landlords, while it became increasingly clear that no amount of tinkering with tenant right or the game laws was going to have much effect in coping with a depression caused by bad seasons, foreign competition and low prices. Protection seemed to hold the only answer, and by the mid 1880s the early enthusiasm aroused by the Alliance was rapidly fading away.

Another shortlived organization, Lord Winchelsea's National Agricultural Union, rashly attempted to combine the interests of the labourers into one body along with those of the landlords and farmers. Exhibiting strong Unionist leanings, the N.A.U. enjoyed a period of influence in the villages after 1892, but failed to survive the death of its founder in 1898. It was six years after this that nine farmers, meeting after the Blankney Hunt Dog Show, each put down a pound to establish the nucleus of the Lincolnshire Farmers' Union. The original moving spirit of this organization was E.W.Howard, a progressive farmer, Unionist supporter and temperance enthusiast, but the transformation in 1908 of the county movement into one of national scope, the National Farmers' Union, was largely the work of Colin Campbell, one of those Scotsmen who had moved into English farming. At this time the idea of forming a new Country Party was being canvassed, a product of the farmers' dissatisfaction with Parliament's neglect of their problems, and particularly their disappointment with the limited provisions of the new Agricultural Holdings Act of 1908. The N.F.U. saw its membership grow from 10,000 in 1910 to 15,000 five years later, though at the latter date the Union represented under a tenth of all farmers in England and Wales – and those the larger ones. It was, however, solely a farmers' organization, and so was quite unlike its predecessors, the Chambers, the Alliance, and the National Agricultural Union. Landlords and their agents, and middlemen like factors and dealers, were not allowed to be members of the N.F.U., which was confined to owner-occupiers and tenant farmers. Adopting the motto, 'Defence not Defiance', the N.F.U. soon became the powerful voice of agriculture: the government heeded it in framing measures to deal with the food shortages in the First World War, and has continued to do so ever since.

The N.F.U. grew up in a period when farming conditions, though not very prosperous, were on the mend. Its rise was clear evidence that the depression had done its work in breaking down the old subordination of farmers to the political leadership of landowners. If the N.F.U. was one form of organizational answer to the problems of these farmers who adopted an independent stance, cooperation was another. Contemporary observers thought that cooperation might well be instrumental in raising standards of output, securing better markets, and reducing the cost of farmers' materials. Rider Haggard, for example, visited Denmark, where the growth of cooperative dairies and bacon factories had enabled a nation of small farmers to capture much of the British market. Did Danish methods hold a lesson for England? On the whole it appeared not. The cooperative cheese and butter factories established in the midlands in the 1870s had few imitators. More farmers were encouraged to enter into contracts to supply milk to newly-established private creameries and to the private producers of dairy foods, condensed milk, and baby products. There was however, a growth of farmers' cooperatives concerned with bulk purchases of seeds, fertilizers, and feeding stuffs. These began in 1867, when market gardeners round London joined in an association. Growth of this type of cooperative was particularly rapid in the early years of the present century, and in 1914 there were some 200 such organizations with about 24,000 members. The less common marketing cooperatives were to be found in dairying and horticultural areas, particularly where there were numbers of smallish men engaged in cultivating the same kinds of produce. In general, however, cooperation never really caught on. Farmers were unable or unwilling to provide the necessary capital and skilled management, and to develop a loyalty to regular cash dealing with the cooperative. That majority of farmers who remained aloof preferred to deal direct with individual middlemen or retailers who seemed to offer better terms; and many clung to the traditional weekly visit to the nearby market town, a visit which was a social as well as business occasion, an opportunity of discussing matters with old friends and associates. English farmers as a whole showed an unwillingness to reveal their affairs to a wider circle, or to lose their individuality by falling in with standardized methods and standardized products.

If the diversity of English farming conditions and production was unfavourable to cooperation, it was also a reason why agriculture was not universally depressed in the quarter-century after 1875. Dairy farmers saw the butter, cheese and bacon markets dominated by the Danes and Irish, but benefitted from the big expansion of the liquid milk trade. Potatoes, market gardens, and orchards were generally profitable, too, as the numbers of urban consumers grew and tended to become better off. Consumption of dairy produce, vegetables, salad stuff and fruit were all closely related to income. Producers of store cattle and fat-stock specialists had little to fear from imported meat so long as the butchers' customers preferred the home-produced article and were prepared to pay more for it. Only those farmers who relied heavily on corn were severely and permanently affected by imports and low prices, though the unusually numerous years of rain and floods, hard winters, cold summers, and droughts, and the consequent shortages of fodder, cheapness of livestock and the disastrous outbreaks of animal disease, all caused distress which was very widespread.

In recent years historians have tended to minimize the effects of the 'great depression' in agriculture, arguing that the numerous farmers who depended on pasture products were not badly hit, if hit at all, and that the evidence of depression conditions given to the two Royal Commissions of enquiry was heavily flavoured by the problems of the corn areas. But this view overlooks, or discounts, the widely pervasive influence of the long series of unfavourable seasons and livestock losses, and neglects the political and social background against which the decline of English agriculture should be set. That farmers all over the country believed themselves depressed is evident from their complaints, and from the memoirs and investigations of writers like Lord Ernle and Rider Haggard. For it was not merely that prices were low and markets uncertain. The farmers found agriculture – not so many years before the premier source of the country's wealth – sacrificed to the urban consumers' interest in cheap food, while agriculture's grievances were neglected by a Parliament in which the landed interest had an ever-declining voice. Contemporary changes in the village, particularly the emancipation of the labourer and his flight from the land – what Liberals and Radicals saw as encouraging signs of progress – were viewed by the farmers as portents of even more difficulties to come. It was little wonder that when things were at their worst many old farmers thought it was time to go. The times bred up a new kind of farmer, one who was strictly economical and severely business-like, who was prepared to bend with the wind, farm cheaply and employ as few hands as possible, and who looked to organization to protect his interests. In this sense the great farming depression was a true watershed in the country's farming history.

Harvesting, reproduced from Copeland's *Agriculture Ancient & Modern*, 1866, after an engraving of a painting by John Linnell, 1857.

4   The Farmworkers

When the farming population was at its peak in 1851 there were 1,284,000 male farm workers and 199,000 females in English agriculture. They were not spread evenly over the countryside, for in pastoral and upland districts, especially in the North and West, there were many small farms and holdings worked solely by the farmer and his family. Even the pasture farms devoted to large-scale fattening for the market employed fewer hands than did farms of comparable size in the arable South and East. It was generally held that while every 25 or 30 acres of arable required a man's labour, the figure for grass was 50 or 60 acres. Another regional difference was that in the pastoral North it was still common for the farmworker to live in the farmhouse with his master, sharing his table, and sleeping in a garret in the roof. The Earnshaws' scripture-quoting Joseph at Wuthering Heights is a fictional representative of a class of farm servants which remained common in remote districts even at the end of the nineteenth century. In the south, however, living-in had largely died out in the previous century, perhaps because it was cheaper to house the labourers in cottages, and not have to feed them, as Cobbett alleged; or, more probably, because the labouring population grew and social habits changed more rapidly among the status-conscious large farmers of the southern counties.

Farmworkers were differentiated also by skills and conditions of work, and the more highly skilled enjoyed the highest status and better rates of pay. Men who acquired a reputation in rather unusual skills might work as independent craftsmen – expert thatchers, drainers, and hedgers – who contracted with the farmers and villagers of the neighbourhood, travelling from place to place, and often doing a little higgling or dealing in provisions on the side. The men and women whose attendance was required on the farm every day, shepherds, the carters who looked after the horses and oxen, the foggers and milkers and dairymaids who tended the dairy, were generally hired by the year as farm servants. In the north they lived in, and in the south they had a cottage by the farm. In some counties, like Hardy's Dorset, they made it a practice to change masters regularly. Towards the end of winter masters and men resorted to the hiring fairs, where the men seeking new masters stood in the market place with some symbol of their trade to indicate the employment required. 'Among these, carters and waggoners were distinguished by having a piece of whipcord twisted round their hats; thatchers wore a fragment of woven straw; shepherds held their sheep-crooks in their hands; and thus the situation required was known to the farmers at a glance.' Gabriel Oak, it may be remembered, failing to find a place as bailiff, quickly bought himself a crook and smock-frock and turned himself into a shepherd. Many farm servants, however, stayed always in the same trade and lived with the same farmer for many long years. Such a one was George Piper, a shepherd whom Rider Haggard met near Andover in 1901:

> Then over seventy years of age, for sixty of them he had been a shepherd, forty years of that time being spent in the employ of a single master. Sunk as he was in eld, it was easy for anyone accustomed to watch his class, to see that in very many cases the services of two men of the present generation would be of less value than those of this shepherd, who knew his sheep and was known of them. There he stood in the cold wind upon the bleak Down crest watching the fold much as the dog does, and now and again passing the hurdles to do some little service to his flock, every one of which he could distinguish from the other. This, too, on a Sunday, the day on which it is so difficult to keep the modern stockman to work, however necessary.

A farm servant who lived in could save part of his wages, and these savings, deposited over some years in a local savings bank, sometimes ran to considerable sums. After a time, the farm servant might decide to marry and set up on his own. Not so with the day labourers, who generally married young and had families to keep on wages which, in mid-century, might in some areas be as low as six or seven shillings a week. Fortunately, the wife was often able to bring something in, and the children too, if they were old enough. Some farmers, indeed, would hire only those men who had a wife and son capable of helping in the fields. Alternatively, the wife took in washing, sold eggs or her own home-made pies and confectionery, or spent her spare time in some village craft such as glove-making, pillow lace or straw-plaiting.

Day labourers' wages varied greatly from the low-paid counties of southern England to the more highly paid counties of the north, the difference reflecting variations in the supply of labour and the alternative occupations available. In 1851, James Caird, surveying English farming for *The Times*, calculated that wages in the north were on average 3s a week or 37 per cent higher than in the south. In Lincolnshire, a middling county, the average wage for a man in 1851 was 11s a week, and women and children could earn 2s a day at harvesting, 1s 9d at lifting potatoes, and 9d at weeding and planting. The villages contained numerous friendly societies, savings banks, coal clubs and clothing clubs. In nearby Nottinghamshire wages were higher, the average income for a family was between 12s and a pound, and the labourers enjoyed the advantage of cheap coal. The situation was much less happy in the low-wage areas. Wages in Devon, even as late as the 1860s, averaged only between 7s and 8s, together with three or four pints of inferior cider. The normal day was 10½ hours, and women's work was paid at only 7d or 8d a day. In southern Wiltshire, the nadir of poor farm wages, men's weekly rates fell from 12s at the end of the French Wars to average only 7s–7s 6d between 1817 and 1844. Skilled men, carters and shepherds, earned another 2s a week, but had to put in additional hours. Over the country as a whole, however, there was a rise in wages as farm labour became less plentiful after mid-century. In 1850 the average figure was 9s 7d (11s 6d in the high-wage areas, 8s 5d in the low). In 1860 it was 11s 7d, 1870 12s, 1880 13s 9d, and by 1914 15s (13s in the low-wage areas).

Figures collected in 1838 by Dr Kay, Assistant Poor Law Commissioner for Norfolk and Suffolk, showed that the average annual income of those labourers with children over the age of ten rose by about £5 a year for each child at work. A Suffolk labourer's family, consisting of wife and five children, spent a weekly income of 10s as follows:

	s	d
2½ stone of flour	6	10½
yeast		3
rent	1	7½
coal		10
candles		3½

leaving 1½d over for clothing, beer, tobacco and all other items.

In Dorset, according to the Royal Commission Report on Labour of 1893–4, ordinary labourers earned 10s a week, and carters, shepherds and cowmen from 11s to 13s. They got an extra 1s 6d or 2s if no cottage was available. Boys received from 4s upwards, and women 9d–10d a day. There was an additional pound a year for fuel in lieu of furze, and coal was hauled free to the cottages by the farmer. Shepherds received extra payments of 1d for each lamb reared (6d for twins), and 12s or 13s for every 100 sheep sheared. Allotments of 20 to 40 perches were available, for which the men paid 3d per perch (£2 an acre), but in case of sickness labouring families had to resort to the parish for the services of a doctor. Hours in summer were six to six (but until eight p.m. at haytime and harvest), and in winter seven to five. A budget for a family consisting of man, wife and five children worked out as follows:

Income :	s	d	Expenditure :	s	d
Man	11	0	Bread	6	3
Boy aged 14	5	0	Bacon	1	8
Boy aged 11	1	6	Cheese	1	0
	17	6	Butter	1	3
			Tea & Sugar	1	9
			Flour		$5\frac{1}{2}$
			Club subscription		9
			Tobacco		3
			Lights & Sundries		9
				14	$1\frac{1}{2}$

Day labourers received part of their wages in kind. The cottage was often free or let at a nominal rent, and the farmers frequently supplied some form of fuel, though it might only be peat, furze, or in Wales, culm, balls of coal-dust. The cottage went with the job, and when the labourer changed master he changed cottage too. This might well put him in the farmer's hands: for fear of losing his home he might be frightened to ask for more wages, request a day off for some important purpose, or even ask for repairs to be made to the cottage. On the other hand, the tied cottage ensured the farmer a workman as it ensured the workman a home. Tied cottages existed in many other occupations, among railwaymen, police, schoolteachers, and factory employees living in the manufacturer's houses. And in areas like Dorset, where the farm hands changed masters every year, the tied cottage does not seem to have deterred them from moving.

Other payments in kind might include milk, a potato patch or vegetable ground, an occasional sack of flour at a standard rate, and perhaps a flitch of bacon. To many of the men the most important consideration was the daily allowance of drink. This was ale, or in the West Country cider, and the quantity allowed might be as high as half a gallon or even more. At harvest time a barrel was placed in a corner of the field and the workers helped themselves. The allowance of drink was much prized. Not only did it make something to look forward to, a pleasant break in a monotonous task, but it helped to wash down the tedious midday fare of bread and cheese and provided valuable nourishment. Temperance reformers might rail against the custom, but drink was a standard part of the wage, and it was difficult to get workers even to start a job without it. Labourers often regarded it as a good ground for staying in a low-paid, arduous employment which offered no prospects. An American farmer, Frederick Law Olmstead, remarked on this when he visited England in 1850. In the tap-room of his inn at Warminster he found

> three fellows with smock-frocks. As I approached, one called to another, who was nearer the fire, to give me his seat, and offered me, with truly rustic grace, his half-emptied pot of beer. I dislike to repulse what is meant for kindness; so I tasted it, and tried to enter into conversation with them. I soon found it was impossible; for I could make nothing of two-thirds of their replies, and I doubted if they could understand me much better. So I contented myself with listening, while they continued to talk or mumble with each other. The subjects of their conversation were beer and 'the girls': of the latter topic they said nothing to be repeated; of the former, they wished the farmers never gave worse drink than that they were now enjoying – 'it was most good for nothing, some of it, what they gave out.' And one told how he had had to drink so much of it once, it had made him clear sick; and then another told how, on the other hand, he had made himself sick one day, when somebody wouldn't give him as much beer as he wanted, by taking a draught of cold water.

Impressed by the poor wages and bad conditions, Olmstead once tried to persuade an English labourer that he and his family would be far better off in the United States. His arguments were all rejected, however, once it was discovered that American farmers did not give their men a free allowance of drink:

> 'And how much beer?'
> 'None at all!'
> 'None at all? ha, ha! he'd not go then – you'd not catch him workin' withouten his drink. No, no! a man 'ould die off soon that gait.'
> It was in vain that we offered fresh meat as an offset to the beer. There was 'strength', he admitted, in beef, but it was

wholly incredible that a man could work on it. A working-man must have zider or beer – there was no use to argue against that. That 'Jesus Christ came into the world to save sinners,' and that 'work without beer is death,' was the alpha and omega of his faith.

The women and children were sometimes employed in gangs under a foreman, who contracted with a farmer to lift potatoes, pick fruit, harvest vegetables, weed and rake up couch grass or clear the ground of large stones. Gangs were especially common in the eastern counties where enclosures had brought new land into cultivation 'and the local supply of labour was inadequate. But they were also found elsewhere, and there were gangs employed in cockling on Morecambe Bay and the Norfolk coast. The work was hard and the hours long. Sometimes the gang was conveyed to the field in the farmer's waggon, but often there was a long tramp through the rain and muddy lanes before work began, and again at the end of the day. In winter snow and icy winds bit at faces, froze feet and fingers, and caused chilblains. In summer the gang was thankful for some shade in which to rest for their meal breaks, and heavy morning dews soaked the skirts of the girls. Farmwormers as a class were relatively healthy and long-lived when compared with many other occupations, but they suffered from rheumatism and similar painful complaints, and became bent and crippled in old age. Characteristically, Victorian reformers were more concerned about the moral dangers of gang work, the degradation of the female workers and loss of 'feminine delicacy', than with its hardships and miserable pay. Young girls were in the fields all day with only low companions – a gangmaster or foreman, perhaps some men to help, and older women, all of possibly doubtful character. It was the moral concern which led to the regulatory Gangs Act of 1867: gang masters had thenceforth to be licensed, and children under the age of eight could no longer be employed. The gangs continued, and indeed the use of casual labour in farming has tended to increase over the years, though the hiring of children was much restricted by the coming of compulsory education and child employment regulations.

Labourers' usual hours were from six to six in summer, with an hour and a half off for meals, and from seven or first light to dusk in winter. Farm servants put in extra hours fetching hay, preparing teams, and tending to the horses and cows, often starting at four or five a.m. These tasks had to be done every day of the week, and Sunday work occupied three or four hours.

Whether day labourers were paid in bad weather was a variable matter. In long periods of snow or frost they might not be required at all, but on the occasional days of heavy rain they were often employed in the barn at threshing or other jobs. Part of Sunday, and meal hours in the week if the allotment were handy, would be spent in raising vegetables, but often the allotment or potato ground was as much as a mile or more off and many hours were spent in tramping to and fro.

Harvest was the busy season of the year. Every man and woman was required from dawn to dusk, and although horse-drawn mechanical reapers came in from about the 1850s they were for long supplementary to hand labour and most of the corn was still cut by scythe, sickle or bagging hook. It was laborious work and slow, and a gang of five, led by a good scytheman, required a day to cut two acres. Frequently Irish harvesting gangs, or English, Welsh and Scots, were hired to help out. Some of these gangs went to the same farms every year, and the farmers came to depend on them, just as the London east-enders travelled down each September to the same Kentish hop gardens. Women and youngsters followed the men to help rake, bind, and stook. Even the mechanical reapers required numerous hands to rake and stook the cut corn out of the way of the machine's return path

Harvest home at Swallowfield, near Reading, 1860.

across the field. When the weather was favourable and the corn was not 'laid' and difficult to cut, harvest had its compensations. Workers made a special contract with the farmers for the harvest: wages were good, and there was plenty of food and drink. And when all the corn was in the stacks there was the harvest home, with all the hands at a long table headed by the farmer and his lady, sometimes the squire himself, and there was fiddling and dancing in the barn. But as time went by the harvest supper was dropped and cash paid in lieu. The plentiful drink in the harvest field led to fights and accidents. And in the age of hand tools it was hard, hard work, and haymaking was just as arduous. 'Hay was similarly made in all its stages by hand, and with a care which preserved its colour and scent. The grass, mown by the scythe, fell into swathes. These were broken up by the haymakers, drawn with the hand-rake into windrows, first single, then double. The double windrows were pulled over once, put first into small cocks, then into larger which were topped up and trimmed so as to be shower proof, and finally arranged in cart rows for pitching and loading. Women, working behind the carts, allowed scarcely a blade to escape their rakes.'

The harvest feast, such as it was, made one of the few breaks in a daily round of work, meagre meals, and sleep. The labourers' diet was especially monotonous, with a heavy reliance on bread – bread and cheese, bread and milk, bread and bacon, bread and dripping – though with greater use of oatmeal and porridge in the north. Northern labourers were better paid, and they often had the great comfort of cheap coal, which made it possible to keep cottages warmer and allowed more hot food to be cooked. In the south fuel was often scarce and expensive, there was less hot food and fewer fires, and the chimneys sometimes smoked so abominably that the door had always to be open when the fire was lit. Milk, unless supplied free by the farmers, was not so much used as might be supposed, and during the early decades of the nineteenth century tea became the common drink, at least of the women and children. Its substitution for beer was decried by some contemporaries who thought the tea less healthful and less sustaining. In extreme poverty burnt toast was soaked in hot water to produce some feeble imitation of tea. A kitchen garden, allotment or potato patch provided vegetables, though in some parishes the labourers complained about the lack of allotments, the farmers being unwilling to release land for the purpose. Where there was a little land vegetables helped to eke out the diet. There was a great belief in the health-giving properties of certain garden stuff, particularly onions and watercress. On his 1901–2 tour of Rural England Rider Haggard met a poor labourer who could recall a diet which consisted of little but bread and onions.

Not far from Blunt's Hall I saw an old labourer named John Lapwood, whose life experience, which I verified by inquiry, is worth preserving. For half a century or more he worked on the Post Hall and Oliver Farms in Witham, and now, by the help of some kind friends, was spending his last days in a little cottage, where he lived with his old wife. We found him – an aged and withered but still an apple-cheeked individual – seated upon a bank, 'enjoying of the sweet air, although it be a bit draughty'. He told me that in his young days wages for horsemen used to be down to 9s a week, and for daymen to 8s, when the weather allowed them to be earned. During the Crimean War bread cost him a shilling a loaf, and other food a proportionate price. He stated that for months at a time he had existed upon nothing but a diet of bread and onions, washed down, when he was lucky, with a little small-beer. These onions he ate until they took the skin off the roof of his mouth, blistering it to whiteness, after which he was obliged to soak them in salt to draw the 'virtue' out of them. They had no tea, but his wife imitated the appearance of that beverage by soaking a burnt crust of bread in boiling water. On this diet he became so feeble that the reek of the muck which it was his duty to turn, made him sick and faint; and often, he said, he would walk home at night from the patch of ground where he grew the onions and some other vegetables, with swimming head and uncertain feet. I asked if his children, of whom there were eight, lived on onions also. He answered no; they had generally a little cheese and butter in the house, but he could not put it into his own stomach when they were hungry and cried for food. 'Things is better now' he added.

The possession of a pig was luxury – Cobbett measured labourers' happiness by the number of their pigs. It was sometimes difficult to find them enough to eat, and often the pig had to be sold to pay off debts or buy clothing. Many labourers were permanently in debt, and relied on their pigs, the extra harvest earnings, or the wife's earnings and the family's additional field work to clear themselves and make it possible to get warm clothes and new boots against the winter. Some managed to pay a few coppers a week into a friendly society or coal club as a means of guarding against a rainy day. But many of these clubs were unsound and they were marked by a high rate of failure.

Observers complained that English women had little idea of how to make the best of what they had. They lacked the skill of continental housewives, who from similar materials could produce a variety of tasty soups and stews. Lack of time and of fuel, and inadequate cooking facilities were perhaps as important here as lack of knowledge. Cobbett opposed potatoes because they needed cooking. Labourers, too, were notoriously conservative in their food habits. During the Napoleonic Wars when harvests failed and bread was very dear, some landowners tried to educate the farmworkers into using rice. Sir Joseph Banks, the famous botanist, imported rice from London and had recipes printed for his Lincolnshire farm people, but to little avail. As time went by, village housewives came to rely more on the newly-appearing village shop and baker's vans. Already by 1850 manufactured bread was widely bought in the countryside, especially in the southern counties. The art of home baking, it was reported, was almost unknown in Kent, Surrey, Sussex and Middlesex, and only Devonshire and Suffolk maintained a reputation for their cottage loaves. Unknown to the country housewife, from the 1880s manufactured bread was made from the new roller-milled flour, whiter and finer than the old stone-ground kind, but largely lacking in valuable proteins and phosphates. The canned condensed milk, also popular towards the end of the century, was made from evaporated skimmed milk deficient in Vitamins A and D and in fats, and helped give children rickets. Country folk were thought by doctors to be under-nourished, and certainly the typical country diet left much to be desired.

The labourers' diet varied greatly from one part of the country to another. This arose partly from the prevalence of regional dishes and habits, but also from differences in the level of wages, the cost and availability of fuel, and the nature and quality of the food given or sold to the men as part of their traditional payment. This food might include wheat, butter, cheese, milk, mutton and bacon, though again the amounts and the quality varied from one district to another, and sometimes the labourer was obliged to pay a high price to the farmer for inferior produce, or even accept meat from diseased animals, which could not be taken to market. In mid-century the living in the areas of lowest wages might be hard indeed. Going through Salisbury Plain in 1850, James Caird found a man's weekly wages to be 7s, with a shilling of this to be paid for his cottage.

We were curious to know how the money was economized, and heard from a labourer the following account of a day's diet. After doing up his horses he takes breakfast, which is made of flour with a little butter, and water 'from the tea-kettle' poured over it. He takes with him to the field a piece of bread and (if he has not a young family, and can afford it) cheese to eat at mid-day. He returns home in the afternoon to a few potatoes, and possibly a little bacon, though only those who are better off can afford this. The supper very commonly consists of bread and water. The appearance of the labourers showed, as might be expected from such meagre diet, a want of that vigour and activity which mark the well-fed ploughmen of the northern and midland counties. Beer is given by the master in hay-time and harvest. Some farmers allow ground for planting potatoes to their labourers, and carry home their fuel – which, on the downs, where there is no wood, is a very expensive article in a labourer's family.

An enquiry conducted in 1863 by Dr Edward Smith indicated that English labourers ate less well than did their fellows in Wales, Scotland and Ireland, particularly because they took less milk. There was a tendency for the best part of the food, especially the meat, to go to the husband, leaving his wife and children little but bread and potatoes. This was markedly so where the family was young, where a vegetable allotment was not to be had, and work for the wife was scarce. Although the wide regional variations in incomes and food habits make average figures not very meaningful, they clearly showed that bread, with $12\frac{1}{4}$ lbs consumed weekly by each adult, and potatoes at 6 lbs, were basic to the labourers' way of life. An average of only 16 oz of meat was eaten by each adult weekly, and many families never had butcher's meat: a sheep's head, pluck, or half a cow's head filled the stewpot, and even provided the best meal of the week, Sunday dinner. Tea, drunk very weak, and often without sugar or milk, was the standard beverage of wife and children, the husband getting his beer or cider in the field. The quantities of milk, butter and cheese consumed were often surprisingly small. Examples provided of typical meals again showed the significance of regional variations:

Lancashire : breakfast – milk, porridge, coffee, bread and butter; dinner – meat and potatoes, or meat pie, rice pudding or a baked pudding; the husband takes ale, bread and cheese; supper – tea, toasted cheese, and bacon instead of butter.

Devon : breakfast and supper – tea-kettle broth (bread, hot

water, salt, and $\frac{1}{2}$ pint of milk), bread and treacle; dinner –
pudding (flour, salt and water), vegetables, and fresh meat; no
bread.

There is the possibility, as Caird hinted, that where wages and
diet were inadequate, the labourers' inferior strength and energy
meant that more men had to be employed for tasks which
occupied fewer hands in the north. Certainly, some southern
labourers were remarked for their slowness of gait and their
measured pace of work. And this may, in part, be an explanation
of the miserable level of wages paid in areas of southern England.
However, as the century wore on and the men's wages advanced,
there were corresponding improvements in their food. By 1902, a
Board of Trade Report showed, many farm labourers' diet was
on a par with, or even above, the average consumption for the
country at large. They were now eating as much or more meat,
bacon, cheese, and sugar, and drinking as much milk and tea,
while jam, margarine, coffee and cocoa were quite common. But
again average figures can give a misleading impression, and
although standards generally had risen greatly there was still a
great deal of inadequate nutrition, as there was among the poor in
the towns; and some of the farm labourers' gains were lost in the
years after 1902 as prices tended to rise faster than wages.

Though the rise in wages towards the end of the nineteenth
century and the fall then in food prices made possible marked
improvements in diet, labourers' incomes were pinched in new
directions. Compulsory education, introduced in the decade after
1870, meant that children's earnings were curtailed, though there
was a good deal of truancy. Equally serious, before school fees
were abolished in 1891, the few pence a week which it cost to send
children to school was a heavy burden on an income that might
well be much below 20s. This was especially the case where there
were several children of school age, though the fees could be
remitted to the very needy. However, wages were advancing, and
clothes and household necessities were getting cheaper. Observers remarked some interesting signs of greater affluence among
country folk. Furniture improved, cottages were less bare, there
was the occasional outing to a fair. Even bicycles and prams began
to be seen, there was carpet on the staircase, possibly the
occasional piano. People got about a little more, men began to
read newspapers and attend political meetings, the old isolation
of village life was breaking down.

Whether housing improved very much it is difficult to say.
Except in some places where, later in the century, population had

declined, cottages were generally in short supply. The basic difficulty, as Rider Haggard pointed out, was that

> no one can afford to build houses which return no interest; because also the land cannot reward the labourer sufficiently to enable him to build his own or by the payment of an adequate rent, to make it profitable for anyone else to build it for him.

At any time in the century a great deal of the housing available was antiquated, cramped, and insanitary. A row of little cottages, with crooked walls and ragged thatch, might look picturesque, but the romantic exterior concealed squalor and wretchedness within. Large families lived in one or two rooms, with earth floors that 'heaved' and were sometimes awash in winter with damp or even flowing with spring water. Neither roof nor walls were rain-proof, dirt and droppings oozed from the thatch, and water had to be fetched in from a pond, pump or rain barrel. One or two privies at the end of the garden might have to serve for eight or ten families. Rider Haggard found that bad housing was a major factor in labour leaving the farms.

> Of course the lowness of the wage and the lack of prospect will always cause a great number, perhaps a majority, of the more enterprising spirits to desert the land, but I am convinced that there are large numbers who would bide in their villages if only they could be sure of constant work and find decent homes in which to live . . . Let anybody who is curious to know leave the main roads and the more populated villages where there are resident gentry . . . Let him examine the hamlets for himself – those of the stamp of Cratfield by Halesworth, for instance – and ask for a few particulars from the parson or from any old fellow whom he meets upon the road. Then, in nine cases out of ten, he will hear that there used to be more houses than there are now, that so many have fallen down and never been rebuilt and that certain young folk who wanted to marry have gone away because they could find no cottage decent enough in which to live . . . There are the dwellings that look so pretty in summer, with roses and ivy creeping about their crumbling stud work and their rotten thatch, but which often enough are scarcely fit to be inhabited by human beings. There, close at hand, perhaps conveniently placed to receive the surface drainage from the road, or even in wet times from the new-manured fields, is a pond, the local supply of drinking water. A little further down the street there

may be houses such as I told of in Whissonsett, their roofs fallen in, their windows broken, their walls cracked.

Gradually they have become uninhabitable and, the owners being unable or unwilling to repair them, they have been suffered to sink to ruin . . .

Conditions, however, varied considerably. In some landlord's villages the houses might be substantial brick dwellings, on two floors, with two sizeable downstairs rooms and two or three bedrooms above, a cellar or pantry, a copper and kitchen range, and a shed for coal or wood. Such houses might not be very new, but they had been built reasonably well in the first place and were kept in good repair by the estate. At Grafham, Huntingdonshire, the Duke of Manchester built cottages with three good bedrooms and a living room 14ft by 12ft, while in 1893 Lord Leconfield rented newly-built houses at North Stoke in Sussex at 1s 6d a week – for four bedrooms, a living room 12ft by 12ft, kitchen, and large garden. Similarly, rows of dwellings erected by country manufacturers for their work-people were generally of a superior kind. Some industrialists, indeed, built model villages, as did Titus Salt, a Bradford textile manufacturer, in 1854. His village, near Bradford, retained a rural aspect for it looked across to open country and a great park. The cheaper cottages at Saltaire had from three to six bedrooms and let at rents of from 2s 4d a week. Unfortunately, when farm rents and profits fell heavily in the later nineteenth century landowners and farmers often lacked the money to build new cottages or keep old ones in good repair, while the introduction of stringent bye-laws raised the cost of building and made it even more uneconomic.

Even on landlords' estates there were some very old cottages, mud and stud hovels which went back to the previous century and before. Sometimes they were let on leases for lives, an archaic and uncertain form of tenure which had the effect of discouraging expenditure on improvements and repairs. Even in the early decades of the nineteenth century many houses run up by village speculators lacked proper foundations and dampcourses and anything but the slightest provision for drainage. Such builders, often petty landowners and tradesmen taking advantage of the increase in numbers, were concerned only with making quick profits from high rents. They made no attempt to build well, or even safely. Cheapness was the only consideration. The walls were constructed of the cheapest kind of brick, highly porous, and often only half a brick thick. They cracked, became damp, and threatened imminent collapse.

First letter from the emigrants, after Faed. This mid-nineteenth century illustration depicts probably the only literate member of the family reading the letter aloud.

Housing in the countryside was rarely plentiful. There was a tendency for the farmworkers to be herded into the oldest and most dilapidated dwellings, as the newer houses, with their higher rents, were occupied by the better-paid craftsmen, industrial workers, railwaymen, and other newcomers. The consequence of population growth was to increase the size of families and hence intensify overcrowding. There were 'close' parishes where the land was in a few hands and the owners were concerned to keep down the labouring population in the interest of low poor rates. Cottages were pulled down as they became vacant and not replaced. The farmers hired their men from neighbouring parishes, the 'open' ones, where the speculative builders and tradesmen thrived.

Those who knew something of the reality which lay behind the romantic, 'natural' façades of rustic hovels, had some hard things to say. Edwin Chadwick, the sanitary reformer, described in 1842 some mud and stud cottages in the Vale of Aylesbury:

The vegetable substances mixed with the mud to make it bind, rapidly decompose, leaving the walls porous. The earth of the floor is full of vegetable matter, and from there being nothing to cut off its contact with the surrounding mould, it is peculiarly liable to damp . . .

Cobden noted Welsh farm labourers as living 'in mud huts, with only one room for sleeping, cooking and living – different ages and sexes herding together. Their cottages have no windows, but a hole through the mud wall to admit the air and light, into which a bundle of rags or turf is thrust at night to stop it up.' A few years later, in 1850, Caird, as *The Times'* special agricultural commissioner, reported on Wark Castle in Northumberland: It was, he said,

> the very picture of slovenliness and neglect. Wretched houses
> piled here and there without order – filth of every kind
> scattered about or heaped up against the walls – horses, cows
> and pigs lodged under the same roof with their owners, and
> entering by the same door – in many cases a pigsty beneath
> the only window of the dwellings – 300 people, 60 horses and
> 50 cows, besides hosts of pigs and poultry – such is the village
> of Wark.

Bad water supplies, inadequate drainage and sanitation, damp draughty rooms, and indifference about the removal of accumulated rubbish – all spelt disease. Diarrhoea, typhus and various other fevers, the dreaded typhoid and cholera sometimes ravaged cottages as severely as they did the scabrous slums of the cities. John Fox, medical officer of the Cerne Poor Law Union in Dorset, reported in 1842 as follows:

> It is somewhat singular that seven cases of typhus occurred
> in one village heretofore famed for the health and general
> cleanliness of its inhabitants and cottages. The first five cases
> occurred in one family, in a detached house on high and dry
> ground, and free from accumulations of vegetable or animal
> matter. The cottage was originally built for a school-room,
> and consists of one room only, about 18ft by 10 and 9 high.
> About one-third part was partitioned off by boards reaching
> to within three feet of the roof, and in this small space were
> three beds, in which six persons slept; had there been two
> bedrooms attached to this one day-room, these cases of typhus
> would not have occurred. The fatal case of typhus occurred in
> a very small village, containing about sixty inhabitants, and
> from its locality it appears favourable to the production of
> typhus, synochus, and acute rheumatism. It stands between
> two hills, with a river running through it, and is occasionally
> flooded. It has extensive water meadows both above and
> below, and a farm-yard in the centre, where there is always a

large quantity of vegetable matter undergoing decomposition. Most of the cases of synochus occurred under circumstances favourable to its production. Most of the cottages being of the worst description, some mere mud hovels, and situated in low and damp places with cesspools or accumulations of filth close to the doors. The mud floors of many are much below the level of the road, and in wet seasons are little better than so much clay. The following shocking case occurred in my practice. In a family consisting of six persons, two had fever; the mud floor of their cottage was at least one foot below the lane; it consisted of one small room only, in the centre of which stood a foot-ladder reaching to the edge of a platform which extended over nearly one-half of the room, and upon which were placed two beds, with space between them for one person only to stand, whilst the outside of each touched the thatch. The head of one of these beds stood within six inches of the edge of the platform, and in this bed one of my unfortunate patients, a boy about 11 years old, was sleeping with his mother, and in a fit of delirium, jumped over the head of his bed and fell to the ground below, a height of about seven feet. The injury to the head and spine was so serious that he lived a few hours only after the accident. In a cottage fit for the residence of a human being this could not have occurred. In many of the cottages, also, where synochus prevailed, the beds stood on the ground-floor, which was damp three parts of the years; scarcely one had a fireplace in the bed-room, and one had a single small pane of glass stuck in the mud wall as its only window, with a large heap of wet and dirty potatoes in one corner. Persons living in such cottages are generally very poor, very dirty, and usually in rags, living almost wholly on bread and potatoes, scarcely ever tasting animal food, and consequently highly susceptible of disease and very unable to contend with it. I am quite sure if such persons were placed in good, comfortable, clean cottages, the improvement in themselves and children would soon be visible, and the exceptions would only be found in a few of the poorest and most wretched, who perhaps had been born in a mud hovel, and had lived in one the first 30 years of their lives.

Fortunately some landowners had an interest in replacing old cottages with new. Their motives were mixed. Sound, neat cottages added to the respectability of the estate and the reputation of its owner. They attracted good tenants to the farms because superior farmers were concerned to get the best labour. Improved housing, it was also believed, had a powerful moral effect, encouraging cleanliness, thrift, and sobriety. Whatever the motives, profit was not one of them. It was virtually impossible to build good cottages to let to farmworkers and get a reasonable return on one's money. But although profit was discounted, it was still important to keep down the cost. Early in the century some landowners were still building in the traditional mud and stud, or wattle and daub, because it was cheaper than brick. Subsequently, with the vogue for the 'picturesque' the *cottage ornée* was popular, though its cost made it more suitable for the rural middle class of professional men rather than labourers. The taste for the quaint overrode common sense, and the excess of ornament, the tiny windows, and deep eaves made for houses that were small, dark, inconvenient, and costly to keep in repair. Later styles, about mid-century, were more practical. They were constructed of brick and slate, and on large estates, such as those of the Duke of Bedford, were produced in quantity to standard designs using prefabricated windows and door frames. His cottages could be built for from £90 to £100 each, and were let at 1s or 1s 6d a week, according to whether they had two or three bedrooms. The Duke's cottages were described as

> very good – very plain indeed, but not ugly. Each holds only one family and is not the least too large for it to avoid the temptation of lodgers, but by their leases the cottagers are also absolutely debarred from taking them. The walls inside are whitened brick, not plastered and the whole is very plain but substantial and well finished. The inhabitants seemed enchanted with them and very dirty people became neat and clean in them.

Housing, however, was only one of the grievances of the labourers, and generally not the one most strongly felt. More serious, because more immediate, were the levels of wages and the prices of food. Wages fell sharply at the end of the Napoleonic Wars; food prices fell too, but there were still violent fluctuations and the occasional years of scarcity and dear bread, as in 1816–18, while unemployment mounted as the soldiers returned home looking for work, and depression among the farmers in 1813–15 caused them to lay off hands. Distress stalked the villages. There had been numerous food riots during the famines of the war years, when mobs attacked millers and corn merchants, and prevented waggons loaded with grain from being moved to the ports. Now bread was still at the core of the unrest, but protests were more against poverty, against inadequate wages, unemployment and restricted parish relief. In East Anglia agitation by depressed farmers against their post-war plight was followed by riots among the labourers. In 1815 rioters in Suffolk smashed farm machinery, and in the following spring there were more incidents in Essex, Huntingdonshire and Suffolk. May saw the troubles concentrated in Norfolk. At Downham Market a crowd attacked William Baldwin's flour mill and helped themselves to flour and meal. Additional plunder included 20 loaves and the contents of the butcher's shops and cooked meat store. The arrival of the yeomanry turned the market place into a battleground before the mob was dispersed. At Littleport the labourers demanded money from the farmers and shopkeepers, wrecked the house of the Rev. Vachell, and armed with bludgeons, pitchforks, and fowling pieces set out to march on Ely. There they intimidated the magistrates, forced the innkeepers to dispense food and drink gratis, and continued to attack millers and shopkeepers until at length the Royston Volunteer Cavalry put an end to the uproar. A special Assizes at Ely sentenced 24 men to death, of whom 19 were reprieved. Discontent was clearly infectious, as was seen when the riots spread from one centre to another, but behind the sporadic, ineffectual outbursts lay the reality of hunger. 'I might as well be hanged as starved', said Richard Rutter, a rioter at Ely – and he was, in fact, transported for life. Said another, William Dawson, when confronted by the Rector of Upwell: 'Here I am between Earth and Sky – so help me God. I would sooner lose my life than go home as I am. Bread I want and bread I will have.'

After the hangings and transportations of 1816 the rioting died away, but many isolated, scattered incidents continued to disturb the peace of the countryside. These were mainly local, petty affairs, individual protests, the paying off of personal scores against tyrannical farmers, reactionary clergy, and harsh parish overseers. The exposed nature of farmers' property and the inefficiency of the police made such crimes as rick-burning, sheep-stealing, and cattle-maiming easy to commit and difficult to prevent. Assailants were unlikely to be detected unless they were careless or boastful. In December 1832, for instance, an aggrieved pauper set fire to an overseer's stacks at Guilden Morden. He had been heard to say that the overseer 'was a damned bad one to the poor', and that 'he wished all the farmers were in hell, he wished they were all to be hung, and he was to be Jack Ketch over them'. Some of the labourers' ire was directed against the itinerant Irish who helped get in the harvest and were seen by native workmen as depriving them of their rightful employment. Near Peterborough in 1831 a gang of 30 labourers, armed with scythes, gathered to attack the Irish. Other very occasional outbursts concerned enclosures, which kept the poor from their traditional access to the commons. The disturbances of this kind at Otmoor were unusually large and prolonged, and on 6th September, 1830 as many as a thousand people tramped over the moor, 'possessioning' it, and hedges and fences were levelled in clandestine nocturnal forays.

A more common grievance at this time was the threshing machine. This labour-saving device had recently made its appearance on the arable farms of southern England and East Anglia, and since it reduced winter employment was seen as a prime cause of distress. In the autumn of 1830 attacks on the machines, accompanied by rick-burning and demands for higher wages, spread rapidly from East Kent westwards, and broke out too in East Anglia and elsewhere. Unpopular employers received mysterious letters, whose blood-curdling threats ostensibly emanated from the mythical 'Captain Swing'. For a while the labourers had things their own way, and frightened farmers responded with concessions. Soon, however, attitudes hardened, the magistrates were reinforced by the military, and this 'last labourers' revolt' was quickly brought to an end. Some 400 threshing machines were destroyed: 19 men suffered on the scaffold, and 500 more were transported, a bitter retribution for riots in which no lives were lost.

Some ten years later disturbances of a different kind appeared in Wales, on the border of Pembrokeshire and Carmarthenshire. These 'Rebecca riots', so-called because the leaders disguised themselves in women's clothing, originated in angry and lethal raids on newly-erected turnpike gates and their keepers. Then the riots moved to attack more general objects of dislike, displayed a strong current of anti-English sentiment, and degenerated into weapons of private hate and vengeance. The farmers, originally sympathetic, turned against the nightly gatherings and outrages, and in time a combination of military repression and peaceful reform of the turnpikes restored order.

As in the towns, the second half of the nineteenth century saw a decline of rioting and more peaceful attempts at reform in the countryside. There was still some machine-breaking, rick-burning and cattle-maiming but from resentment expressed in blind, mindless assaults on individuals and their property, the labourers gradually moved towards constructive ways of mending their lot. Friendly societies and benefit clubs, which had appeared quite early in the century, provided a useful outlet for reformist energies, and incidentally offered facilities for saving and some small degree of security against losses caused by sickness and death. The clubs met regularly in the village alehouse, and these gatherings, it is suggested, though nominally peaceable, were occasions when grievances were aired in an atmosphere of beery recklessness, and were the origin of a number of the riots which marked the early decades of the century. Benefit clubs, like village cooperative stores, could play a part in improving amenities, and gave villagers some sense of managing their own lives. But often the membership was too small and too unstable for success, members fell out in bad times, and as a result income often failed to match outgoings and financial collapse ensued.

A hint of a trend towards unionism, expressed in the form of little local 'turn-outs', began to be seen as early as the 1830s. In subsequent decades there were occasional attempts at harvest strikes, and sometimes demands for higher wages achieved temporary success. By the beginning of the 1870s conditions were more favourable for large-scale organization. Industrial unions had shown what could be done in other occupations, and the isolation and ignorance of the country worker were gradually breaking down. Railways, visits to towns, newspapers, the penny post, and the activities of emigration agents all tended to bring the rural labourer into the current of contemporary life. Sporadic union activity sprang up in Kent, Buckinghamshire, Hertfordshire, Herefordshire, and Lincolnshire, and in 1872 the movement gathered further strength. It was on 14th February of that year that Joseph Arch, champion hedger and mower, and self-educated Methodist lay-preacher, addressed the men of Wellesbourne under a chestnut tree. Arch was chosen to head the Warwickshire union, and in the following year the local organizations coalesced to form a national body, 150,000 strong. Its main strength lay in the low-wage counties south of Trent, and its growth owed much to men of Arch's stamp – self-educated men, quite a number of them Nonconformist lay-preachers, with a sprinkling of village teachers, shopkeepers and journalists. Not surprisingly, the union had a strongly moral and intellectual aspect, with much emphasis placed on education and temperance, and it embraced such radical demands as extension of the franchise and nationalization of the land.

Though some farmers and their landlords were sympathetic, many were not. The conservative were shocked by the union's radicalism, and alarmed by the sudden upsurge of demands for independence and advancement among the dull drudges and

97

'clodpates' of yesteryear. By 1874 the farmers were replying to union demands with lockouts, blackleg labour, and evictions of union supporters from their cottages. Poor men without work and without homes had no resort to fall back on, they could not keep up their subscriptions, and union membership fell. Farm workers were peculiarly exposed to retaliation by their employers, for there were often many men and but few farmers to give them work. The fall in grain prices in 1875–76, too, encouraged farmers to look for economies in labour, and this together with disunity within the labourers' movement hastened the collapse. By 1879 little remained of the great enthusiasm of seven years before. The 'revolt of the field' had failed, and its leaders turned to political action for a new road forward. When things improved in the late 1880s union feeling once more sprang into life, only to flicker out in the depressed years of 1893 and 1894. The true foundations for a permanent union were built only in the environment of rising prices and wages-lag before 1914, and the beginnings were minuscule indeed. True, the 7,000 members of 1911 more than quadrupled in the next three years, but even then they represented only a pitiful proportion of the total numbers still on the land. Many more years were to elapse before an agricultural labourers' union would have the power of making a real impression on the men's lives.

At first sight it is difficult to understand why bad conditions did not encourage rapid movement off the land at an early date, at least in the southern counties where wages were very low. The growth of industry and of large urban communities certainly exercised an attractive force, though mainly in their immediate neighbourhood, and it was only gradually that movement became more than local and the work of emigration agents bore fruit. Some men, certainly, went off to find seasonal work at haymaking or harvest, or in town maltings and breweries. In general farm workers were illiterate or nearly so, and often ignorant, dull-witted and suspicious of new ideas. They lacked the specialized skills which would ensure them well-paid jobs in industry, and the jobs they could get – as soldiers, railway porters, builders' labourers, carters, grooms – were not much better than those they left behind. Above all they lacked the means to move, living as many of them did on the edge of subsistence, with the burden of young and large families, and often in debt. Proximity to some large centre of employment was an important influence on migration, and there are indications that much of the movement which occurred in the earlier nineteenth century was short distance, within a radius of 20 or 30 miles from the great cities. In the more remote areas of the deep countryside only the most enterprising or most desperate thought of moving before the spread of railways, newspapers and other alien influences gradually broke down the barriers of fear and isolation.

Migration, therefore, was not very widespread until the second half of the century. Poverty, custom, ignorance, kept country labourers set in their ways. Their ignorance was profound. When Canon Girdlestone, as late as 1866, began to organize the migration of poor labouring families from his parish of Halberton in north Devon to industrial towns in the north, he had to consign the travellers to the care of the railway company as if they were so many parcels. Some of them had never travelled more than a few miles in their lives, and believed Manchester to lie across the ocean. 'Full and plain directions' to be shown to the railway officials, were 'given to the simple travellers . . . written on a piece of paper in a large and legible hand.' For migration to take place it needed someone to give a lead, provide funds, and arrange all the details of new jobs and the means of getting to them. Sometimes this was a conscientious clergyman, like Girdlestone, sometimes a landowner beset by unemployed crofters, like the Duchess of Sutherland, sometimes it was the organizer of a village emigration society, whose members paid into a fund until there was enough to draw lots and decide which family was to go. Agents employed by shipping companies, American railroads, land companies and state governments placed advertisements in newspapers, held public meetings, and generally aroused interest in emigration. It was not always easy, for apart from the limitations of ignorance and poverty, the farmers opposed these ideas: they generally disliked anything which made labour less plentiful or more independent. If, as sometimes happened, a villager emigrated, made good, and wrote back to relations and friends, the impact might be considerable. Improvements in railways and shipping helped by reducing the cost, danger, and time involved in the journey. But on the whole it was a slow process, and it was late in the century before migration from the more remote parts of the country became very large.

So limited a degree of mobility in a period of fairly rapid population growth made for difficult problems. Pools of surplus labour accumulated, especially in southern England, where there was less expansion of industry to take up the slack. The decline of some old rural industries, such as iron-making in the weald of Kent and Sussex and in the Forest of Dean, the decay of the old cloth industry of East Anglia and the West Country, and the eventual decline of hand trades like framework-knitting in the midlands, helped to create unemployment. Sometimes new occupations sprang up in partial compensation. Market gardens and nurseries increased, brick works developed on a large scale in Bedfordshire, and in Cambridgeshire during the later nineteenth century the mining of coprolites for making fertilizer was of some importance. In Norwich the production of wire netting on machines not very dissimilar to the old cloth looms became a valuable trade, much of the netting being exported to farmers in Australia.

Surplus labour, when unrelieved by some local expansion of industry, spelled underemployment and destitution, and especially in winter when farm work was less plentiful. Then families often depended entirely on what the women could earn. They were better off in heavily-wooded areas where fuel was cheap and there was plenty of wood cutting and other winter work to be had. Even labourers in full employment were poor by contemporary standards. Life was a continual struggle to manage, to find the money for next winter's boots, to keep food in the larder, to stay abreast of debts. True, labourers drank beer and smoked pipes, their wives occasionally spent a few pence on a trifle of dress, a gimcrack brooch, or trinkets hawked round by pedlars. The children might have a halfpenny for sweets or go to a fair or peepshow. But these inconsiderable luxuries were themselves the concomitant of poverty, for they made poverty bearable. Any serious accident, illness, or death in the family was a disaster – for unless the friendly society helped out there were no spare funds to meet it. Then one borrowed from neighbours or looked for charity. There was indeed charity, but it did not go far enough. The few people of some wealth, the squire, parson, doctor and large farmers, put their hands in their pockets when times were especially hard. There was some customary help: blankets at Christmas, clothing for the destitute – that sort of thing. A few squires paid for a doctor to attend on the poor gratis, but generally the landowners directed their help towards their own tenants and servants. Among the well-to-do there was a growing conviction that indiscriminate charity was no solution and might even be positively harmful. What was needed, it was thought, was to encourage curative measures such as better education and self-help through thrift and temperance.

There was of course the Poor Law. It had been reformed in 1834 in the interests of thinning the ranks of persistent paupers demoralized through living on relief, and of reducing the financial burden on the ratepayers; and the nature of the reform was greatly influenced by the problem of surplus labour in the

Woodlanders from Puslinch, South Devon, photographed in the 1890s.

countryside. The New Poor Law proposed that all relief should be given in the workhouse, and to this end many new workhouses were built, supervised by Boards of Guardians, who were responsible for a group of parishes known as a union. The union workhouse was a grim establishment, where the comfort and diet were of the sparsest and the discipline of the harshest. Strict rules, enforced by the ex-sergeant-majors who were often appointed to the post of workhouse master, prohibited the mixing of the sexes and enjoined silence at mealtimes. Families entering the workhouse were broken up, and the men put to the hard, dusty and humiliating work of breaking stones for the roads or crushing bones to make bone meal for the farmers. The prime object was to discourage pauperism. The harshness of the 'house', based on the principle of 'less eligibility', was designed to deter all but the desperate from seeking relief, and to encourage all who could to find themselves work. But this assumed that work was there if only the labourer was obliged to look for it, and worked hard to keep it when he got it. In those parts of southern England where agriculture and industry stagnated, where obstinate reserves of surplus labour gathered and festered, this was rarely the case. The Poor Law, where it was applied in all its rigour, became as one historian has remarked irrelevant to the problem of poverty. It did not seek to relieve the poor; it rejected them.

In practice, however, it was difficult to enforce the new regime. Boards of Guardians were too humane, or perhaps too fearful of the possible consequences, to act as harshly as the Act prescribed. After all, it was not so many years since labourers in the eastern counties had marched under the banner of 'Bread or Blood', and as recently as 1830–31 the followers of Captain Swing had smashed threshing machines and burned down ricks in demanding an extra shilling a week. Nocturnal rick-burning, maiming of cattle, attacks on unpopular overseers and farmers, still continued – as unconnected outrages, the work of angry individuals nursing private grievances. The Swing riots were indeed the 'last labourers' revolt', in the sense of an organized or general protest. But unrest remained, to surface occasionally in sporadic incidents of arson or violence.

Whether or no the Guardians felt the need for restraint, it was difficult to make the new Act work. It was virtually impossible in a public institution to make the conditions of life worse than in the lowest paid occupation outside. Further, the cost of providing for paupers in the workhouse, though low enough in all conscience, might still be higher than in those non-institutional forms of relief which the workhouse was supposed to replace. Hence outdoor relief, as these other forms were called, tended to persist. Widows, for instance, still received some little help with their rent or fuel to keep them from entering the house; and some farmers, as Caird noticed, preferred to employ extra men, whom they really did not need, rather than leave them to the mercies of the union and have their own poor rates increased.

Before 1834 a variety of schemes had been devised to overcome the problem of surplus labour. Emigration societies were formed, to pay the passage of families to America. Men were employed, apparently not very effectively, on repairing the roads, or occasionally on working a parish farm by spade labour. There was the 'roundsman' system, by which the able-bodied unemployed were sent round the parish to find employment. Most effective, but not appreciated by the reformers of 1834, was the 'labour-rate' device, by which farmers agreed to share the surplus hands among themselves in return for a reduction in their rates. This had the merit of providing the men with a living wage while relieving the parish of the surplus labour, and at the same time providing the farmer with extra manpower for undertaking improvements such as drainage and raising the general standards of his farming. The notorious Speenhamland system, it has been shown, was much less commonly used after the high wartime prices had passed away. 'Speenhamland parishes' relieved the inadequately-paid by supplementing wages on the basis of a crude cost of living scale. Whether, as contemporaries claimed, it tended to keep wages down, and encouraged early marriage and a high birth rate among the labourers, seem doubtful. At all events, detailed study has shown that it was largely superseded by other forms of relief at least twenty years before it was abolished by the Act of 1834.

The advocates of the New Poor Law put all forms of outdoor relief under the same general condemnation. They demoralized the labourers, discouraged the hard-working and encouraged the idle, created a heavy burden of poor rates, and above all interfered with the free working of the labour market. It was this last – the free labour market – which the Act of 1834 was supposed to restore. To what extent it succeeded it is impossible to say, for very soon the general advance of the economy began to increase the availability of employment, promoted higher mobility, and so led to the gradual dissipation of the rural labour surplus. Railway building, very active in the middle 1840s and 1850s, was particularly important in this respect. Not only did it mean that hands were needed for the barrow and shovel work of earth moving and track construction, but also that the permanent railway staff required more and more men, as porters, drivers, guards and signalmen. An average of 100,000 men laboured for twenty years to create some 10,000 miles of track, while more important for farm labourers, railway staff grew from 65,000 in 1851 to 174,000 thirty years later. The railways hastened the decline of some rural industries but stimulated others, not least agriculture itself, as well as mines, brickworks, limekilns and quarries. As the economy expanded the rural surplus gradually disappeared, and by degrees turned into the labour shortage which marked parts of the countryside towards the end of the century.

Before then, from the 1870s, there was growing concern about what contemporaries called the flight from the land. Landowners and farmers, beset by low prices, were afraid of rising labour costs, and saw scarcer labour as leading to declining standards of farming; cheap labour was as essential to a farming system that was still only partially mechanized as it was to the country house and its way of life. Reformers concerned about urban conditions saw the influx of country labour as adding to the unemployment and overcrowding of the towns. Strategists pointed out that town-dwellers were unfit for soldiering, and that migration was draining the countryside of the nation's reservoir of able-bodied men – and the recruiting figures for the Boer War brought this home. These appalling statistics shows that nearly half of army volunteers in industrial towns proved to be under-sized, exhibited various physical defects, or were suffering from active disease. No wonder that two-thirds of the London police force was recruited from farmworkers, while in respect of longevity few occupations, and those largely of a middle-class character, could show a degree of superiority over that of the humble country labourer. Lastly, some attention was paid to the rural myth, the idea that country life was the true, the good, the simple life, that farming was the one natural and essential industry, and that the countryside was the seat of traditional virtues, the fount of morality and honesty, while city life demoralized and corrupted.

There was great discussion, much controversy, a few plans, but little action. What did the labourer need to tie him to his village? Clearly he needed better wages, better housing, better conditions – though it was disputed how bad these really were. Above all he needed land. Look at the continent. There was still a stable and numerous peasantry, having a large share of the soil, and responsible for a large share of its product. Land was the key. It would give the labourer a stake in the country, something to work for, something to stay for. And so came the Smallholdings Acts.

Access to land had long been an issue in the countryside. Enthusiasm for allotments, and the larger units known as cow pastures, developed in the late eighteenth century as a response to growing rural poverty. The possibility of keeping a cow, or at least of growing vegetables, it was argued, gave the labourer an incentive to be industrious and frugal. Where there was land of this kind there was less resort to the parish for relief. In fact, it was often a rule of those who let allotments that the labourer must give up his bit of land if he sought poor relief. Allotment societies grew up in the early decades of the nineteenth century, supported largely by enthusiastic country clergy. The landowners were also generally in favour, and it was the farmers who were hostile, arguing that allotments made the men too independent, invited thefts of seed and fertiliser, and caused them to spend their strength on their own land rather than on the farmers'. At all events, allotments became fairly commonplace, especially in southern England. A lot depended on the willingness of owners and farmers to set land aside and on the enterprise of some public-spirited parson or estate agent. Wiltshire was particularly notable for its allotment schemes, and as early as 1833–4 a survey of 26 parishes in the county showed there to be some 1450 cottagers who held allotments, averaging in size a little under a quarter of an acre, rented at sums ranging from 4s to 15s. Wiltshire was exceptionally well provided, but allotments gradually spread elsewhere, and in 1893 it was reported from neighbouring Dorset, for instance, that half the labourers there had them. They were harder to find in the north, perhaps because suitable land was scarcer, and because northern labourers, with their superior wages, had less need of them.

Allotments, however, were merely a supplement to a labourer's wages: they were never intended to provide .him with an alternative means of getting a living. The Smallholdings Acts of 1892 and 1908 were intended to keep people on the land by turning them into small-scale farmers, in imitation of the continental peasantry. The labourer was to become an independent cultivator, a specialist producer of the small man's products – vegetables, market-garden stuff, soft fruit, poultry and eggs. The scheme ran into many difficulties. In the beginning it was difficult to persuade the County Councils, on which the large farmers were well represented, to take the necessary local initiative. Then the land selected for smallholdings was often unsuitable: it needed to be a fertile and easily-worked loam, with good access to nearby towns or very near a railway station. Those farmworkers who were sufficiently enterprising to take on a smallholding had to know what to produce and how to go about it. They had to be prepared to work very hard at busy seasons, especially when it was a matter of catching the market with early crops. They also had to have a business sense, to have ambition to reach beyond the limited possibilities of nearby market-towns and exploit the huge potential demand of the cities. Above all, they needed some initial stock of capital in order to get a start and withstand the occasional losses and setbacks, and credit facilities were few or non-existent. Few labourers could hope to fit this bill, and few in fact attempted to do so. Less than a third of the applications for smallholdings under the Act of 1908 came from farm labourers. The number of smallholdings created, even after further extension of the legislation following the First World War, was tiny relation to the still great numbers of full-time labourers: in the 1920s there were under 30,000 smallholders and some 650,000 agricultural labourers. And, even so, many of the holdings were not occupied by farmworkers at all, but by existing farmers seeking additional land or by tradesmen who required grazing for their draught animals.

The rural proletariat was a shrinking one, but it remained a proletariat. In the forty years between 1871 and 1911 the proportion of the national work force engaged in agriculture nearly halved. In 1911 the number of full-time hired workers in English farming stood at 665,000, but represented only 7.6 per cent of the total. Wages were higher, hours of work had fallen slightly, the womenfolk went out to work less often and the children had more years at school, and living standards, though very low, had improved. Since 1884 the farmworkers had enjoyed the right to vote and were beginning to be wooed by politicians. The yellow and blue vans bearing emissaries of the parties crisscrossed the countryside to garner votes. The villager, too, could help elect his parish council, and could even serve on it. All this made little difference. The farm labourer remained a low-paid rustic drudge, an ignorant simpleton, good for the stock jokes in *Punch*. It is probable that the quality of farm labour actually declined – certainly farmers said so. Many of the old skills were falling into disuse and were disappearing. The most intelligent and ambitious had migrated to the towns or gone abroad. The brighter children, now a little better educated, sometimes caught the kindly eye of a teacher or parson and were helped to a better job in the city. Even the traditional country tales and folk songs, which changed from village to village, were fast going from memory. Cecil Sharp and fellow-enthusiasts went round the countryside committing them to paper before they were completely lost.

Slowly the farm worker adapted to the industrial age. The truth was that the countryside gave him but a poor living and little to look forward to. The semi-feudal control of the landed class was passing away but it was being replaced by that of the large farmers and business men who sat on the county and rural district councils. The countryman's vote could do little to change national policies or influence the structure of society, even if he really understood the nature of the issues fought over at election time. His answer, expressed hesitantly and often with regret, was to leave. And so the drift from the land continued, leaving the villages to be populated by a new stratum of middle-class residents from the towns and to respond to the needs of a growing number of tourists. It was a long drawn-out process, and by 1914, when the Great War led to an accelerated pace of change, it still had far to go. But before this the results were already visible: a lost country population, and a farming system that was to be the most highly mechanized in the world.

5 Industrial Workers in the Countryside

The industrial revolution, it is not always realized, created industrial villages as well as industrial towns. Textiles, mining, quarrying, brick-making and other kinds of manufacture were the dominating occupations of numerous villages, even in southern England. In the Redruth area of Cornwall, for instance, there was china clay; paper, bricks and cement came to monopolize the Thames-side villages of North Kent and those in the Medway valley; and many country towns and large villages across the country witnessed the arrival of workshops concerned with agricultural engineering. Quite often these industries developed in communities where only a hamlet, if that, existed before. The communities were sometimes isolated, off the beaten track, and self-sufficient. Where there was the domination of a single occupation it produced a common bond which seems to have made the inhabitants inward-looking, with their own rough code of standards, and their own shared suspicions of the outside world. Such was the community of Headington Quarry, described by Raphael Samuel in a recent volume. This village, originally a squatters' settlement on the waste, maintained a link with the outside world through the women who took in washing from Oxford colleges and hotels, the menfolk fetching it weekly by trap or hand-cart.

In the late eighteenth century, and early decades of the nineteenth, villages grew up around new textile factories in Lancashire, the West Riding, and the dales of Derbyshire. Arkwright located the first cotton mill at the village of Cromford, on the Derwent, and nearer Derby a small town grew up round the mills established by his associate, Jedediah Strutt, at Belper. Water power, provided by the fast-flowing rivers, was the original attraction of these locations, but many mills contrived to keep going when later the large steam-powered mills developed in the towns. Hand trades, too, spread out from urban centres to bring great changes to many villages. Nailmaking, carried on in little forges attached to the houses, spread in the scattered communities of the Black Country, and framework-knitting stretched out from midland towns to change the rustic character of villages such as Ruddington near Nottingham, and Wigston

Magna, just outside Leicester. New influences came rapidly to bear. Population expanded, houses and shops multiplied. The old-fashioned cottages of the farm people were overshadowed by new brick houses having the characteristic long range of upper-storey windows needed to give light for operation of the stocking frames. The rhythm of village life now responded more to the erratic ups and downs of commerce than to the annual round of the seasons.

The industrial revolution is often thought of as primarily a series of technical changes in the sources of power and methods of production, a matter of steam engines, canals, railways, factories and power-driven machinery. In fact, for the first hundred years or so of the 'revolution', steam power and factories were quite exceptional over much the greater part of industry. A great deal of the industrial expansion took the form of the extension of existing hand trades, some of which have survived into the twentieth century. Most of them, however, eventually gave way before the growing efficiency of the powered machine, though their decline was usually protracted. It took time to overcome the technical weaknesses of the early powered machines and to improve the range and quality of their products. It was not until the 1830s that the power loom was fully competitive even in the coarser types of cloth, and at that time there were some half-million men working at hand looms. The flexibility and cheapness of hand labour also went far to offset the greater productivity of machinery. Thus hand-nailing, largely carried on by women and girls, long survived the first development of a nail-making machine, as did handloom weaving and framework-knitting the first introduction of power looms and powered knitting frames. The collapse of many hand trades did not come until the 1840s or 1850s, and in some cases much later. Furthermore, some new factory trades still required the assistance of domestic workers. Cheap clothing, such as shirts and dresses, was cut out *en masse* in factories, but it was hand workers who sewed and trimmed the finished garments. The making of shoes and gloves, too, was on the same basis. Factory-made lace, also, had to be gone over by hand in the home to rectify the small holes and imperfections left by the machine.

Some hand trades continued throughout the nineteenth century, and there were many villages outside the new industrial areas where old crafts lingered on. Straw-plaiting was found in villages stretching from Buckinghamshire through south Bedfordshire to Suffolk; pillow lace was more widely scattered in the area round north Bedfordshire, in Buckinghamshire and Northamptonshire, and also round Honiton in Devon; glove-making was important in Oxfordshire round Woodstock, and in parts of the West Country; Dorset was noted for its string, cordage, nets, rope, sailcloth and sacking, and round Shaftesbury and Blandford shirt-buttons were made; in East Anglia by the nineteenth century the old cloth industries had declined and largely disappeared in the face of competition from the West Riding, while in the West Country cloth-making moved into factories, though these were still located in small towns and villages. Hand-woven cloth still managed to survive in Wales and the North. Flax mills remained common in many areas, producing yarns to be converted into bags and sacking on cottage looms. In Cottenham, Cambridgeshire, at the end of the nineteenth century, all the women were employed in the market gardens in the summer and in the unusual occupation of making swansdown in the winter.

These trades were very largely the preserve of the womenfolk, but numerous crafts belonged to the men. In large villages shoemakers were commonplace, and it seems they were often men of some education, and were likely to be at the centre of any political discussion or agitation. The 1400 people who made up the large village of Bere in Dorset in 1841 supported as many as 18 cobblers. The making of wicker baskets, hurdles, boxes and hampers was very widely spread, though some villages gained a reputation for a certain product, as East Stour in Dorset did for its baskets. Residents at Shelford in Nottinghamshire can still remember willows being specially grown for basketry, and recall a rod yard where rods were peeled, and the thick rods set aside for sending to Manchester where bobbins were made from them. In general, wooded areas tended to give rise to a greater variety of occupations than was usual in districts of large arable farms. The woods offered work in thinning, cutting, clearing and planting, and fostered woodyards and workshops where were made fencing, hurdles, gates, tubs, barrels, hoops, thatching spars, brushes and the like. Large hoops, made in the woods of West Surrey, were exported to the tropics for sugar hogsheads. The woods, too, offered fuel and game for those willing to take the risks of trespassing. It was for these reasons that Cobbett remarked on the difference between the ragged and dirty labourers of Thanet and those in his familiar woodlands of Hampshire and Sussex. 'Invariably have I observed', he said, 'that the richer the soil, and the more destitute of woods, that is to say, the more purely a corn country, the more miserable the labourers.'

But even in corn country there were often quarries, brickworks and little local potteries. Quarries were widely found wherever there was sand and gravel suitable for building and repair of the roads. Stone was also much quarried for the new town halls and other monumental buildings with which the rich industrial cities marked their coming of age. Other quarrying activity concerned fuller's earth and the rarer kinds of stone. At East Bridgford in Nottinghamshire, for example, a kind of gypsum, known as satin spar, was used for making ornaments, inscribed 'a present from Niagara.' The clay for making bricks and pottery was ground by horse mills, and the finished products were shipped to market by a convenient river wharf or canal. The wives and children often helped the menfolk in the brick fields.

Everywhere flour mills, bone mills, corn and meal warehouses, tanyards, and leather-dressing shops were to be found. Along the coast agricultural employments were supplemented by fishing, and there was a breed of amphibious husbandmen who cultivated smallholdings when they were not manning little inshore fishing boats. There were salmon netters on the tidal rivers; stake nets were a feature of the gently shelving shores of parts of Wales and Lancashire. Oysters were widely cultivated – in the nineteenth century they were commonly sold in working-class areas – and there were numerous crabbers and lobster men. Many women were employed in winkling and cockling; there were the mussel rakers of the Exe, and the cockle gatherers of Stiffkey in Norfolk, 'with skirts tucked up, broad straw hats on head, and deep baskets slung across shoulder'. The country towns and larger villages all contained their building craftsmen, bricklayers, plasterers, carpenters and glaziers. Joinery shops produced doors and window frames, and cabinet-makers made furniture to order. Again, certain villages became noted for their specialist wood working, as Buckleberry Common in Berkshire was well-known for its bowl-turning. Clog-making was a feature of villages in Wales and Lancashire. In an age dependent on the horse and cart there had to be numerous horse breeders, meal men and farriers, as well as smiths, saddlers, harness-makers and wheelwrights. In 1851 there were 30,000 wheelwrights, and as many as 112,000 blacksmiths – more than all the men engaged in the great iron works. Some smiths branched out into making implements or undertook fancy wrought iron work for gates, lanterns and other purposes. This craft was particularly strong in the weald of Sussex, where the old charcoal iron industry had finally died out at the beginning of the nineteenth century. For a long time village furnaces still produced the metal parts of agricultural implements, from shepherds' crooks to ploughshares, but they were gradually replaced by specialist implement makers who, in turn, gradually gave way to the large manufacturers, firms like Ransome of Ipswich and Garrett of Leiston. As the farm machinery industry grew so the old village implement-makers turned to acting as agents for the large firms and went round the farms repairing machines and replacing worn parts.

Although the impact of the railways and the superior productivity of the factories meant the eventual disappearance of many country occupations, some of these still survived into the twentieth century, and indeed were joined by a number of new ones. Long before then their importance for the employment of country people already varied greatly from one district to another, and in general they had become more markedly a feature of the southern agricultural counties. This naturally followed from the industrial changes which led to so much of the midlands and north becoming dominated by coal, iron, shipbuilding and factories. Furthermore, the slow pace of migration of rural families in the south meant that labour supply was rarely a serious problem in the survival of a local enterprise. When they failed it was mainly as the result of a change in fashion, an influx of cheap imports, or the competition of factory-made substitutes.

J. L. Green's survey of rural industries in the closing years of the old century shows a great many in decline or completely disappeared. In Bedfordshire, for example, Luton was still the centre of the sewing of straw hats and bonnets, work performed by the village womenfolk while the men migrated to the towns to engage in the finishing processes. Straw-plaiting, which 'used to be carried on vigorously, and was a very lucrative business in the neighbourhood of Ampthill', was now 'scarcely worth doing'. But in the villages around Biddenham, those adjoining Northamptonshire, the shoe trade had 'become a considerable industry, and had absorbed many who were employed on the land'. Pillow lace had much declined in the north of the county, but in the Woburn district numbers were engaged in the preparation of fuller's earth. In the cottages around Potton 'threading beads for ladies mantles, etc.' had taken the place of straw-plaiting and lace-making. Market gardening was also important, while an iron foundry and the making of parchment, boots, shoes, and leggings employed a number of people.

Berkshire could boast very few rural industries. Though a paper mill and a chair-frame factory existed near Thatcham, the former manufacture of velvets, ribbons and men's clothing in the neighbourhood of Newbury had gone. Berkshire once had a name for its cloth, and teazles were still to be seen growing wild which had 'once been cultivated, and used in the preparation of the surface of the cloth'. It was now rather uncommon to meet women 'who are either willing or physically competent to do field-work. Formerly at harvest time they earned considerable sums in reaping and tying the corn, in hoeing the turnips, and in making the hay.' Large numbers of women and children, however, were still busy during the acorn harvest, when a woman could earn between 3s 4d and 5s a day. Women could also be seen in the autumn collecting leaves in bags for use in their gardens and as bedding for pigs. Hurdle-making was fast disappearing as imported withies came in so cheap as to make the growing of osiers uneconomic. Bell-founding had long since disappeared from Blewbury and Cholsey, and 'quite half the malthouses' had been shut up as a result of the concentration of the brewing industry. Fortunately, iron foundries, mainly for agricultural implements, prospered at Wantage, Compton, Wallingford, Newbury and Hungerford, and a clothing factory at Abingdon. The establishment in the county of Wellington College and the Broadmoor Asylum had encouraged a growth of employment.

In Oxfordshire, wool-combing, and the making of shoes and slippers for the shopkeepers of Banbury, had quite died out. The vicar of Sibford had assisted some forty or fifty people to emigrate to Canada, New Zealand and Australia, and they were supposed to be 'doing well'. Weaving and lace-making had declined, though around Chipping Norton some gloving and cloth-making continued. Banbury, famous for its plush as well as its cakes, still had an old mill which had the honour of supplying the continental courts with plush. The plushes and velvets were mostly made of mohair (goat's hair), and were chiefly used for covering furniture, and for making curtains, livery breeches, and the coats of gamekeepers, farm labourers and bargemen. There was also a tweed factory, and about the town girths, braces, belts, garters, dog collars and similar articles were made 'in great quantities'. A box factory started in 1871 with four or five hands had grown into an extensive business employing eighty. The town also had cabinet-making, basket work, gloves, and hosiery, though the hand-made rope industry was nearly at an end. Nearby at Bodicote was a farm specializing in growing medicinal herbs. Glove-making was still important round Burford, Charlbury and Woodstock, and blankets round Witney. A chair-making trade was established at Whitchurch, Stokenchurch and a few other places. Shoemaking was fairly widespread, and also to be found were huckaback-weaving, damask-weaving, straw hats and bonnets, axle-making at Deddington, dyeing at Broughton, and paper-making at North Newington.

In Somerset stocking-knitting and brush-making had largely disappeared. Paper mills gave employment to a number of villagers, as did gloves at Glastonbury, shoemaking at Street, and silk, satin and velvet manufactories at Croscombe and Shepton Mallet. The weaving of webbing, once a great industry in East Coker, could now scarcely 'stand on its feet'. A local grievance concerned the pulling down of cottages, which meant that workers in East Coker had to live at a distance. Around Yeovil women took in gloving, being furnished by the manufacturers with sewing machines, for which they paid large sums by instalments. Some of the village girls went to Yeovil to work in the collar factories, and laundry work for the middle classes was 'considerable'. Old eight-day clocks to be seen in the area showed the names of local makers, and a few of the clockmakers still survived. The main industries at Castle Cary were haircloth weaving and string. Salmon and herring were important at Porlock, Minehead and Watchet. At Taunton teazles were still grown. But in general, the county's old trades of woollen, worsted, and silk textiles, gloves, lace, linen, sailcloth, shirt collars, brushes, bricks and drain pipes, bath stone and other quarrying, had much declined.

So long as rural transport, and a good deal of town transport too, depended on the horse, a great many people continued to get their living by rearing horses, producing feed for them, and making carts, waggons, vans, and all the necessary equipment and accoutrements. The country's horse population, indeed, did not reach its peak of $3\frac{1}{2}$ millions until the early years of the present century, though it declined rapidly from the 1930s under the competition of the motor vehicle. Until the appearance of the bicycle, and later rural bus services, many country people remained physically isolated, and the craftsmen and shopkeepers of market towns and large villages enjoyed a high degree of local monopoly. The railways first began to break down this monopoly in mid-century, but railway stations were often inconveniently located, and for a long period rail fares were too high for the majority of villagers. Railways certainly brought some changes: they made possible the expansion of dairying, fruit production and market gardening, and they brought into the countryside cheaper coal, factory-made goods, imported products, and newspapers. Eventually they helped bring about the collapse of old rural industries which had flourished for centuries, and so made a major impact on the lives of many villagers.

But the process was generally a slow one, and railways were slow too in influencing migration from the countryside, which was one factor in the long survival of many hand trades. Unless a girl moved to the towns or found work locally as a domestic servant or dairymaid, there was little alternative to a hand trade. This being so, parents sent their girls to a craft school to acquire the skills needed for making the traditional products of the district. In the country lace-making areas there were little lace schools held in cottage kitchens and living rooms, where a well-skilled woman presided with strict discipline over her class of a dozen or twenty young girls. The pupils started young, often at the age of four or five, as it was thought that only thus could they acquire the essential deftness of finger. Pamela Horn tells us of the cramped, badly-ventilated, and often unheated conditions in which the children sat for hours at a time, keeping warm with little individual pots containing hot charcoal or ashes placed by their feet. Pillow lace, long established in north Bedfordshire, and the neighbouring counties, and also in Devon, was an important trade. In 1851 there were as many as 10,487 female lace workers recorded in Buckinghamshire, 10,322 in Northampton-shire, 5734 in Bedfordshire, and 5478 in Devon. In each county, several hundred of these were girls aged between five and nine, and many more – from nearly a thousand to over two thousand – were of ten to fourteen years. Except in Bedfordshire, the following two decades saw gradual decline in the numbers, the consequence of changes in fashion and the growing competion of the cheaper machine-made lace.

Pillow lace was produced by the systematic and rapid manipulation of bobbins. The stiff parchment pattern of the article to be made was first fixed to a hard pillow, which was supported by the worker's knees or partly by a three-legged pillow horse. The pattern itself was marked out by pins, and the threads were wound on bobbins of bone or wood. The ground of the lace was formed by twisting and crossing the threads, while the pattern was made by the interweaving of a much thicker thread. The long hours spent in a bent position, and often in an unhealthy atmosphere, with evening work done by the inadequate light of rushes or candles, were very bad for the workers, and especially for young girls. The earnings, however, were important to the family's income, though they varied considerably with the state of the trade and the skill of the worker. In the early 1860s, a girl of 13 might earn 2s 6d or 3s a week, when her father might get only 10s on the farm. The lace schools generally made little attempt to provide a general education, and consequently the girls trained in them were often unable to read or write properly. Not until the 1870s, with the introduction of compulsory

From an advertisement for a harvester, 1897.

elementary education and the raising of the minimum age for employment to ten, did the standard of the girls' education show much improvement. But it was the eventual collapse of the industry itself in the face of changed fashions and increased competition from the machine-made substitute which finally brought to an end both the lace schools and the employment of very young children. In its heyday lace was a significant element in the country people's way of life. Many women kept up their work after marriage, and even into advanced age, until declining eyesight and stiffening fingers forced them to give it up.

Similarly important were straw-plaiting and glove-making. Straw-plaiting was predominant in those parts of Bedfordshire and Buckinghamshire not taken up by lace, as well as in Essex, Hertfordshire, and Suffolk. It was particularly significant in south Bedfordshire where the 10,054 female workers in the trade in 1851 had more than doubled twenty years later. But not long after that an influx of cheap foreign plait, from Italy, China, and later Japan, together with changes in fashion, caused a rapid collapse. As in the lace-making industry, a large proportion of the workers – over 16 per cent in Bedfordshire in 1871 – was aged between five and fourteen. Straw-plaiting was unlike lace, however, in the degree of skill involved. It was usually learned at home, and when children were sent at four to a plait school it was usually to be kept hard at work making plait for their parents to sell. Children spent many hours, too, plaiting at home, and even occupied themselves on their way walking to and from school. The lengths of plait, made up in a variety of patterns, were often sold in a nearby market to those who specialized in making the finished article. The plait was wound and stitched together to produce bags, baskets, hats and bonnets, which found a market in the towns. In the trade's heyday straw-plaiters could make as much or more money as did farm labourers, and the farmers of the area grew a special type of wheat which produced a straw suitable for the work.

When mother and children were all occupied in making as much plait as possible, home comforts were often neglected. The trade enabled young workers to gain an early financial independence and leave home, and it was no doubt a combination of these things which accounted for the high rate of illegitimate births prevalent in straw-plaiting villages. The children's education was sadly neglected, and before 1870 the parents could not be induced to send their children to school unless plaiting was made part of the curriculum. Even after that date the trade was a cause of irregular attendance, especially among girls, and the employment of very young children remained a feature of the plaiting trade.

Glove-making, too, employed considerable numbers in parts of the West Country. Somerset had 8050 glovers in 1851 (1683 of them below the age of fifteen), and Devon had 3103. The trade was notable also around Woodstock in Oxfordshire, and in areas of Worcestershire and Herefordshire. Children began to learn it from about seven or eight, working at home early and late, or sometimes doing a twelve-hour day in a local factory from the age of ten. Though principally a female trade, whole families were sometimes engaged. The father cut out the leather, and mother and children did the sewing, using the glovers' brass 'donkey' to hold the glove firm and keep the stitches even. As in the other hand trades the rates of pay were miserably low. In 1864 3s 6d or 3s 9d was paid for a dozen pair of 'best men's' gloves, and three workers, mother and two daughters, could make six pairs a day.

In West Oxfordshire, an area famous for its gloves since at least the sixteenth century, the trade was concentrated in villages on the edge of Wychwood Forest. Leafield, for instance, had 153 female glovers in 1851, 69 of whom were aged under 21, while Hanborough had 149, of whom 52 were between the ages of 8 and 19. One woman usually acted as carrier for the whole village. In 1871 Sarah Surmer of Stonesfield took the bundles of completed gloves into Woodstock by the weekly waggon, and brought back supplies of raw materials. Naturally, the local leather industry extended beyond gloves into saddlery, breeches, gaiters, boots and shoes. The Burford firm of William Wiggins appeared in the trade directories first as makers of gloves, breeches, and gaiters, and subsequently as leather dressers, carriers and china dealers, then as fellmongers and tanners, and later still as boot and shoe manufacturers and butchers. Their tannery in Witney Street was worked until the First World War.

Many operations went into the production of gloves. The skins had first to be tanned, sorted, dyed and finished, the processes varying with the type and quality of the skins, and the kinds of gloves for which they were intended. Then a highly skilled cutter cut the skins into rectangles, using shears or large scissors. A slitter or webber next took the rectangles of leather and cut these into the gloves' component parts, using steel punches or 'webbs'. The next operation was to 'point' or apply decoration, either by hand or using a multi-needle machine. Finally, the parts had to be sewn together, lined, bound, and ironed. It was the later processes in which outworkers were engaged, though small family businesses might undertake all of them, with one worker doing several different operations. Even today some outworkers are still employed in the area, the work being distributed by van instead of by the former 'bag woman'.

The glove trade, like others, experienced severe fluctuations. There was a particularly difficult period after 1826, when despite the intervention of Mr Dent, the eminent glover of Worcester, cheap French gloves were allowed to compete in the English market. In time the small family businesses tended to decline, and the trade was dominated by large manufacturers who employed scores, sometimes hundreds, of outworkers. Samuel Pritchett of Market Street, Charlbury, the largest Oxfordshire employer in 1851 (who was listed also as a farmer, leather dresser, draper and grocer), employed 28 grounders, 8 bleachers, 16 cutters, 8 layers-out and ironers, 8 boys, and as many as 820 females. Eventually the small workshops were replaced by factories, such as that built by Messrs Fownes at Charlbury in 1895. As in boots and shoes, machinery, particularly machines adapted from the Singer sewing machine, became important in speeding up the work.

The larger employers of outworkers sometimes developed into major firms which have continued as a force in the industry to the present. Dents of Worcester is an example in gloves, and Clarks in shoes. Cyrus Clark, of a family of Quaker yeomen, started as a fellmonger and wool-stapler in Street, Somerset. In 1825 he set up on his own, and developed a popular line in warm wool-lined slippers. The growth of the business in shoe production was characterized by the employment of outworkers, who stitched the uppers and soles already cut out by machine in the factory.

None of these hand trades normally produced more than a pittance. A single woman – making gloves for $3\frac{1}{4}$d a pair – might perhaps just be able to live on the earnings so long as the trade thrived. Usually, the work was supplementary to a family income, enabling housewife and daughters, sometimes also the young boys, to eke out the pay of the husband. Families might do quite well so long as the trade was prosperous. But these hand occupations were frequently subject to periodical setbacks: they relied upon the market economy and were not immune from the forces which, in the country at large, determined prosperity or slump. Changes in fashion or a growth of the numbers in the trade caused periodical gluts; then there were months of enforced idleness, hunger and distress. As an occupation, farm work was more reliable, though even there large farmers often turned hands away when times were bad. Perhaps it was the uncertainty of many village occupations which encouraged girls to take up domestic service, badly paid though it was, and the men, when they moved to the towns, to opt for relatively secure, if still low-paid, jobs. Security, the prospect of a small pension, and the glamour of a uniform, attracted them into the army, the police or railway service. Otherwise, they seem to have liked jobs which had some connection with the soil or with animals, and they became grooms, coachmen, carters and gardeners. Of course, lack of education and skills restricted the choices open to them, but on the whole they do not seem to have liked factories or large industrial concerns.

There were, however, expanding industries in the countryside, other than the hand trades, which gave men and boys an alternative to work on the land. Brick-making, as we have noted, was very widespread, but there grew up major concentrations in southern counties, in districts of Sussex, north Kent, and especially south of Bedford in Bedfordshire. Cement works appeared around Portland Bill on the south coast, along the Medway valley, and near Rugby. In the railway era, small market towns and villages developed engine and waggon works and marshalling yards, as at Swindon in Wiltshire, Toton in south Derbyshire and Ashford in east Kent. Rural textile factories, mostly survivors of the water-power days, were of local import-ance in Derbyshire, the southwest and the north. Naval dock-yards provided important growth points in southern counties at Portsmouth, Devonport, Chatham and Sheerness. The railway-created seaside resorts, like Blackpool, Southend, Skegness and

Folkestone, were added to the older ones of the coaching age, Brighton, Weymouth, Sidmouth and Scarborough, to provide expanding opportunities for market-gardeners, fruit-growers and carters, and openings for waiters, beach attendants and domestic servants.

In Cornwall the china clay industry assumed peculiar importance as the number of workings grew and output climbed from the 11,000 tons of 1827 to the 773,000 tons of 1910. In the middle of the century about 7000 men were employed, many of them small leaseholders who worked a few acres in their spare time. By the late 1870s clay workers were paid 2s 6d for a day of $7\frac{1}{2}$ hours, and subsequently the depression in both tin mining and farming encouraged more men to enter the clay works. It was hard labour. A man reckoned to shift 20 tons or more of sand or clay in a day, using only his shovel, and there was much toil in breaking up the clay, pushing the heavy waggons, and loading barrels which might weigh half a ton. There was often a long walk to and from work, and after work in the summer men 'used to go out and turn up a bit of garden to last over the winter'.

An association between mining and land was not confined to china clay. Coal mining communities could be said to have 'one root in the mines, the other in the land'. In late Victorian times many of the pitmen in rural east Cumberland had an acre or two for a cow, and the practice of renting land went back to at least the later eighteenth century. In 1836, for instance, miners' cottages were described as having 'cow grassings and cow houses attached'. This may have been a valuable means of attracting men to these rather remote mines, and of inducing them to stay once there. Certainly mine owners, and also early factory owners elsewhere, took in waste land and established farms especially to supply these nascent industrial communities. In east Cumberland Lord Carlisle had a number of farms, at Kirkhouse, Bowbank and elsewhere. Oats and hay produced on the farms provided fodder for the colliery horses, and some of the grain and livestock was sold direct to the pitmen. Centrally-placed farms also provided convenient bases for the offices, workshops, stables and storehouses needed to service scattered and isolated groups of mines.

Whether these industrial communities provided very much of an attraction to country workers is uncertain. The conditions of work were unfamiliar, arduous, and often dangerous. Miners sometimes worked in water up to their waists, and there were numerous accidents from roof falls and explosions. If farm wages were lower, and many farm workers lacked the means of keeping a cow, yet their occupations offered the compensation of easier, cleaner, and less risky work. Moreover, the housing in industrial hamlets was often little or no better than in farming villages. A Cornishman who about 1890 left a farm to work in the clay pits never forgot the cottage he was given: 'You could see the stars between the slates. My wife wept when she came in . . .' It had only one room, no kitchen, no ceiling, an asphalt floor, and 'a little shed at the side for the washing'. In the east Cumberland colliery settlements some of the early cottages had been adapted from byres and farm buildings. New houses were built in due course, but as late as 1890, though the one-room dwellings had almost gone, there were still many with only two rooms, lacking a piped water supply, and characteristically dark and 'lamentably damp'. As many as 205 of the homes inspected in 1887 had more than two persons per room. Large families, and the presence of relations and lodgers, added to limited accommodation in creating over-crowding. Nevertheless, availability of cow grazings and easy access to the open country were amenities that equally over-crowded families in the towns did not enjoy.

A great many of the mines of the time had been opened on land belonging to the aristocracy and gentry. For the most part these pits were leased by contractors who ran the mines and paid the landowner a royalty on the quantity of coal raised. In some instances, however, the pits, and also ironworks and related businesses, were operated directly by the landowner himself, through the medium of his agents and managers. Where this was the case the proprietor was obliged to take some interest in the technical problems of mines and works, and especially in those accidents and breakdowns which might cause stoppages and financial loss. Some aristocratic owners, too, displayed a concern for their workforce unusual for the age, with the consequence that the workers' housing, village amenities, and working conditions were all superior to those generally prevailing. The management of Earl Fitzwilliam's mines in south Yorkshire, for example, showed an unusual concern for the men's safety, and while this was obviously the most vital need, there were many other advantages which the Fitzwilliam miners enjoyed. Indeed, as Graham Mee remarks in a recent study, 'it is very doubtful if any group of miners were in receipt of a more generous and comprehensive set of benefits in the first half of the nineteenth century'.

A superior standard of housing was certainly one of these benefits. The Commissioner appointed under the Mines Act of 1842, Seymour Tremenheere, produced a highly favourable report on the pitmen's houses at the Fitzwilliams' Elsecar mine:

> Those at Elsecar consist of four rooms and a pantry, a small
> back court, ash-pit, a pigsty, and a garden; the small space
> before the front door is walled round, and kept neat with
> flowers or paving stones; a low gate preventing the children
> from straying into the road. Proper conveniences are attached
> to every six or seven houses, and kept perfectly clean. The
> gardens of 500 yards of ground each, are cultivated with much
> care. The rent for cottage and garden is 2s a week. Each man
> can also hire an additional 300 yards for potato ground . . .

Educational facilities, too, were not neglected: the Fitzwilliams
supported a Mechanics Institute, a library, and schools. Those
rather few employees who lived so long as to be beyond useful
work were relieved by a small pension, and pensions were also
provided for widows. Despite the concern for safety in the mines
shown by the Earl and his managers, there were occasional fatal
accidents, some of them arising from the men's own disregard for
safety regulations. The pensions paid to widows varied in amount
with circumstances, and the Earl himself took a close interest in
the matter, writing, for instance:

> I think she is left with one child – what have I given to the
> widows of those who were crushed by a fall of coal about a
> year ago – what were their circumstances and what are hers?

The rural communities which were supported by coal mines and
isolated factories and ironworks tended to be self-contained.
Sons followed fathers down the pit, and strangers were uncommon and were not easily accepted. The Carlisle mines in east
Cumberland were typical in that the small number of newcomers
came very largely from neighbouring parishes and rarely from far
afield. Though these workers had links with the land, grazing
their own cows, digging potatoes, and keeping their pigs, their
livelihood was strange and alien to the inhabitants of neighbouring agricultural villages. The kinds of industry with which they
were familiar were those ancient crafts like cloth-making, clothing, leather tanning or shoemaking, which had always been
carried on in the home or small workshop, and were often the
part-time occupation of the womenfolk, subsidiary to a living
from the land. But in time even these traditional trades changed
their character, and declined and disappeared altogether. Factories, rural offshoots of the industrial revolution, made their

A 10hp self-propelled traction engine 'Hero' manufactured by Tasker's of Andover in 1869. It is shown travelling to the Southampton Show, preceded by a man with a red flag. Notice too the steersman at the wheel at the front, and the stoker at the back.

appearance in country towns and villages, though frequently very modest in size when compared with the great establishments of the industrial cities. Sometimes the cottage hand worker was able to adapt his or her skill to the needs of machinery and sit long hours at the factory bench instead of at the cottage door. Often, however, the works were of a kind and scale quite beyond the experience of the old traditional crafts. Such were the bigger foundries, cement works, and canning and jam factories, while massive flour mills, breweries and paper mills superseded the parochial mills and brew-houses of the past. Some areas saw a considerable growth of employment in large works and factories. In North Devon, not an area that might be thought of as remarkable for industrial growth, there were by the 1880s a butter factory, two plough works, and a leather-dressing establishment. In addition there were saw and turning mills, brick and pottery works, shipbuilding at Appledore, a foundry at Barnstaple employing over 50, a lace factory with 250 men, women, and children employed, and three collar factories at Bideford with as many as a thousand hands.

Though the great brewing firms of London and Burton-on-Trent had long dominated the industry, provincial firms also grew in size, and from a base in a country town now supplied and controlled many of the country inns which formerly brewed their own beer. Such were – or are – Strong of Romsey in Hampshire,

Style and Winch, Fremlin's and Mason's, all of Maidstone, and Shepherd Neame of Faversham, Kent. Canneries and jam factories encouraged a growth of smallholders in their immediate neighbourhood, and the vegetables and fruit had a ready market at the works on their doorstep. In Cambridgeshire, during the agricultural depression, Messrs Chivers & Son transformed the villages of Histon and Trumpington.

> Mr Chivers, sen. – who resides in a comfortable white brick residence on the village green – started a jam factory, and to it are brought all sorts of fruit from the whole district. The working men are prosperous and contented. Formerly there was a deal of poverty. Mr Chivers commenced business, he said, with three acres of land; some friends helped him, in due course, to purchase 150 during the first ten years of his business. Now he has some 500 . . . The working men of Histon, in numerous cases, do not hesitate to pay 50s to 60s an acre for land; whilst a few miles off, in the adjoining county of Essex, land cannot even be let rent free in numerous parts. On the other side of the Colne Valley is a farm which, a few years since, could not be let or sold to anyone. Mr Chivers, however, has now transformed it into a veritable Arcadia.

Jam-making concerns not only spread new forms of cultivation but also offered opportunities of supplementary earnings in the busy seasons. At the beginning of the twentieth century the Tiptree Fruit Farm in Essex, source of the famous Tiptree jams, occupied some 430 acres, and was paying women from 5s to 8s a day to pick strawberries, and 1s 4d a day to draw straw beneath the plants.

Country towns also saw the growth of makers of agricultural implements and machinery. Lincoln, for instance, became the home of numerous firms, some of which achieved international reputations for their products. Among the smaller manufacturers was John Cooke, who began by inventing a successful plough, moved to Lincoln, and in 1857 opened a works which at his death thirty years later was employing 70 men. The Robey brothers established a substantial business making portable steam engines, steam ploughs and threshing machines, while William Foster, in the same line of work, had 200 men under him by 1885. Clayton and Shuttleworth Ltd created a much greater concern with wide international markets, and by 1870 employed 1200 men making 1000 steam engines and 900 threshing machines a year. Another company to assume great importance was founded by Ruston,

Burton and Proctor. Ruston was the leading figure and built up a famous manufacture of portable engines, steam locomotives, excavators, road rollers and tractors. By 1912 the Ruston firm employed 5200 men and 315 office staff. In 1851 only 62 men and boys in Lincoln were recorded as engaged in iron manufacturing; by 1870 this number had grown to 2500, and by the end of the century that number had doubled.

On a much smaller scale the same story was repeated in other market towns. Even tiny, sleepy Dorchester saw in 1870 the establishment of Francis Eddison's Steam Ploughing Works. There were many on the farms round Dorchester who entertained grave doubts about the wisdom of steam ploughing the chalky soils, and indeed in dry weather clouds of dust enveloped the steersman, who 'had to toil in goggles with a handkerchief tied over his mouth', as Barbara Kerr tells us. An attempt at hiring out steam-plough sets to suspicious and conservative farmers had already come to grief before Eddison's arrival. But his energy and persistence succeeded, and he was the first contractor to operate on a county-wide basis. However, though some local men found employment in his concern, its backbone consisted of skilled hands from the north, and especially from Eddison's own home of Leeds. The works whistle, wakening the men at 5.45, disturbed the ancient quiet of Dorchester, and Thomas Hardy was one of the residents who complained about this unwelcome industrial irruption. But steam ploughing created extra work at a time when agriculture was in the doldrums, and carters, in particular, gained additional earnings hauling coal and water to the fields where the engines were working. And as Eddison cushioned the impact of seasonal demand and farm depression by moving into road rollers, a small but useful area of work for mechanically-minded country lads was opened.

As new sources of employment appeared in the country towns and the old village trades decayed, so village communities tended to fill the role of dormitories and satellites. The expansion of the population and business of the towns also provided country people with openings other than those in factories and foundries, as shop assistants, carters, office workers and domestic servants. Villagers travelled to work by train or bicycle, and inevitably there was a drift of people making their homes in the towns where they earned their living. Nineteenth-century urbanization was not simply a matter of the creation of vast new conglomerations dominated by belching factory chimneys; the old cathedral cities and market-towns also expanded, if in a far less spectacular manner. Thus Lincoln, whose growth of industrial activity was closely connected with the land, rose from a modest 7205 souls in 1801 to reach 57,294 in 1911; Ipswich, similarly, increased from 11,000 to 74,000 in the same period; Oxford from 12,000 to 53,000; Reading from 10,000 to 88,000; and York from 17,000 to 82,000. These, however, were examples of the more remarkable instances of urban revival. There were many other old towns which experienced a much more modest pace of change or even saw long periods of stagnation. Bath, for instance, which climbed rapidly from 33,000 to 51,000 in the thirty years after 1801, saw its growth slowly fizzle out and its numbers decline in the later nineteenth century; Cambridge by 1871 had doubled its 10,000 inhabitants of 1801, but then took another forty years to add a further 10,000; and King's Lynn took a whole century merely to double its 1801 figure of 10,000.

Many smaller towns and rural districts showed even smaller increases. In the 110 years between 1801 and 1911 the total population of England and Wales multiplied four-fold. But this overall increase was the product of a combination of high growth in London and the major cities, more modest growth in the lesser towns, and near stagnation in many small country towns. Numerous villages did not grow at all, or even declined. The combined population of six English counties with the slowest rates of population increase, Cornwall, Huntingdonshire, Oxfordshire, Rutland, Westmorland and Wiltshire, was 583,000 in 1801, and 944,000 in 1911, a rise of only 62 per cent in over a century, or less than a sixth of the national average increase. The process of urbanization had already gone far by 1851, when the town population had just overtaken the country-dwellers; by 1881 there were more than twice the number of people in the towns as in the country.

But observers at the turn of the century had no need of statistics to see what had happened, and was still happening. They noted, like J.L.Green, the decay of the old rural trades, they listened, like Rider Haggard, to the farmers' complaints of a growing shortage of hands, especially of good men; and, like F.G.Heath and William Savage, they waxed indignant over abandoned cottages, fallen into ruin, and the neglected state of many of those still inhabited. Free trade and the changes in farming had much to do with the situation, the superior wages and amenities of the towns even more. The growth of modern industry and the development of urban society drew the countryman from the land and from his ancient trades; the cottage loom was silenced, and if the country housewives had not yet quite laid aside their lace and gloves, there too, the end was not far off.

6 The Land Agents

The nineteenth-century land agent had ancient forbears, going back to the medieval bailiff or steward of manors. Indeed, the term 'steward' survived into the early nineteenth century, when it was still quite common to use the description 'land steward' for the man placed in charge of the proprietor's landed property. Sometimes the land steward was also the house steward and had responsibility for running the mansion, but generally the two posts were separate and distinct.

There were, in fact, two kinds of land agent, the full-time salaried official who ran the large estate, and the independent professional man who, for a commission, looked after small estates or the detached properties of a large landowner. The full-time official was the direct descendant of the former steward, while the independent land or estate agent had come to replace the local attorney or farmer who earlier had been entrusted with the supervision of small or isolated properties. In both branches it was a profession in which lawyers had always been strong, in part because the sale, purchase and management of land gave rise to numerous legal problems with which a lawyer was best equipped to deal. Solicitors remained strongly entrenched in the business of land agency, though towards the end of the nineteenth century they were giving place to surveyors. This was especially marked after the founding of the Institution of Surveyors in 1868, when a supply of professionally trained land agents became available. But long before this the surveyor was becoming a recognized specialist in land measurement and valuation, and his services were in great demand in the era of parliamentary enclosure of open fields and commons after the middle eighteenth century. The enclosure commissioners themselves, originally described in Enclosure Acts as farmers or simply 'gentlemen', were increasingly replaced by surveyors in the later enclosures.

Competence in both law and surveying was obviously important for men charged with the responsibility for landed property, but these by no means exhausted the list of desirable qualifications. The authors of treatises of estate management claimed that no agent should be without a thorough knowledge of every kind of rural undertaking – including the culture of wastes and of timber, methods of irrigation, drainage, embanking, the building of canals, laying-out and repair of roads, construction of mills and engines and of rural architecture – to say nothing of familiarity with economics, statistics, accounting and banking. But generally an understanding of soils, and the kinds of farming best suited to them, were more important requisites. The agent had to be able to judge whether a tenant's farming was appropriate and whether it met the usual standards of the district. Tenants had to be prevented from damaging the land by taking exhausting crops, and sometimes the farmers were bound by their agreements to follow the agent's advice in these matters. Frequently agents were directly involved in farming themselves, having responsibility for the proprietor's home farm and often running a farm of their own, let to them at a low or nominal rent as one of their perquisites. Kersey Cooper, agent for the Duke of Grafton, not only looked after the Duke's home farm but also 1300 acres of his own. He managed an estate of 14,000 acres and saw to the mansion as well, but still found time to visit the weekly markets and spend a day or two with the Suffolk hounds.

The period was one which saw a growth of interest in the application of science to agriculture, and increasingly experiments, especially ones concerning fertilizers, were published in the farming journals and were making farming less a matter of simple trial and error. The theories of Liebig were discussed by scientifically-minded landowners and farmers, and at Rothamsted the famous team of Gilbert and Lawes carried out carefully controlled trials to test the effects on plant growth of various kinds and quantities of fertilizer. The new 'artificial' fertilizer, superphosphate, was developed by a process of treating coprolites or phosphate rock with sulphuric acid, and in 1842 Lawes opened at Deptford the first factory for manufacturing superphosphate. Agents were expected to have informed opinions on the scientific controversies of the day and an understanding of the merits of the widening range of fertilizers available.

The application of 'artificials', as well as of guano imported from South America, and the use also of the older kinds of manures brought into the farm was expensive, if only because of the high cost of carriage. Farmers were reluctant to invest heavily in fertilizing their land if their fields were badly drained and it was likely that much of their outlay would be thrown away. Expensive pedigree stock would be placed at risk if grazed on ill-drained pastures. Further, the use of the growing range of factory-made implements and machines, such as drills, cultivators, horse-hoes, hay tedders, and reapers, was discouraged by waterlogged soils where the trampling of the horses might do much harm. Drainage, therefore, was seen as the essential pre-requisite of high farming. It was the foundation of greater efficiency and the first means by which the land was to be made capable of bearing richer crops, and hence higher rents. Leading agents of the great estates were among the most enthusiastic advocates of the methods of high farming, and hence of drainage. Andrew Thompson, one of three brothers prominent as agents and experts on land improvement, argued that drainage was the indispensable basis for other advances 'in the shape of improved cultivation and manures, of improved buildings, and frequently a fresh arrangement of the fields'. Arguing that land improvement was an obligation laid upon the conscientious owner, agents persuaded their employers to find large sums for subsoil drainage. The invention in the early 1840s of efficient mobile tile and pipe machines, which could make the tiles on the site, lowered the cost of under-drainage and helped to push it forward. Land Drainage Companies were formed to advance loans to landowners, proprietors of wet clay lands were encouraged to drain by the government's cheap loans offered as compensation for Corn Law Repeal. But, at some £4 to £8 per acre, drainage still remained a costly investment. Frequently the expense was shared between landlord and tenant, the landlord providing the tiles and the tenant the labour. Alternatively, the landlord undertook the whole investment but added five per cent of his outlay to the rent. It is estimated that some £24 m. was spent on under-drainage and associated improvements to buildings in the thirty years after 1846.

There was little point in spending large sums on drainage if the farm buildings were antiquated and inadequate. Farmers interested in practising the best modes of high farming wanted well-planned dairies, housing suited to the efficient fattening of bullocks, farmyards designed to collect the manure for use in the fields, and barns adapted to the use of steam power for threshing, root-slicing and chaff-cutting. And a farmer of this kind would not be satisfied with a cramped or inconvenient farmhouse for himself. High farming, therefore, required the landowner to invest heavily in bricks and mortar, and here again the agent's expertise would be called upon for suitable designs and the supervision of construction. A knowledge of building work and road construction had always been part of the agent's qualifications, and became even more important in the era of enclosure and high farming, when the consolidation and improvement of farms required many new buildings and service roads. In addition, there were always repairs to be made at the end of a lease, or alterations to suit a new tenant. Flood control and the maintenance of river banks were frequently of importance, and in coastal areas there had to be repairs to sea walls damaged by storms. The agent, too, kept a wary eye on the proceedings of canal and river navigation companies, to see that the boatmen caused no damage to crop or fences, and that farms were not affected by changes in the water levels. When the railways appeared the agents were much involved in negotiations over routes, rights of way, sales of land, and the location of the stations. The farmers had to be satisfied on questions of access to lands cut in two by the tracks, and railway contractors were known to be not above making unauthorized deviations from their line or taking up excessive amounts of land with their embankments.

Much of an agent's time was absorbed by day-to-day dealings with tenants. He listened to their grievances, enquired into demands for repairs, considered whether husbandry covenants had been breached, and examined the justice of proposed rent reductions. The collection of rents each spring and autumn gave rise to problems. Farmers normally paid their rents six months in arrear. On large estates, particularly, they were often allowed to carry longer arrears, sometimes for periods of years. Some tenants were notorious for finding excuses for delay – the unfavourable nature of the seasons, losses of livestock, low prices in the markets, heavy outlays on improvements. Sometimes they failed to appear on the appointed day, or paid in only a part of what was due, saying they would send the rest later. Agents reported a 'good rent day' if all the payments were got in and there were few complaints. H.V.Tippet, agent to the Earl of Scarbrough, reported of the June 1874 collection:

> Our rent day at Tickhill went off fairly yesterday. All paid up
> – a fair amount of grumbling but nothing serious except
> Cuthbert who states that he will give notice to quit in August
> unless your Lordship will reduce his rent £50 per annum, and
> have the rabbits killed . . .

There was always a danger of small occupiers absconding with their rents unpaid, and the agent kept a watch on tenants known to be in difficulties, to see they were not selling off their cattle or implements in order to forestall a warrant of distress. The payment of tithes was especially unpopular with the farmers, and their collection, too, was fraught with difficulties.

Through all this the agent had to try and maintain good relations with the farmers. Landowners disliked having their management complained of, especially when they looked to the farmers' support at election time. They would not, however, put up with 'unsteady' tenants, those who gained an unsavoury reputation for drunkenness or licentious behaviour. Such men reflected on the respectability of the estate and the credit of its owner, and were given short shrift. But frequent changes of tenants were to be avoided: short tenancies led to bad farming and excessive outlays on repairs, and entailed the risk that farms might fall into hand, with consequent trouble and loss. Good landlords thought they had an obligation to be 'easy' over fixing the rents, and they often made reductions to old or specially deserving tenant. Undeserving ones, however, were refused. One of Lord Scarbrough's tenants was refused a reduction since his farm was 'full of twitch and altogether unfit to grow anything. The fences are neglected and full of gaps.' In bad times temporary rent abatements were adopted by common consent, the lesser proprietors following the lead of the greater. Leases were rarely interpreted very strictly, except where there was clear evidence that the buildings had been neglected or the land damaged by an improper course of crops. Legal disputes between landlord and tenant were therefore unusual. Where the landlord was a keen sportsman the well-to-do tenants were often invited to ride with the hunt or make up shooting parties. There was customarily a tenants' dinner after rent day, and the farmers were invited to the house for celebrations called to mark some special occasion, such as a wartime victory or the coming of age of the owner's heir. Landowners went out of their way to keep old tenants, and allowed farms to be passed on to relations, though necessarily new occupiers had to be found from time to time. Where farms were let on lease there was a fairly general expectation that the end of the term would see a change of tenant. An important part of an agent's responsibility was to seek out new tenants and look into their suitability for the farm in question. References were taken up with previous landlords, and the farmer's professional reputation and command of capital were carefully investigated. It was frequently the case that a farmer who offered less rent than other applicants, but who possessed more capital and experience, was the one preferred.

Another consideration that might be relevant was the farmer's political views. A docile, complaisant man was to be preferred where the landlord had strong interests in politics or sport. The Earl of Yarborough, as R.J.Olney tells us, once asked that the tenant of one of his more important farms should be 'not of a too *political party man*, or one that would make himself too busy in parochial matters or a dissenter'. The Earl also adopted a strict attitude towards his tenants' social behaviour. He was displeased to hear that one of the occupiers had held a shoot on the day of his father's funeral, and he expressed the hope that another would give up steeple-chasing, which he regarded as a low amusement. When one of his tenants evicted a labourer from a cottage, the Earl evicted the tenant from his farm; however, he showed his regard for the offender's family, one long connected with the estate, by offering the vacant farm to the man's brother.

Where landowners, like the Earl of Yarborough, took a keen personal interest in the running of his estate, the agent might be little more than a go-between who referred all matters of importance to his principal. Sometimes, however, distance from the landowner's mansion gave a local agent some degree of independence, though he was expected to keep the owner well-informed of the current situation in the neighbourhood. Thomas Dungworth, the Earl of Scarbrough's rather aptly-named Lincolnshire agent, looked after his Glentworth estate, had a home in the mansion there, and occupied a holding worth £152 a year. When the price fall at the end of the Napoleonic Wars caused the tenants to claim a rent reduction, Dungworth marshalled facts and figures to support their case:

> The Farmers' embarrassment at this time has not *wholly* and *altogether* been occasioned by the Pressure of the times alone, in paying High Rents – Heavy Taxes, and the low prices of Grain and Cattle but has *partly* been affected by the Failure of the Wheat Crop which has been very materially Injured by the Mill-dew or Blight, which has caused a very great deficiency in Quantity, as well as that of a mean quality . . .

Lord Scarbrough, however, was a landlord who found the post-1815 pressure for rent reductions difficult to accept. In his view the farmers should have been less extravagant in their palmy days and put something aside for less favourable times:

> Had they not given Dinners, with different sorts of Wine, drove their Gigs and sent their daughters to Boarding Schools at 40 and 50 gns a year instead of teaching them to be good Housewife's at Home. They would now have had something to spare for worse Times and not endeavour to make the *whole* Burden fall on the landlord.

In the event, as T.W.Beastall notes in his recent study of the Scarbrough estates, the Earl decided that a return of £600 to the tenants would be sufficient compensation for their distress. He had already reduced his rents by 16½ per cent in 1816, and had made a comparison of them with those of other Lincolnshire proprietors, the Earl of Yarborough and Lord Manners, and he had taken advice from Earl Fitzwilliam.

From time to time there was a call for a general report on the condition of an estate, in order to determine whether improvements were desirable and whether the rents should be revised. Such a report might include a detailed consideration of the soils, the farming, drainage, the availability of markets, transport facilities and many other aspects of the property. In 1845 William Downes carried out a survey of this kind for the eighth Earl Scarbrough. Despite all of the recent difficulties, Downes reported, there still existed on the Lincolnshire estate 'a set of practical farmers, who may bid defiance to the rest of England . . . but here as in other quarters are to be found minds full of prejudice which reason can scarcely turn.' At Skegness (later to be developed by the ninth Earl as a new seaside resort) Downes noted that the agricultural land offered good prospects for profitable farming. The soil was rich alluvial deposit, well suited to both pasture and crops. Markets were readily available at Spilsby, Wainfleet and Partney, the famous horse fair at Horncastle was not far off, and the roads were good. Drainage arrangements were satisfactory, and since the sea had receded there was little danger of flooding. There were plentiful supplies of brick earth, stone and shingle. The land tax was heavy, however, and there was a drainage rate of 1s an acre, though fortunately the poor rates were low. Hedges were needed to provide more shelter for stock, but he thought that, in general, the advantages of the property made it possible to raise its value by 25 per cent.

Where industrial enterprises developed on estates it was vital to find agents who understood them. The landowner who knew nothing of coal mines or iron works was very much in his agent's hands. The sixth Earl Scarbrough, for instance, found the technical details of a new mine lease quite beyond him. Writing to his coal agent in Durham he confessed that he was unable to make decisions on 'the *underground* work, which it is not to be suppos'd I can understand'. He was obliged to rely entirely on his agent's reputation as an expert, since 'many of the Propositions are describ'd in such technical Terms (peculiar, I suppose, to the Coal Trade) that you may imagine, I do not understand them but wherever I do, I perfectly approve of yr. answers . . .'

Another Yorkshire owner, the fifth Earl Fitzwilliam, went out of his way to obtain an understanding of mines, steam engines and industrial management. This was especially valuable to him as his enterprises were not leased out but were managed directly by his estate staff, and the Earl assumed overall control. No purchases were to be made, or 'new or extraordinary works were to be commenced', without his prior approval, and strict regulations were issued for the checking of bills and the regular examination of books and ledgers. But as Graham Mee shows in his study of the Fitzwilliam industrial enterprises, the structure of management was only gradually adapted to the industrial branches of the estate. For many years the House Steward, Joshua Biram, was responsible for the collieries, assisted only by an overlooker, two underground stewards or underlookers, and a banksman at each pit. In addition he had responsibility for the farm, smithy, garden, stables, park and house. It was not until 1833, when Benjamin Biram succeeded his father, that the posts of house steward and colliery manager were separated. Even then the duties of the Superintendent, as he was now known, combined the diverse functions that nowadays would be carried out by a colliery manager, mining engineer, accountant, sales manager and personnel manager.

It appears that the running of the six collieries, with their 350 miners and labourers, absorbed most of the Superintendent's attention. The Birams, indeed, were eminent mining engineers. Their plans enabled successive Earls Fitzwilliam to work their Barnsley seam for eighty years without requiring new capital works for pumping. Joshua Biram was employed as an arbitrator in disputes between landowners and colliery owners, and his son acted in a similar capacity in cases concerning collieries and the owners of canals and railways. Benjamin Biram's opinion was sought by coroners who tried to determine the causes of a number of disastrous pit explosions, and in 1849 he was one of a number of leading mining engineers who gave evidence to the House of Lords Select Committee on Accidents in Coal Mines. Benjamin was at least partially responsible for the good safety record of the Fitzwilliam mines, towards which his own inventions made a valuable contribution. He patented a safety lamp and a winding system, and his design of ventilating fan was much used. His patented rotating vane anemometer, an instrument for measuring the speed of air currents, was still manufactured as the Davis Biram anemometer as recently as 1965.

The Birams, however, were exceptionally able mine managers, and it was more common for owners of collieries to have great difficulty in finding capable and efficient mineral agents. In the early decades of the century, according to the Select Committee

Report, under a half of the men placed in charge of mines in the Black Country could be considered well educated, and not a few were illiterate. Professional training and qualifications were still not commonplace, and proprietors had to take their agents very much on trust, relying on their experience and personal reputation. Many, undoubtedly, were incompetent. The Dudley properties, for instance, declined seriously under the supervision of Francis Downing, a promoted clerk, who despite his lack of technical knowledge was placed in charge of both the farming and the large industrial enterprises of the estate. In 1836, when the Dudley estates were in the hands of trustees, two mining engineers were called in to make a report. They noted an alarming situation, with shafts in bad repair, a lack of plans of the workings, and coal taken from beyond the boundaries of the estate. Subsequently, James Loch, at this time the most eminent of landowners' agents and financial advisers, was called in. He endorsed the mining report, and recommended the replacement of Downing by a professional engineer. Loch reported, too, that the agricultural parts of the estate were sadly neglected: the farmers lacked enterprise, and the dilapidated conditions of the farms 'generally exceed what in my experience in any other part of the country I ever met with'.

The career of James Loch linked him with some of the wealthiest and most influential men of the age. As a law student at Edinburgh he associated with a talented group which included Francis Horner, Sydney Smith, John Murray and Henry Brougham. He qualified and practised as a lawyer, and subsequently emerged as the best-known estate manager of his day, consulted by leading proprietors such as the Howards of Castle Howard, the Earl of Ellesmere, and the Dudley Trust. He was a Member of Parliament for 25 years, and his advice was sought by Peel, Grey, Huskisson and Brougham. He might well have made a career in politics but found his true *métier* as director of the affairs of great landowners. His most important role was as Chief Agent to the Sutherland family, a position he held from 1812 to his death in 1855. It was in this powerful capacity that he became known as 'the Duke's Premier' and 'the Sutherland Metternich'. He controlled not only the family's estates in Staffordshire, Shropshire and Yorkshire, but also the extensive property in Sutherland. The inheritance by the Sutherland family of the Bridgewater Canal took Loch into the complex problems of waterways and railway competition. The Canal was enormously important, producing revenues of some £75,000 a year, and it was from the surplus of their canal and estate income in England that the

Sutherlands financed the relocation of the Sutherland crofters displaced by the sheep clearances in the highlands. Large sums were devoted to establishing the crofters in coastal settlements, industrial enterprises were fostered, and harbours and roads improved – over £79,000 was spent on roads alone. The belief was that the coastal economy of northern Scotland could be fertilized with imported technology and skills, for example those of the Staffordshire coal miners introduced into the region. This confidence, unfortunately, proved to be misplaced. The fall in prices of the local products, the uncertainty of the fisheries, the failure of industrial enterprises, and the overcrowding of the new settlements as population continued to grow, all showed that the 'coastal economy' was less viable than originally supposed. In the end the Sutherlands had to encourage the crofters' emigration to America and Australia as the only way out.

Loch regarded his Sutherland responsibilities as comparable with the task of ruling a small country. 'The property of a great English Nobleman', he asserted, 'must be managed on the same principle as a little kingdom, not like the affairs of a little Merchant. The future and lasting interest and honour of the family as well as their immediate income must be kept in view – while a merchant thinks only of his daily profits and his own immediate life interest.' Great estates could not be run simply as businesses, Loch argued. The consequence of this view was that the Sutherland tenants, like those on other great estates, enjoyed rents which were deliberately kept below the average of the area, and so held their lands on easier terms than their neighbours. It was, said Loch, 'fit and proper that those who hold of a great man should do so.'

Not all agents had such lofty principles as Loch, or were as proficient in their work as the Birams. Men capable of undertaking great responsibilities were scarce, and numbers of agents were incompetent or even dishonest. A distrust of stewards went far back into earlier centuries, and doubts about their ability and probity were certainly reasons why many landed proprietors disliked having farms fall into hand and were reluctant to assume the direct management of mines or industrial works. Although elaborate systems were devised for the supervision of staff and the checking of their accounts, it was almost an impossibility to ensure that no fraud occurred. It was difficult, for instance, to be certain that money said to have been spent on repairs had been so laid out, or that all the expenditure was strictly essential. Dishonest agents often found ready collaborators among local suppliers and tradesmen. And men placed in charge of properties detached from the main body of the estates necessarily enjoyed some freedom of action, while their activities might be subject to inspection only very infrequently. A common failing was the prevalence of delays in the completion of accounts and the remittance of cash balances. Local agents sometimes used the balances for their own purposes, and there was always risk of embezzlement. Often, however, it was merely that the agent was dilatory rather than dishonest. When he was a farmer or, in the case of industrial works, an engineer, then accounting might not be his strong point. If pressed for his accounts and balances such a man was inclined to excuse himself on the ground of illness or pressure of business. The manager of Earl Fitzwilliam's Elsecar ironworks, Henry Hartop, replied in 1843 to a demand for his accounts by saying that his mind had given way 'beneath the pressure, to so great an extent, as to make it impossible for me to balance the Elsecar Books correctly'. Shortly after writing this he gave up the job, but it was another seven years before the estate received his accounts.

In practice it was often difficult to distinguish genuine incompetence from dishonesty. But there were certainly some crooked agents who deliberately set out to feather their nests at the landlords' expense. Generally this occurred where the proprietor, too wrapped up in politics, sport, or the *beau monde*, spent very little time at home and could not be bothered to examine his accounts. The Irish agents of absentee landowners were renowned for their rapacity. They embezzled the rents, got the estate into a tangle of debts, and secured a financial stranglehold on the property in the process. In County Cork the appropriately-named Alfred Cleverly made away with some £24,000 of Lord Mountcashel's money, and his depredations even extended to his lordship's plate, his gold snuff-boxes, his trinkets and his yacht.

Equally corrupt and treacherous men could be found much nearer home. Barbara Kerr writes in her *Bound to the Soil* of the peculations of Robert Short Waters, agent to the seventh Earl of Shaftesbury. Owing to the Earl's wide-ranging interests in factory and mining legislation, and his preoccupation with the reform of housing, lunatic asylums, and the climbing chimney boys, the management of his large Dorset estate was neglected. For ten years Waters ran the properties unchecked. An able, ambitious man, Waters was appointed as agent in 1845 at the early age of 23, presumably on the strength of the experience gained by working with his father, who was agent to a number of owners. Waters installed himself in a farm of 240 acres and built handsome stables for the purpose of indulging his interest in horse breeding. Here he enjoyed 'a comfortable establishment with three maid servants and a groom'. He kept packs of hounds and well-filled wine cellars, went racing, and was said to live 'at a rate of £2000 a year with an income of £500'. Revenues totalling some £21,000 a year passed through his hands, and he took it upon himself to grant long leases and spend heavily on improvements. As a critic of the country's industrial system, the Earl was anxious that, in return, his estate should not be attacked for its backwardness. He was particularly enthusiastic for extensive drainage works to be undertaken, and for new cottages to be provided for the farmworkers. Though absorbed by his many concerns with legislation and reform, the Earl was soon aware of a need for stricter financial control of his affairs, but the introduction of a system of separate accounts merely allowed Waters to conceal his activities and spread additional confusion. The Earl's auditor found it difficult or impossible to check the agent's figures, and indeed the expenditure on drainage was never audited at all, since the only account kept by Waters took the form of casual jottings in his diary.

The costly drainage works enabled Waters to falsify the sums spent on bricks, tiles and timber, and to cover items used on his own farm. He took advantage of the cupidity of local contractors, and augmented his salary by £430 by getting himself made agent and surveyor to the Land Drainage Company. He extracted arrears of rent from a tenant, while recording them in his books as written off. His office clerk, increasingly worried by the frauds in which he was involved, threatened to commit suicide. Waters eventually dismissed the clerk, after first trying to persuade him to emigrate, and then making an attempt to get him certified as a lunatic. Eventually, in 1863, the Earl took action. Plagued by overdrafts and by rumours of his agent's high living, he requested Waters's resignation. A new auditor found that no books had been balanced for seven years, and the more recent accounts in utter chaos. Waters responded to the crisis by taking the offensive. He brought a suit in Chancery against Shaftesbury, alleging that he had advanced from his own pocket sums still unpaid. The criminal charges brought against Waters by the Earl became enmeshed in the Chancery case, and the enormous complexities of the agent's tangled web of accounts delayed proceedings. In the end Shaftesbury agreed to a dropping of legal proceedings on both sides. Waters went off to a lucrative job abroad, while Shaftesbury struggled for the rest of his life to put things right and clear up the debts. He still continued his philanthropic activities. 'Philanthropy', he said feelingly, 'combined with a peerage, reduced a man to the lowest point.'

As against unprincipled plunderers of the Cleverly or Waters kind, there were the conscientious agents who rendered their masters a lifetime of devoted service. Such men came to identify themselves with the estate, and saw their every action as affecting the family's reputation and its future. Sometimes they went much beyond mere responsibility for property management and played an important role in the guiding of the family finances. Francis Blaikie, who was agent to the celebrated farming pioneer, Coke of Norfolk, felt morally obliged to concern himself with his employer's long-term financial position. He was the more concerned to do so because Coke himself was inclined to be careless over money matters and had little regard for his future income and outgoings. 'I am quite appalled with the present and future prospect of Mr Coke's affairs', Blaikie wrote to the family lawyer in 1822. 'Would to God Mr Coke could but see these matters in the same light that I do . . .' He tried to ensure that the capital derived from sales of land was not treated as income but was re-invested, for otherwise 'Mr Coke's pecuniary resources will be alarmingly narrowed, and the blame will ultimately be attached to both you and myself – I have the matter much at heart.' When there was an urgent need for economy, as in 1822, Blaikie took a cut in salary from £650 to £550.

He was also a very competent and energetic manager of the Coke farms, as Dr Parker, the modern authority on Coke, tells us. Blaikie believed he had a responsibility for diffusing his specialised knowledge of farming matters, and he distributed his own agricultural pamphlets to the tenants. He further publicized his ideas by entering questions in the *Farmers Journal* under a variety of assumed names, so as to be able to send in the replies. He gave detailed advice to tenants, and was the inventor of an inverted horse-hoe, designed to clean away the weeds without smothering the rows of growing plants. When in 1816 he first took up his duties at Holkham, he made a general report on the farms and the tenantry, and drafted a volume concerning the general forms of leases and covenants. His advice extended to farm buildings as well as husbandry, and he tried to instil among tenants who fell into arrear a sense of their ingratitude towards their 'indulgent and kind landlord'. So impressive were Blaikie's 'clear head and correct judgment' that Coke's lawyer, Philip Hanrott of Lincoln's Inn, advised Coke that the agent should be brought into all discussions of the family's financial affairs.

Outstanding agents of exceptional gifts and knowledge could

be found on leading estates at any time in the nineteenth century. Some had trained for their work as pupils of an established official, like John Beasley, the Spencers' agent at Althorp, or H.W.Keary, the Holkham agent in the mid-nineteenth century. Quite frequently the expertise was handed down with the post from father to son, and an estate might be run for a long period by two or three generations of the same family. The general tendency was for the agent to spend most or all of his working life in the service of one employer. This was one reason, in addition to agents' origins and social conservatism, why they identified themselves so closely with the estate and its long-term future. Christopher Haedy, from 1839 to 1859 chief agent or auditor of the Bedford estates, well earned his high salary of £1800 and a London house, as Professor Spring tells us. Haedy spent several hours a day hearing tenants' complaints, and while at Woburn kept 'the morning to out of door work and the evening for pen and ink work'. He declined an invitation to dine with the Duke because the loss of an evening would throw out his routine. In addition to the normal run of estate duties, Haedy was familiar with the qualities of the domestic staff and their responsibilities. He made all the arrangements for the sixth Duke's funeral, decided the order of procession when the Queen and Prince Albert paid a visit to Woburn in 1841, and hired detectives to guard against the appearance of London thieves. He even went so far as making trials to see whether candles costing 2s 1d a pound were as good as those usually purchased at 3s. When he came to lay down his responsibility he wrote a memorandum: 'I retire from the Auditorship with the pleasing consciousness that your Grace's estate and affairs are in a condition as prosperous as can well be desired.'

Experienced agents of great estates were respected for their knowledge of rural affairs, and they were prominent among those called to give evidence to Royal Commissions enquiring into agricultural conditions. Herbert Smith, the well-known agent to Lord Lansdowne and Lord Crewe, and author of a treatise, *The Principles of Landed Estate Management*, was consulted by Rider Haggard during his tour at the beginning of the twentieth century. He was 'perhaps the most able and interesting' of the gentlemen whom Haggard met in Wiltshire, and was especially informative on the labour situation:

He told me that the labour position was bad; that 'we cannot get half enough labour, and what we do get is very inferior.' Yet on these estates of 14,000 acres there is an ample supply of excellent cottages at a low rent – 1s to 2s a week, I believe. Also, there are reading-rooms and libraries, and the largest system of allotments in England, amounting in all to about 600 acres, though, with reference to them, he added: 'Alas! many, of these which formerly were well cultivated, are now going out of cultivation for lack of tenants.'

Agents like Blaikie, Haedy and Herbert Smith ranked as high-level professionals in the world of estate management. There were also, however, numerous amateurs, and it was common form among farming experts to sneer at those agents who were family relations, friends, or retired army officers, with no special training or experience. But it was overlooked that such 'amateurs' were often the younger sons of landowners or large farmers, had been brought up in a farming environment, and had experience of running a farm of their own. The most distinguished amateur of this kind was Rowland Prothero, later Lord Ernle, who rose to be President of the Board of Agriculture during and after the First World War. Prothero left Oxford in 1876 after winning a Fellowship at All Souls. He began a career in the law but had to abandon it when threatened with blindness. For several years he followed an outdoor life, wandering on foot through France, and thus gained a partial recovery of his sight. He decided, however, not to return to the law but to take up a literary career. He published several volumes of letters and journals as well as farming books, and in 1894 was appointed editor of the *Quarterly*. Five years later he suddenly made an entirely new departure, gave up the *Quarterly*, and became agent-in-chief to the tenth Duke of Bedford. As he wrote in his memoirs:

> The transition from the pen to the ploughshare did not seem to me unnatural. It only meant that one of my oldest and strongest interests had asserted itself. Such newspapers as noticed my change of employment were inclined to comment less on my folly than on the Duke of Bedford's rashness. My few intimate friends knew my feelings and understood how strong was the lure of the land. Others condoled with me on what they thought a descent in the social scale . . .
>
> Apart from this predisposing influence in favour of accepting the agency, the terms were tempting. The salary and the retiring pension attached to it were generous. But it was the offer of a country house in Bedfordshire, under very pleasing conditions, which I think turned the scale. My wife and I, who went down together to see it, fell in love with Oakley at first sight. The Duke told me that the more time I

was able to spend in the country, the better he would be pleased. He added that he wished me to occupy the house on the same terms on which his father had held it during the twenty-five years when he had been MP for Bedfordshire, before succeeding his cousin as ninth Duke. The result of this arrangement was that I found myself the possessor of many attractive perquisites. The house was offered me free of rent and rates. A staff of three indoor servants were permanently maintained at the Duke's expense. He paid the wages of the seven gardeners and three keepers. The house was heated and lighted at his cost. Cream, milk and butter were supplied every day from the dairy at Woburn. Game and the produce of the garden were at my disposal. Port, whisky and mineral waters were an allowance and I was given the run of a cellar of Vintage Hocks . . . Another country house was placed at my disposal on similar terms on the Duke's estates in Cambridgeshire . . .

While chief agent to the Bedford estate, Prothero managed to keep up his writing in his spare time. It was in 1912 that he published his well-known *English Farming Past and Present*, which reached a sixth edition in 1961. In 1914 he entered Parliament as Member for the University of Oxford. During the War he made his mark on several important committees, and in 1916 was appointed President of the Board of Agriculture and

Rent audit, 1832. From Jeffreys Taylor *The Farm*.

Fisheries in Lloyd George's coalition ministry. He was largely responsible for the introduction of guaranteed prices for farm produce and the great wartime expansion in home-produced food supplies, and he also set up the Agricultural Wages Board and established a minimum wage for the farm labourer. Despite his age and poor health he was persuaded by Lloyd George to stay on until September 1919, but was disappointed to see much of his work undone after his resignation. Created Lord Ernle in 1919, he continued his literary output in retirement; he died in 1937 at the age of 85.

Few agents rose to the heights achieved by Prothero. Efficient men were respected members of the rural community whose advice was sought on farming matters and who enjoyed close relations with the leading businessmen of the district. They sometimes took a prominent part in agricultural societies, and occasionally were elevated to the Justices' Bench. There was Thomas Sopwith, chief agent to the Beaumont family, whose varied interests and abilities brought him a Fellowship of the Royal Geographical Society. But generally the social status of agents was not very high. They might dine occasionally with their employer, and joined in hunts and shooting parties, but otherwise were not usually found much in aristocratic company. Their remuneration was respectable if not excessive: something between £500 and £1000 a year was the common level in mid-century, though they often enjoyed valuable perquisites such as a house rent-free, with perhaps some shooting and a farm at a nominal rent. Those who acted as free-lance agents for smaller landowners charged a percentage of the rental. In 1831 Christopher Comyns Parker, a land agent of Woodham Mortimer, near Maldon, Essex, charged 2½ per cent of the rental for valuing land or houses, and an additional 2½ per cent if required to find a tenant. For valuing tithes, marking, measuring and selling timber, supervision of repairs and settling accounts he charged 5 per cent. Other commissions, such as valuations of stock and crops, earned a fee of 5 guineas a day.

The operation of a private land agency was arduous, and was seldom free of anxiety in the depression years after 1875. Mr Alfred J. Burrows, a retired land agent, remembered that his father produced a large booklet to advise farmers on *The Agricultural Depression and How to Meet It*. Near Michaelmas, he wrote, one learned to dread the arrival of tenants bearing notice of quitting. Then it was a matter of persuading them to accept a reduction in rent or some other concession, and so induce them to tear up their notice. Rent audits were held at the village inn at about eleven in the morning. Mr Burrows clearly recalled one man, 'the last farmer I remember to wear a smock frock. His standing grievance was damage by rabbits. As he worked up his grievance, so he worked his smock off over his head, and then sat down to write his cheque.' The audit was followed at three by a dinner, the agent presiding at the long table:

> Before him was a round of roast beef, weighing about 25 pounds. At the other end of the table was one of the principal tenants, faced by an equally big round of boiled beef. Plum pudding followed with brandy sauce. The invariable after-dinner drink was punch, whiskey at one end, rum at the other.

John Oxley Parker, the son of Christopher Comyns Parker and successor to his practice, was entertained by an old farmer who 'always places me in the post of honour by his side at dinner, but it is rather troublesome. He is so deaf that he cannot hear a sound, and everything must be written on a little slate by his side.' This was not, however, the most hazardous aspect of a land agent's life. The various outdoor engagements, and the journeys through weather fair and foul and over indifferent roads, presented serious risk of accidents. In his diary John Oxley Parker recorded numerous incidents, from a wound in the cheek received when shooting, to falls from horses and upsets in his gig or cart. On 27 March 1850, for instance, he recorded: 'Mare frightened and ran away . . . Escaped, but cart upset and broken'; and again on 24 July 1854: 'Irish horse fell down, broke both shafts, threw us out, but no mischief except to shafts.'

The properties managed by the two Parkers included many of the largest estates in south and east Essex as well as number of scattered single farms. The diaries in which they recorded their daily activities, the journeys undertaken and the business settled, give a very clear idea of the energy which the work required: Christopher Comyns Parker's entries for one day in May 1826 read as follows:

> May 2nd Called at Laindon Watch Farm – saw bark measured off – 137 yds. Offered Mr Maling the Topwood and stackwood at £1 per Hd – told Mr Maling to draw Trees to the back of Barn.
> Called at Laindon Hills Hall – marked 18 Trees more in Wood – looked to work of those felled.
> Attended Rev. Wm. Armstrong at Standford-le-hope to meet Parishioners to receive for yrs Tithe, looked over Glebe Land

with view of letting same, recd instructions to have Barn and Premises put into proper repair see Mr A's Tithe A/c Books.

Attended Mr Turner respecting Farm – he did not appear inclined to take the Farm at the Rent asked, wished me to see his Uncle Mr Saml Turner previous to offering Farm to other persons.

John Oxley Parker, the son, had a similar account of a February day in 1843:

> February 2nd, 1843. At Wallasey Island to look on Shearwood's Farm – Lord Wynford's. Mr Allen [the tenant] not there on account of the weather. Went over land – found same in improved state of cultivation. The Wall in good order – 1 man and 2 boys replacing chalk and stone – abt week's work – requires one load Piles one ld. of Stone and one ld. of Chalk dropped along the Wall where wanted and laid in with judgment to make same in most substantial condition – new Gates wanted – Buildings, Sluices etc. bad – Tiling and Thatch requiring repair. House want 2 coats of tarring and brick open Gutter to be laid in cement round the House to throw off water – same now soaks through the underpinning.

The elder Parker found time to run his own farm of 2000 acres in addition to supervising 20,000 acres farmed by others. In April 1836 he was among those knowledgeable authorities called to give evidence before a Commons Select Committee enquiring into the depressed state of agriculture. His son was a founder and committee member of the Essex Agricultural Association, which began its career with a first Show at Chelmsford in 1858. The nature of the Parkers' work brought them into close contact with the business interests of the Essex market towns. John Oxley Parker was on the boards of a number of insurance companies, and in 1859 he joined the banking firm of Sparrow Tufnell & Co., which had branches at Braintree, Chelmsford, Maldon and elsewhere. He opened a new branch of the Bank at Southend, and as time went by became increasingly immersed in the banking business. Whenever his journeys took him to Ongar or Southend he would call in at the Bank's branches there and check the till. Through his land agency he was much involved in railway development in the county, and in 1856 he was one of the prime movers in Sir Morton Peto's abortive attempt to build a line from Tilbury to Colchester. An interest in machinery encouraged him also to join in a firm founded to market a device known as the 'Darby Pedestrian Steam Digger'.

Estate management necessitated many hours at the desk, dealing with correspondence, examining leases, and casting accounts. But it also involved long days out of doors, journeying to meet owners and tenants, tramping through fields and woods, and standing in muddy farmyards. It was no career for the delicate, nor for those who did not care to dispute points with blunt and belligerent farmers. John Grey of Dilston, agent to the Greenwich Hospital estates, recalled the toilsome nature of the work when he took it up in the 1830s. He was responsible for properties scattered over an enormous stretch of country – almost to Carlisle in the west, Newcastle in the east, and Berwick-on-Tweed in the north:

> I was almost killed in the first year and a half; for I rode over every farm and every field and I made a report every night when I came home of its value and its capabilities, whether you could employ water power instead of horse power, and so on. This was a thing that every one could not have done, but I had been brought up in the country, and seven or eight hours in the saddle was no great matter to me.

The owners of landed estates owed a great deal to the arduous labours of their agents. Not all of them were entirely competent, and some were far from honest. But the majority rendered their employers many years of devoted service. They strove for greater efficiency, higher revenues, and improved resistance of the estate to the shocks of misfortune. They may be criticised for encouraging landowners to adopt unbusinesslike attitudes, believing with James Loch that great owners had an obligation to let their land on easy terms. They showed, too, a tendency to give too much support to costly involvement in drainage schemes and new buildings, to persuade landlords of the desirability of undertaking further expenditures on their land when, too often, the long-term economic prospects under free trade did not warrant them. But this is only to say that they were caught up, like so many others, in the nineteenth-century enthusiasm for new techniques and improved ways of doing things. They were also, perhaps, too easily convinced of the superiority of land as an investment, though here the great agricultural depression had a disillusioning effect. However, even if their strategic judgment was not always of the soundest, they were forward-looking in their concern for efficiency and technical advance. At the least they must be reckoned as among the progressive forces influencing agriculture in the modern age.

7 Professional People

In addition to tradesmen, craftsmen, and labourers, country towns and large villages housed a surprising variety of professional people. Buckingham, for instance, had at the end of the eighteenth century a banker, an attorney and his clerk, three ministers of the Church and a Dissenting minister, together with three surgeons, and two schoolmasters. In addition, the town possessed a variety of businesses: a stationer, liquor merchant, a mercer, lace dealer, seven grocers, a carrier, eight victuallers, twelve butchers, a tallow dealer, printer, and a tea dealer. Aylesbury, at the same time, boasted three clergymen, four attorneys, one physician and two surgeons, as well as schoolmasters and an even wider range of tradesmen and craftsmen.

The clergyman deserves to be singled out for special consideration. He had a high social standing, even when his income hardly consorted with it. (The majority of nineteenth-century clergymen had an income of less than £400 a year.) He held an office which went far back in time – indeed, the line of his predecessors might be traced back beyond the origins of the parish church itself. In part, the minister's standing arose from his spiritual authority, though some of his influence could be ascribed to the fact that he was one of the few really well educated persons in the community. Hence his opinion was in high regard and his advice was widely sought; the poorer people were glad to have him witness wills, provide references and write important letters on their behalf. More significant, perhaps, was the fact that the parson was often related to the squire, or if not, then to some family of consequence. Persons of rank stopped at the parsonage house, and the minister dined out at the great houses of the district. The well-connected Sydney Smith, from 1806 to 1829 Rector of Foston-le-Clay, near Leeds, received many distinguished visitors at his 'second-rate inn', as he called his rebuilt rectory; they included The Earl and Countess of Carlisle, Lord and Lady Holland, Sir Humphrey Davy, and Henry Luttrell. Lord Tankerville sent the Rector the gift of a whole buck for his larder, and Lord Lauderdale an embarrassingly large quantity – 230 lbs – of salt fish.

Not infrequently, leading parsons were members of the

Justices' Bench and, indeed, were among its most energetic members. Clerical magistrates were renowned for their rigour in enforcing the law and their zeal in pursuing wrongdoers. Some clergy were also enterprising farmers of their glebe, and were noted for their interest in new techniques of cultivation. The Reverend S.Smith of Lois Weeden, near Towcester, was something of a farming crank, growing his wheat without benefit of manure or fertilizers. He adopted a system of planting wheat in narrow strips, separated by strips of fallow of the same size, hand-dug, two spits deep. Each year he alternated wheat and fallow, and was able to show that in this manner he could produce as much grain as his more conventional neighbours. The Reverend Mr Huxtable, Rector of Sutton Waldron, was a self-taught farmer who developed his own design of housing for stock. He put all his beasts under cover, believing that dryness and warmth promoted fattening and saved fodder, and he kept a thermometer always on the wall to check the temperature of the cattle house. 'Let us keep our cattle warm and dry and well fed and we shall seldom feel the cramp in our pockets', was his slogan. The floors of his cattle houses were sparred so that the dung fell on a layer of sawdust and burnt clay, and an irrigation system carried off the liquid manure to the fields.

A large proportion of Anglican livings were in the gift of landowners, whose families had acquired the advowson at the time of the Reformation. In such parishes the incumbent was often a relation of the squire or his wife, or was a man specially selected for the congenial nature of his religious and political views, and perhaps for his interest in sport. Many so selected had little sense of a calling. This was what E.L.Stanley called 'the essential wickedness' of family livings, where the spiritual welfare of thousands was 'made over to bolster up the finances of a younger son'. Some clergy were absentees who rarely visited their parishes and left them in the care of a wretchedly-paid curate. Sometime the parson's income was augmented by joining livings together, and one of the churches, if not both of them, allowed to moulder into decay. This, however, was more a feature of the early decades of the nineteenth century, for the proportion of absentee clergymen not attending to their parish duties declined from nearly a half of all beneficed clergy to under a sixth between 1810 and 1850. Aristocratic clergymen sought out livings in the best sporting districts, and were not above advertising publicly for a post where the hunting was good and the duties light. They were among the most ardent followers of the hunt, spending several days a week in the saddle, not excepting Lent. Nor were the clergy always strict upholders of the law. In coastal areas they had been known to engage in smuggling, perhaps in league with their sexton and local victuallers. Though large-scale smuggling was on the decline in the early nineteenth century it was not so very long since Parson Woodforde rose in the morning to the welcome sight of the contraband brandy left on his doorstep overnight by his friends among the smugglers.

Generally, however, parsons were becoming more respectable and more pious. It is interesting that their social standing tended to decline as new professions appeared in the community, and the clergy gradually lost their pre-eminence in education and culture. It is significant, too, that their numbers declined on the Justices' Bench, reducing the clerical presence which had become so marked in the previous century. The proliferation of professions and the wider prospects of a satisfying career in the civil service, commerce, or the colonies, meant that the Church was less automatically the choice of an impecunious younger son. The established Church had lost much ground in the century before 1830, when Nonconformist chapels grew rapidly. After 1830 there was some recovery: the number of Church of England clergy rose from just under 15,000 in 1831 to over 23,000 in 1911, while the proportion of communicants in the population also rose slightly. Nonconformity had its greatest strength among artisans, labourers and tradesmen, and in the countryside its strongholds were in parishes dominated by small freeholders rather than in those controlled by the gentry; it was most likely to be found in upland, pastoral and forested regions where farming tended to be small in scale and industrial occupations were numerous – as in Wales, much of the West Country and the north of England. As a consequence, the Church of England became more evidently the resort of the wealthier classes. Perhaps, too, the image of the Church was not helped by the attitude of aristocratic ladies like Maria Josepha, Lady Stanley, who thought rather more of her *'charming* Pew – large, square, high, lined . . .' than of the merits of the clergyman.

Most country parishes came to have two ministers, an Anglican and a Nonconformist. Unlike the former, whose origins, education and tastes were those of the gentry, the latter sprang from a lower level in the social scale. The Anglican dined with the squire, while the Dissenter went to tea with the tenant. 'People who would never think of presuming to ask the rector to eat with them will familiarly invite the Minister to take "pot luck" at table', wrote P.Anderson Graham.

On Sundays you shall find in the church, if not the squire, at any rate his household, the ladies of it almost certainly and the servants. Most of the large tenants come too with their dependants. The game-keeper's stalwart figure fills a seat, for though not conversant with doctrines, he and the other officials of the estate take a pride in thus evincing their loyalty to the established order of things. And with these must be numbered a sprinkling of the very poor, who hobble up the aisle, making a fine show of rheumatic pains and not forgetting the prospect of Christmas coals. In the chapel gather 'ungenteel' farmers, usually the smaller tenants, artisans, and shopkeepers, with a sprinkling of 'free' labourers and farm-servants. The congregation taken in the bulk is worth much less money than that in the parish church, and the dissenting parson is in many ways the same as his hearers. 'Oh, we don't mind the minister, he is just like one of ourselves', the cottager will say.

Between Anglican and Nonconformist existed an avowed rivalry. The Nonconformist minister was almost invariably an aggressive radical, a supporter of reform movements, and a keen advocate of the disestablishment of the Church. Excluded from the upper circles and their pastimes, he had little respect for the Game Laws, and begrudged the parson his greater scholarship and ampler opportunities. When the Minister visited the cottagers and sympathized with them in their hardships, the Rector pointed to the difficulty of making farming pay and the impossibility of paying higher wages. The Minister, in his turn, argued that land carried too many burdens, not forgetting the gentry's rents and the Rector's tithes. The village school, fostered and regulated by the Rector, was a sore point with the Minister, for he regarded it as a nursery for the Church of England. The Churchman blamed the Dissenter for promoting radical views among the poor, for stirring up antagonism towards the established order, and for widening the gulf between the labourers and the Church. In truth, there was a powerful alliance between radicalism and dissent, though many of the poor were simply indifferent to either creed. Frequently they adopted a mercenary attitude: 'When Hodge is young he will ofttimes give full scope to his fancy and go to chapel – if it happens that he likes the preaching – but when age and pain steal upon him he becomes crafty and worships where the loaves are.' But mostly, religion simply did not interest him – village happenings, his wages, allotments, even politics – were far more real and immediate.

The tithe was a sore point in many a village, especially when the proceeds went not to the support of the Church but into the pocket of a lay impropriator. At the time of the Tithe Commutation Act of 1836 the annual value of all tithes was estimated at about £4m., and of this sum nearly a quarter was in the hands of lay impropriators. Under the Act the Tithe Commission apportioned the sum to be levied between the various occupiers in the parish and assessed the value in terms of a rent-charge, usually based on a seven-year running average of the prices of wheat, barley and oats. Payment of tithe had never been popular with farmers. It was regarded as a tax on improvement, since the more efficiently one farmed the more one paid. Before 1836, when the tithe was still sometimes paid in kind, the farmers had plenty of scope for being difficult about it. A Hampshire farmer once informed the tithe-owner that he was about to draw his turnips.When the tithe-owner's men and waggons were gathered by the field the farmer appeared, drew ten turnips, gave one to the tithe-owner's man, and said he would let his master know when he would draw any more. And in the Isle of Thanet a farmer once treated the impropriator's men with even deeper scorn. He 'flung them a plum and sometimes an apple and sometimes a turnip or a rosemary sprig and sometimes sent them away and laughed at them . . .'

Tithe was an acute grievance in Wales, especially as the small or vicarial tithes went to the support of an alien Church. After 1836 there were complaints about the new assessments, and some farmers did not really understand the idea of the seven-year average. In fact, the new payments were not unfair, but they came at a time when farmers were depressed and short of cash. The annoyance felt over tithe was a main factor in the unrest which culminated in the Rebecca riots of the 1840s. The grievance rankled on in the later decades of the century, and came to a head again in 1885–6 when, significantly, there was a sharp fall in the prices of stock and farmers were in financial difficulty. In September 1886 aggrieved farmers met at Ruthin and formed an Anti-Tithe League. Demand for abatements shifted to outright opposition to any payment of tithe. As Mr Dunbabin tells us, there was strong feeling, and numerous distraints had to be levied for non-payment. Haystacks seized for tithe were festooned with placards and clerical effigies. Sometimes distraints were resisted, and the auctioneer was greeted with buckets of filth or had the bulls let loose on him. At Llangwm in 1887 the bailiffs were forcibly prevented from taking away seized cattle; the auctioneer was compelled to promise never to undertake any similar

'The Village Choir Rehearsing the Christmas Anthem', drawn by A.Hunt.
From the Christmas Number of the *Illustrated London News*, 1863.

business, and then sent off down the road with his coat turned as a
mark of repentance.

Hostility to the Anglican Church was the strongest element in
the Welsh agitation. The farmers proved to be pliable tools in the
hands of the Nonconformist preachers. It was no accident that
the upsurge of anti-tithe feeling occurred in the district dominated by the most influential of Welsh Methodist leaders, the
Reverend Thomas Gee. One South Wales farmer argued that
over forty years he had paid £800 to a church he had never
entered. In Llanarmon, a centre of the anti-tithe agitation, there
were as few as thirty Anglican communicants in a population of
1600. The 'Tithe War' was fed by currents of Welsh nationalist
sentiment, but support for it depended to some extent on the
nature of farming conditions and the enthusiasm aroused among
farmworkers, lime-burners, lead miners and other labourers.
Eventually, the Tithe Act of 1891 enabled unpaid tithe to be
recovered through the County Courts, and liability to pay was
transferred from the occupier to the owner of the land. Thus
a grievance was removed from the farmers, though only at the
expense of laying an additional burden on landowners at a time

when rents had fallen, often to extremely low levels.

Though the tithe was a peculiarly oppressive problem in Wales, where the majority of the population attended the Nonconformist chapels, it was also much disliked in England. In hard times, particularly, it was difficult to get it paid. When, for example, the wet seasons and crop blights of the late 1820s and early 1830s drove some farmers into bankruptcy, they often left their farms with tithe unpaid. In October 1831 Dr Hawkins, Provost of Oriel College, received a petition signed by 32 of the farmers of Purleigh in Essex. In the previous three years the farmers there had been granted remittance of part of the tithe, and now they were obliged to ask for the concession for a fourth year. Christopher Comyns Parker, the local land agent responsible for collecting the College's tithe, confirmed that the farmers were in difficulty. They had suffered three wet seasons in a row, he said, and now their crops had been visited with an unexpected blight. The heavy nature of their soil prevented them from abandoning crops in favour of stock, so, in the circumstances, he recommended a further abatement of 15 per cent of the tithe. He went on to comment:

> The combination of bad seasons and the bad spirit of the times make the arranging and receiving of Tithes a most irksome charge but I must as I have heretofore done struggle thro' the difficulties endeavouring to give satisfaction to all parties. . . . When I ask for arrears I am shown a sample of blighted corn which the millers will not buy. I had with me this morning one of Mr Green's labourers of Purleigh Hall who stated that he did not believe his Master's crop would make sufficient to pay the Labourers until next harvest.

If the exactions of lay impropriators were unpopular with the farmers, the incumbents themselves were often estranged from their flock. It was complained that clergy who farmed their glebe employed no more men nor paid better wages than anyone else. Severity on the Bench, coupled with a sportsman's hostility towards poachers, alienated many of the poor. In the riots of 1830–31 parsons were among the unpopular figures who received threatening letters penned by the mysterious Captain Swing, and their ricks were not immune from the attention of arsonists.

There had always been some conscientious clergy, men who did their best to maintain a spiritual influence in the parish, and who tried to amend the conditions of the poor. Some took up their pens, as did Charles Kingsley and the less well-known William

Tuckwell, a Warwickshire parson, who campaigned uncompromisingly for a better life for the labourers. Among the various local projects on which the clergy busied themselves were the founding of schools and adult classes, organization of 'penny readings', and provision of reading rooms and lending libraries. They established savings clubs, coal clubs, and clothing and boot clubs, with the clergyman's wife or daughter acting as treasurer. Sometimes the parson's lady provided tunics and caps, frocks and bonnets, by way of school uniform, while the parson himself bought prizes for the best pupils, and arrived at the school at Christmas laden with oranges and nuts for the whole school. Occasionally a parson troubled to buy essential goods in bulk so as to enable the poor to buy them at wholesale prices. At Alton-Barnes in Wiltshire, Augustus Hare kept a shop in the rectory barn, where clothing and materials were sold at two-thirds of the cost price, and at Stoneleigh in Warwickshire the Honourable and Reverend J.W.Leigh had a complete co-operative store.

Cottage improvement and sanitary reform were major concerns of nineteenth-century clergy. Homes which were damp, vermin-infested, cramped and fetid, which lacked the essentials of pure water and proper sanitation, were not conducive to morality, industry and happiness. They were homes, as Charles Girdlestone said, 'in which the virtues taught in Christian schools and Churches can scarcely fail to droop and wither'. In this sphere the clergy were handicapped by the cost of providing new, sanitary cottages and the unprofitable nature of the investment when labourers were too poor to pay an adequate rent. Reformers had to work through the indifferent agents of great estates or farmers who thought the existing cottages quite good enough; and often the most defective cottages were those put up by small speculators or owned by the labourers themselves.

Among the various services performed by clergymen was that of dispensing medicines and help in sickness. Sydney Smith, the celebrated parson-humourist, was regarded as the 'village doctor'. Smith had attended medical lectures as a student at Edinburgh, and when there were epidemics he ransacked the resources of his considerable private store of medicines and treated both his family and the parish with his own prescriptions. 'I am performing miracles in my parish with garlic for whooping-cough', he wrote on one occasion. However, he recognized his limitations, and scarlet fever was one of them. One winter, when he buried as many as fifteen of his parishioners instead of the usual one or two, he wrote: 'You will naturally suppose I have killed all these people by doctoring them; but scarlet-fever awes me, and is above my aim. I leave it to the professional and graduated homicides . . .' He was what the common people called a 'bould preacher' – 'for I like to have my arms free, and to thump the pulpit'.

> When I began to thump the cushion of my pulpit, on first coming to Foston, as is my wont when I preach, the accumulated dust of a hundred and fifty years made such a cloud, that for some minutes I lost sight of my congregation.

A great eccentric, Smith took up a highly individual style of farming, directed his labourers with the help of a telescope and speaking-trumpet, and invented a 'universal scratcher' for his cattle. But he provided gardens for the cottagers, and studied Count Rumford's recipes to discover the best means of producing cheaply food for the poor.

With the upsurge of evangelism and renewed piety, which began towards the end of the eighteenth century, and with, too, the competition arising from the growing presence of Nonconformist chapels, the clergy became more than ever devoted to good works. Some, like Thomas Pearce, Vicar of Modern, Dorset from 1853 to 1882, were appalled by insanitary, dilapidated cottages and the ravages of disease. He had the experience of hearing one unfortunate despatched into eternity with the chiding remark, 'Don't make such a fuss about it; get on with your dying; you will soon be all right.' Pearce sank new wells at his own expense, and started village clubs and a school. Others, like Henry Deane, a friend of Newman, restored and rebuilt churches. He aimed at more space and light, and swept away box pews, profane ornaments, and unworthy parish clerks. Deane also gave his support to schools, and augmented the meagre stipends of two curacies.

Sometimes a parson saw his call to a neglected parish as a great challenge, an opportunity of bringing civilization to the benighted. Charles Kingsley, the author of *Hereward the Wake* and *Westward Ho!*, spent the greater part of his life as Rector of the Hampshire parish of Eversley. He found a church nearly empty, the farmers' sheep grazing in the churchyard, and a rectory unrepaired for over a century. Kingsley made a point of familiarizing himself with every soul in the parish. He was a tireless friend to the poor, and spent long hours in cottages where there were sick. He was especially aroused by the prevalence of disease and the complacent attitude of cottage owners and the authorities. In 1849 an extremely virulent outbreak of 'low fever' and the national threat of cholera caused him to deliver a series of sermons on the question 'Who causes Pestilence?' Kingsley founded boot and coal clubs, a loan fund, and a lending library. A promising youngster was sent off to Winchester Training College to become a schoolmaster. There was no school in the parish, but Kingsley held adult classes in his rectory. In the winter his adult school and cottage readings took up six evenings a week.

A less eminent civilizer of neglected parishes was the Reverend J.T.Huntley, who in 1845 took up the ministry of Binbrook in the Lindsey wolds. The previous incumbent had been non-resident, and spent elsewhere the £400 yielded by the two livings. Huntley found one church a ruin and the other 'the most wretched hovel I have ever seen'. He hurried on a number of changes in order to try and raise the funds for the restoration of the 'hovel', but his campaign met opposition from the Nonconformists, who had a strong grip on the parish. The Methodists could muster a congregation three times the size of that in the church, and Huntley over-reached himself. He ran into debt to the extent of £4000; the living was sequestrated, Huntley departed, and Binbrook reverted to the care of curates.

Many Church of England clergymen concerned themselves with the problem of poverty, which was a particularly acute problem in some rural areas in southern England during the early decades of the nineteenth century. High poor rates were a standing grievance among the farmers, and when the seasons were unfavourable formed an excuse for demanding a reduction in tithe. More relevant, to the parson, perhaps, was the widespread belief that parish relief demoralized the poor. The badly-supervised work given to paupers on the roads was said to encourage idleness and crime, while relief allocated to men with large families was supposed to promote early marriage and a high birth rate. Faced with these criticisms, parish authorities experimented with various forms of relief, and clergymen were especially prominent in advancing schemes for providing labourers with allotments. The idea was that the produce derived from cultivating a bit of land would not only supplement the cottage diet but would give the labourer a spare-time interest and serve to keep him out of the alehouse. It was thought that allotments could provide a means of reducing the poor rates, and indeed some schemes included the rule that the allotment was to be given up if the tenant sought assistance from the parish. William Wilberforce and the Bishop of Durham, together with Sir Thomas Bernard, were the founders in 1796 of the Society for Bettering the Conditions and Increasing the Comforts of the

Poor. More influential in the cause of allotments was the Labourers' Friend Society, established in 1830 by the Bishop of Bath and Wells, and later revived by Sidney Godolphin Osborne and Lord Ashley.

Between 1795 and 1835 as many as 184 pamphlets proposing allotment schemes were published, a substantial number of them coming from the pens of clergymen. An early scheme suggested by the Reverend J.G.Sherer of Droxford, Hampshire, called for one per cent of all land to be set aside for allotments by authority of Parliament. The plots, he said, should be let at a fair rent, and should not exceed half an acre in size so as to avoid distracting the labourer from his normal employment. The Reverend Stephen Demainbray, Rector of Broad Somerford in Wiltshire, told the 1843 Select Committee that he had started allotments in his parish as far back as 1806. When in that year the parish was enclosed he ensured that land was allotted to the cottages, and he let out a portion of his glebe as smallholdings. His example had been followed in other parishes in Wiltshire, with the result that agrarian unrest and outrages were unknown. Parliament, however, moved only to encourage the growth of allotments, not to enforce them. Permissive legislation passed in 1819 and 1831, after outbreaks of rioting, allowed parishes to acquire land for the purpose of letting it to labourers. By 1833 an enquiry established that allotment schemes were known in 42 per cent of all parishes, though the proportion varied greatly from one county to another, and in many instances only a handful of labourers had allotment land. The counties with most allotments were mainly in the south, and included, in addition to Lincolnshire and Warwickshire, Bedfordshire, Oxfordshire, Hampshire, Wiltshire, Dorset and Devon.

Allotments and gardens, together with better cottages, schools, and savings clubs, all played some part in relieving poverty. But the basic cause, low wages, remained. In many parishes there seemed little prospect of the labourers' conditions being much changed unless their numbers were diminished. The harsh economics of supply and demand determined that when labour was plentiful wages must be barely sufficient for subsistence. It was an appreciation of this fundamental problem that led a number of clergy to advocate measures for reducing the labour surplus. Prominent churchmen supported J.R.Godley's scheme for settling the Canterbury district of New Zealand's South Island. On a much more modest scale, the Reverend Edward Girdlestone braved the hostility of the farmers of Halberton and sent poor labouring families to start a new life in the industrial north of England. If he was not very much imitated it was because few parishes incumbents could afford to cross the squire and his wealthier tenants. Their interest was in cheap and docile labour, and they were suspicious of any move which might make labourers more scarce or independent. Further, any suggestion of radical views on the part of the parson was liable to make him ostracised by people of means.

It was not entirely fortuitous, therefore, that it was a Nonconformist, George Rodgers, Congregational Minister of Stalbridge in Dorset, who inspired one of the most ambitious of private migration projects. In 1872 Rodgers journeyed out to Minnesota in order to inspect lands thought to be suitable for establishing a colony of English emigrants. He chose a site a few miles from Glyndon, a temperance settlement situated 12 miles east of the Red River on land owned by the Northern Pacific Railroad. Glyndon already possessed five stores, three hotels and twenty 'substantial buildings', and its temperance character appealed to the English minister. Rodgers returned to the West Country telling of Minnesota wages as high as 10s a day, and board and lodgings costing only 12s a week. With the assistance of the Northern Pacific's agent in England, Rodgers placed advertisements in papers and collected together a band of 80 prospective settlers from the Yeovil area. They left for Minnesota in March 1873. The project, however, fell far short of complete success. Too many of the emigrants were not farmers but clerks and shopkeepers, or were too old to adapt readily to the strange conditions of a new country. The Minnesota winter was fierce, wood was scarce, the water bad, and the settlement was remote from large markets. Within a few months half of the settlers had

Distraining for £70 arrears of tithe at Pentre Ffynon Farm, Whitford. This illustration from the *Graphic* of 21 January 1888 depicts an episode during the tithe agitation in Wales.

abandoned New Yeovil, as the colony was called, and eventually the area was settled by hardier Germans and Scandinavians.

The most common reaction of clergymen to rural poverty and ignorance was to establish a school. It was rarely a light undertaking. Subscriptions were not always easy to raise, and as J.S.Henslow said, 'All schemes, educational, recreational, or however tending to elevate [the labourer] in the social scale, are positively distasteful to some of the employers of labour . . .' Henslow, professor of botany at Cambridge and sponsor of Darwin and his epoch-making voyage on HMS *Beagle*, retired to the living of Hitcham in Suffolk. There he received so little help from the parishioners that he built a school and paid the teacher out of his own pocket. Even if funds were forthcoming, expenses might increase, and the parson was usually expected to make good any deficiency out of his own pocket. He had a general responsibility for the school, and usually provided the religious instruction. He or his wife were there each day to see that everything was in order. Evidence given to the Newcastle Commission of 1861 showed that the more largely agricultural counties, such as Wiltshire, Westmorland, Oxfordshire, Rutland, Essex and Dorset, had generally the highest proportion of children enrolled in elementary schools, while industrialized and highly urbanized counties came near the bottom of the list. An investigation of the sources of school funds extending over 168 parishes found that clergymen each contributed an average of £10 10s a year, nearly twice the sum subscribed by landowners, and eleven times that by the farmers.

Education was seen as a means of instilling habits of responsibility, sobriety and frugality among the poor. A central role was given to religious instruction, which often took up an hour of every day. In her *Lark Rise*, Flora Thompson recalled that

> Every morning at ten o'clock the Rector arrived to take the older children for Scripture. He was a parson of the old school; a commanding figure, tall and stout, with white hair, ruddy cheeks and an aristocratically beaked nose, and he was as far as possible removed by birth, education, and worldly circumstances from the lambs of his flock. He spoke to them from a great height, physical, mental, and spiritual . . .
>
> His lesson consisted of Bible reading, turn and turn about round the class, of reciting from memory the names of the kings of Israel and repeating the Church Catechism. After that, he would deliver a little lecture on morals and behaviour. The children must not lie or steal or be discontented or

envious. God had placed them just where they were in the social order and given them their own especial work to do; to envy others or to try to change their own lot in life was a sin of which he hoped they would never be guilty.

Village schools built and maintained by local subscription on a site given by the squire and run by the parish incumbent were bound to have a bias, social and political, as well as religious. It was for this reason that the school became an issue which inflamed the hostility existing between chapel and Church. When school rates were introduced, Methodists, Baptists and Congregationalists had no option but to help pay for a school, which as it was complained at Tysoe, 'must always have a member of the Church of England for headmaster – worth as much as two curates to the Church.' But it was only the ardent Nonconformists who felt this strongly. The majority of English countrymen accepted the school for what it was, and could evince neither warmth nor antipathy for the religious teaching it offered. They were indifferent, apathetic, because religion of any sort had little meaning in their lives. The parson represented nothing that was real or important to them. He was merely 'the paid guardian of a national respectability, the village censor of men and morals'. Perhaps this was because, too often, it was 'the overworked scholar, the worn-out townsman, the social star' who was rewarded by a few quiet years in a rural parish. Only men who were prepared to devote long years of hard work to getting to know and understand the countryman could make an impact. The vicar often tried very hard. He made a point of visiting every cottage, no matter how distant or how gruff his reception; he spoke kindly to the sick and aged, listened to the stories of ill luck and hardship, and left behind the occasional shilling or two; he made sure the Church's presence was felt at the farmers' club, the parish meeting, and the annual dinner of the benefit society; his wife presided at the flower show, organized the savings clubs, and spent much of her spare time pondering how to stretch her husband's frequently miserable stipend.

But all this made little difference. In part the villagers' apathy was itself the result of a growing political consciousness, a first glimmering awareness of the place of the country and countrymen in the national life, and a slowly developing understanding that religion, whether Church or chapel, had little to do with the bread-and-butter issues which really mattered. So it was, as Richard Jefferies remarked, that the backbone of the labouring population ignored the Church:

They cleaned their boots on a Sunday morning while the bells were ringing, and walked down to their allotments, and came home and ate their cabbage, and were as oblivious of the vicar as the wind that blew. They had no present quarrel with the Church; no complaint whatever; nor apparently any old memory or grudge; yet there was a something, a blank space as it were, between them and the Church.

As more schools were established in the countryside the school-teacher became a familiar figure in the community. As yet he hardly existed as a professional person. At the beginning of the century the schoolmaster ranked below even the carrier, the blacksmith, butcher, cordwainer, tailor and wheel-wright. Later on, schoolteaching was still only somewhat on a par with a trade – if slightly more respectable because the teacher was expected to dress creditably, if plainly, and to lead a blameless existence. Long years devoted to a single school made the teacher a well-known, respected, and sometimes loved figure. In Joseph Ashby's Tysoe, Mr Dodge ran the school for thirty-nine years, with his wife acting as sewing mistress and filling in when pupil-teachers were laid low by illness. 'Without the Dodges it could never have been said that every child could read and figure and every girl could mend,' wrote Miss Ashby. When the couple retired in 1905, 250 villagers turned up with a brass band to the tea given in the old tithe barn. The vicar, chief speaker on this important occasion, recalled the day when the Dodges had first come to the village. They had promised their lives to the work of the school, he said, and they had given them. When the old schoolmaster spoke in reply he recalled that some two thousand children had passed through his hands. Two hundred of the 214 children now in school were the offsprings of men and women he had taught. He had been there a long time and ideas on education were changing. Teachers were now encouraged to make their own schemes, and to move outside the restrictions of the classroom. But he had been brought up in the old regime and it was too late for him to change. 'The County Council had said it was time for him to go, and they were right.'

When Mr Dodge had started on his long career at Tysoe there was a monitor who taught the infants their alphabet, and later on to say their tables. Noise was characteristic of school. All six standards were gathered together, infants chanted, several older children read aloud at once, teachers scolded. Occasionally the hubbub subsided when the master rang his bell, and then gradually the crescendo of din would mount again. Some

'The Village School': engraved after the picture by A.Rankley exhibited at the Royal Academy in 1856.

children worked at sums on their slates, while others got restive waiting their turn to read while the poor readers stumbled painfully over every word. When the girls were engaged on sewing, the boys did extra sums or dictation. The master rapped with his stick at those who were idle or lost their place, and wrongdoers were kept in half an hour after school. Thrashings were commonplace. Twice a year the inspector, a much feared and sometimes irascible gentleman, arrived to conduct examinations. This was a day of great import for on the results might depend the master's reputation and salary, and on them too rested the question of which children would be allowed to leave school at eleven or twelve – a matter of large concern to their parents. That day saw the master in his best suit, calling out the children to be tested, and frowning anxiously when they hesitated or became confused. The schoolmistress at Fordlow, as described by Flora Thompson, was

> a small, neat little body with a pale, slightly pock-marked face, snaky black curls hanging down to her shoulders, and eyebrows arched into a perpetual inquiry. She wore in school stiffly starched, holland aprons with bibs, one embroidered

with red one week, and one with blue the next, and was seldom seen without a posy of flowers pinned on her breast and another tucked into her hair.

Every morning, when school had assembled, and Governess, with her starched apron and bobbing curls appeared in the doorway, there was a great rustling and scraping of curtseying and pulling of forelocks. 'Good morning, children.' 'Good morning, ma'am,' were the formal, old-fashioned greetings. Then under her determined fingers the harmonium wheezed out 'Once in Royal', or 'We are but little children weak', prayers followed, and the day's work began . . .

The writing lesson consisted of the copying of copper-plate maxims: 'A fool and his money are soon parted'; 'Waste not, want not'; 'Count ten before you speak', and so on. Once a week composition would be set, usually in the form of writing a letter describing some recent event. This was regarded chiefly as a spelling test.

History was not taught formally: but history readers were in use containing such picturesque stories as those of King Alfred and the cakes, King Canute commanding the waves, the loss of the White Ship, and Raleigh spreading his cloak for Queen Elizabeth.

It became a common criticism in the later nineteenth century that the education provided in schools and adult classes was unrelated to the lives and interests of country people. Though in some areas there were effective schemes for evening classes, many young-sters simply whiled an evening away doing a little woodwork or hearing about the wonders of astronomy or some pet interest of the parson. In school the emphasis on the three R's and on learning by rote certainly made for a narrow, dull, unimaginative kind of education. Nevertheless, the system had its merits. It has to be remembered that children of eleven were already near the end of their schooldays. They came from homes where there was rarely a book or any thoughtful conversation, and their parents might be almost, if not quite, illiterate. School gave them the essential elementary skills of learning, and the assumption was that they could go on, if they chose, to enter on a wider world of knowledge. Some adults brought up under this system continued throughout their lives to be able to compose a well-phrased letter in a properly-formed hand; with a little practice they could cast up accounts and work out quantities; they sometimes acquired an appreciation of the riches contained in books, and became avid readers of a far from contemptible range of authors. For the majority, no doubt, the system failed: the skills rusted rapidly, and the world of literature was represented merely by an occasional popular newspaper. Country schools failed to keep labour happy in the countryside. In particular, they failed to provide a countervailing interest to the attractions of the brighter, more convivial life of the towns, the shops, the crowds on a Saturday evening, and the pleasures of the cheap theatres and music halls. Perhaps this was because so many of the teachers were themselves townsmen – and often the duller townsmen at that, or why did they take country posts? – and thus lacked any real understanding or appreciation of country life.

One of the problems faced by teachers was poor attendance. There were some parents who firmly believed that education was the key to advancement, and sent their children to school regularly, even when they were ill and should have been in bed. But school log books tell of much absenteeism, the boys employed with their fathers at busy seasons, and girls kept at home to mind the baby or help with some plaiting, glove-making, or other chore. Poor parents badly missed their children's earnings, and thought school an undue burden when children were old enough to work. They refused to purchase school books, and sometimes resisted the 'home lessons' which children were supposed to learn in the evenings, ready for the next day. The farmers were willing accomplices, readily employing children when they knew they should be at school. Farmers were generally unsympathetic to the whole idea of giving young farmworkers a good education, for fear they would become dissatisfied and go off to the towns. School boards and magistrates were often infected by the same prejudice, and as a result little attempt was made to help the teachers by enforcing attendance.

But there were other reasons for poor attendance. Children might be kept at home, especially in bad weather, because they had no sound boots, or their feet were too sore with chilblains to get their boots on. The children could not go to school barefoot, and parents might need a week or two to find the money for new shoes. Also, children often lacked proper clothing to keep out wind and weather. The schoolrooms, too, were sometimes of a makeshift kind – consisting of a cottage, an aisle of the church, the vicar's loft or even his stable – and were deficient in heating and sanitary arrangements. The little 'dame schools', held in a private sitting room or kitchen, were preferred by some parents as warmer than the school. Mostly the children brought their 'bread and seam' (lard) for their lunch break, though occasionally the vicar's lady or the master's wife provided soup or a hot drink. The master's wife was often expected to keep the school clean, but was allowed the help of some of the children who swept, lit fires, and scrubbed out lavatories. Sometimes a board of managers employed a charwoman to relieve the master's wife of these duties.

By the later nineteenth century there were few well-populated rural parishes without a resident clergyman and a teacher. Other professional people, the solicitor, doctor, veterinary surgeon, land agent and auctioneer, were to be found only in the larger villages and market towns. But though professional men, they often had a country background, and sometimes held a direct interest in farming and the land. The country auctioneer and valuer, for one, had to have the confidence of the farmers, and this could be acquired only by showing a competent knowledge of the various branches of agriculture. Auctioneers, consequently, were often farmers or farmers' sons. In addition to presiding at the weekly markets, they were called in to sell off farm stock when a farmer retired or bankrupted; and they were consulted by owners and farmers anxious to buy stock or have valuations made for purpose of probate and legacy duties.

Auctioneers joined those other professional men, the land agents, doctors and veterinary surgeons, whose work took them over wide stretches of country in all kinds of weather. Doctors were then, as now, worse off, since they had to turn out in all conditions, and not infrequently at dead of night. To travel some miles on horseback through rain and snow, or drive in the limited protection of a gig down muddy lanes and up icy hills, called for devotion and endurance. Perhaps that was why numbers of country doctors were retired Army and Navy surgeons, men used to hardship and to working in bad conditions. Village doctors had to turn their hands to any emergency, extracting teeth by the roadside, delivering babies in a cottage attic, and sometimes carrying out an urgent amputation on a kitchen table. They were not generally the most expert or the most respected of their profession (though one was the famous Edward Jenner, the discoverer of vaccination); and they had a larger share of the trials of medical work and a less ample income, for a great many of their patients were among the poorest-paid classes in the country.

More highly respected and much more prosperous was the country solicitor. He did not have to go to his clients, nor, when he did, was he received at the servants' entrance, as was sometimes the case when the doctor was called to the squire's household. The solicitor's clients came to him, and were prepared to wait to see him, often for a good long time – seated in his clerk's room on the ground floor of what had once been a gentleman's house in the main street. Country towns, explained Richard Jefferies, were by the 1880s pretty much given over to offices, shops, hotels and workshops. The wealthy people had moved out to distant villas with lawns and pleasure grounds.

While waiting for the solicitor to be free, the client in Richard Jefferies' account sits patiently, surveying the brass copying press, letter scales, piles of papers, Post Office directory and railway time-table scattered round the room. Over a small table is a map, 'dusty and dingy, of some estate laid out for building purposes'. On the other side of the room a framed advertisement sets out the numerous advantages of a certain insurance company, and ranged along the wall are posters announcing sales by auction, farms to be let, houses to be had on lease, shares in a local bank, or a gas works for sale.

The hand of the clock moves slowly, and the half-heard talk and jests of the junior clerks – one of whom you suspect of making a pen and ink sketch of you – mingle with the ceaseless scrape of the senior's pen, and the low buzz of two black flies that circle for ever round and round just beneath the grimy ceiling. Occasionally noises of the street penetrate; the rumble of loaded waggons, the tramp of nailed shoes, or the sharp quick sound of a trotting horse's hoofs.

The tedium is interrupted by numerous callers: first a labourer comes about a mortgage on his cottage, then a young farmer who collects the rates for his parish. Others appear: a tradesman, a builder, a squire and magistrate, footmen and grooms with messages – it is easy to tell the positions they occupy by the degree of attention they receive from the clerks.

Callers come still more thickly; another solicitor, well-to-do, and treated with the utmost deference; more tradesmen; farmers; two or three auctioneers, in quick succession; the well-brushed editor of a local paper; a second attorney, none too well dressed, with scrubby chin and face suspiciously cloudy, with an odour of spirits and water and tobacco clinging to his rusty coat. He belongs to a disappearing type of country lawyer, and is the wreck, perhaps, of high hopes and good opportunities. Yet, wreck as he is, when he gets up at the Petty Sessions to defend some labourer, the bench of magistrates listen to his maundering argument as deferentially as if he were a Q.C.

Eventually the business upstairs is over, the directors of some company are shown out, the client ushered in. While the solicitor finishes a little note on his previous matter, there is leisure to glance around his room, noting the

shelves of calf-bound law books; piles of japanned deed-boxes, some marked in white letters 'Trustees of,' or 'Executors of,' and pigeon-holes full of papers seem to quite hide the walls . . . But the large table, which almost fills the centre of the room, quickly draws the attention from everything else.

It is on that table that all the business is done; all the energies of the place are controlled and directed from thence.

At the first glance it appears to support a mere chaotic mass of papers. They completely conceal it, except just at the edge. Bundles of letters tied with thin red tape, letters loose, letters unopened; parchment deeds with the seals and signatures just visible; deeds with the top and the words, 'This indenture', alone showing out from the confusion; deeds neatly folded; broad manuscript briefs; papers fastened with brass fasteners; papers hastily pinned together; old newspapers marked and underlined in red ink; a large sectional map, half unrolled and hanging over the edge; a small deed-box, the lid open, and full of blue paper in oblong strips; a tall porcupine-quill pen handle sticking up like a spire; pocket books; books open; books with half-a-dozen papers in them for markers; altogether an utter chaos . . .

The business is such that . . . this great house can hardly contain it . . . The tenants resort to the solicitor for farms, for improvements, reductions, leases, to negotiate advances, to insure, for the various affairs of life. The clergyman comes on questions that arise out of his benefice, the church-yard, ecclesiastical privileges, the schools, and about his own property. The labourer comes about his cottage and garden – an estate as important to him as his three thousand acres to the squire – or as a witness. The tradesman, the builder, the banker come for financial as well as legal objects . . . Local government needs his assistance. He may sit in an official position in the County Court, or at the bench of the Petty Sessions . . .

The all-important work of registering voters fills up the space between one election and another. At the election his offices are like the head-quarters of an army. He may represent some ancient college, or corporation with lands of vast extent. Ladies with a little capital go home content when he has invested their money in mortgage of real property . . .

The later nineteenth century saw a remarkable growth of education and training, the setting of standards, and the recognition of qualifications, all of which became the hallmarks of the professions. The church and the law, of course, were fully established long before. The clergy had become educated and respectable, if not always moral and responsible, in the course of the sixteenth and seventeenth centuries. The mysterious working of the law had always required expert advice because money and property were at stake, and the Inns of Court had provided a professional training of sorts since medieval times. The science of medicine made much slower progress, and the true causes and proper treatment of even common diseases were still shrouded in myth and doubt during the greater part of the nineteenth century. 'The President of the College of Physicians', remarked *The Times* in 1856, 'is so nearly on a level with the meanest herbalist', that the opinion of the very greatest names in the profession possessed little real value. Two years later, when the Medical Register was established by law, it was estimated that only a third of British practitioners possessed formal qualifications. It was not until 1867 that Lister published his principles of the anti-septic treatment of wounds, to be adopted tardily in the following decade, and it was as late as 1882 that Koch discovered the tubercle bacillus. Consequently, it was only gradually that the qualified doctor and surgeon replaced the herbalist and apothecary. The professional character of the veterinary surgeon, also, only began to be established after the foundation of the Royal College of Veterinary Surgeons in 1844.

Land agents, and auctioneers and valuers too, moved only slowly towards professional status. In education, qualified teachers were in increased supply as training colleges grew in the second half of the century, but the village school remained a sanctuary of the unqualified. The countryside, more than the towns, was a bastion of amateurism, where even the gentry families employed their servants to bleed them, resorted to traditional herbal remedies, and sent for the village farrier to pull a tooth. In the village it was often the case that certain untrained individuals acquired a reputation for their skill in medicine, and expertise in treating sick animals. The amateur land agent persisted, as he still does, and it was late in the day before the unqualified umpire gave way to the professional valuer.

By the opening of the twentieth century the most important of the specialized services – law, medicine, veterinary science, education, land agency, the valuing and auctioning of property – were largely in expert and trained hands. If the country members of professions enjoyed less prestige than did their colleagues in the cities, this was partly because they were generally less well qualified and less well rewarded. In terms of experience, however, they might have the edge, for the country lawyer and doctor, for example, had to be able to deal single-handed with a very wide range of problems. Moreover, they were the more valuable to their clientele, indeed indispensable, since they were there and available when their urban counterparts were out of range. And their especial reward was the great fund of respect which was theirs in the small, and still personal, rural community.

Inhabitants of Stratton, Cornwall, 1887. Back row (left to right): Clerk (agent for the Grenville property), watchmaker, cordwainer, carpenter, shoemaker, ironmonger (and owner of scratch pack of hounds). Front row (seated, left to right): Blacksmith, barber and precentor of the Wesleyan Chapel, auctioneer and printer, shoemaker, labourer who had been a drummer boy at Waterloo.

8   Tradesmen and Craftsmen

Tradesmen and craftsmen played a vital role in the countryside, providing goods and services which were essential to the efficient functioning of the community. The dividing line between tradesmen and craftsmen was not very distinct, for both could be seen as employing specialized skills and knowledge in the running of a business. 'Tradesman' however, suggests perhaps something more of a dealer or middleman, and 'craftsman' a skilled artisan, a blacksmith or wheelwright, for instance, producing useful products in his workshop. Some craftsmen had quite large establishments, employing several journeymen and apprentices, and became the working managers of substantial businesses. Sometimes, like the blacksmiths, they turned to the making of agricultural implements, established a local reputation for their wares, and built up a considerable manufacture, graduating eventually to using steam power in a factory building.

Before the late nineteenth century one of the most widely found country characters was the miller, perenially white and dusty from his flour sifter. He often combined milling with a trade in corn, and sometimes developed a large middleman's business. In addition to grinding the farmers' corn on commission, he dealt on his own account, buying and selling, and arranging shipments to distant markets. Corn-growing areas once had numerous mills, for the capacity of each was small and transport costs were a consideration. There were two main types of windmill. The main structure of the wooden post mill was pivoted on a massive crown or centre post, which in turn was mounted on two great timber beams crossed at right angles and resting on brick piers. From these 'cross trees' a number of sloping beams, called quarter bars, held the crown post in position. The sails were kept in the eye of the wind by pushing the whole superstructure of the mill round on its pivot on the crown post. A long tail beam projected from the side of the mill opposite the sails and came nearly to the ground, often supported by a wheel. This was used to turn the mill, an operation which might have to be done several times a day manually or with the aid of a horse. The wheel had travelled round the mill so many times that it wore a circular rut in the ground. Uncertain, shifting winds meant a good deal of labour in turning the mill, but in the eighteenth century a fantail, consisting of a wheel with six or eight vanes, was added to turn the mill automatically as the wind changed. The tower or smock mill, often much larger than the post mill, consisted of a brick or stone tower, or sometimes an eight-sided wooden tower, supporting a movable mill top. The sails were kept in the wind by the flyer wheel mounted above the mill top behind the sails.

Most windmills had four sails, each of which might be twenty feet long or more. They could be trimmed to meet different states of weather – 'full sail,' 'threequarters', 'half' or 'quarter' – a chain and pulley device enabled the miller to adjust the wooden slats on the sails so as to increase or reduce the surface exposed to the wind. A braked cogwheel was used to stop the sails, though in a high wind it might be necessary to wait for a lull before the brake was effective. At night the sails were usually chained in position. By a system of geared cogwheels the sails turned the mill stones, which were fed with grain through funnels from an upper storey; the ground meal in turn was funnelled from under the stones to a lower floor. There the flour was milled and sifted away from the middlings and bran, and fed into sacks ready for dispatch. Much of the machinery of the old mills was wooden and needed constant attention and frequent replacement. This was the province of the millwright, who was called in to replace faulty wheels or broken cogs; he also supplied the miller with dressing machines and bolting cloths, as well as new mill stones brought from Derbyshire or Cornwall, or imported from France.

Where there was a fast-flowing stream providing a sufficient head of water would be found water mills, taking their power from an overshot or undershot wheel. A recurrent difficulty was that useful streams often served a variety of purposes, not only providing power for corn mills, and possibly other mills used for brewing, iron-slitting or cloth-fulling, but also serving the farmers for drainage and irrigation. Navigation companies might have an interest in the stream for water carriage, and objected to the dams and weirs which mill-owners erected to provide a more constant head of water. The operation of these dams not only obstructed the free passage of boats but affected water levels, sometimes causing unexpected flooding or alternatively making the river too shallow for navigation. The history of rivers is scored with the persistent controversies which raged round the competing interests of landowners, millers, farmers, navigation companies and drainage commissioners. However, both wind and water power diminished in importance as steam engines came into use

Old English tavern scene, showing the use made of the chimney corner.

in corn mills about the end of the eighteenth century. The engine might be portable or stationary, and at first was usually supplementary to the main source of power, used when the weather was calm or the river was low. Purpose-built steam mills seem not to have been common until well on into the nineteenth century, and especially after 1850. Their appearance, no doubt, was linked with the increased availability of water-borne coal supplies and the later extension of the railway system in the second half of the century.

After 1875 corn milling was revolutionized by the onset of the new process of roller milling. Here the grain, instead of being ground between mill stones, was crushed by a series of porcelain or chilled-iron rollers in a system of gradual reduction. The roller process originated in central Europe, and rapidly became established in England after 1879 when the first automatic roller mill was opened in Manchester. For a while the traditional mills kept their stones and installed rollers only to process the middlings left after the fine flour had been extracted. However, the introduction of roller milling coincided with increased imports of foreign grain, which was of the 'hard' variety, better suited to the roller process than the English 'soft' wheat. The combined influence of rollers and imported wheat was to permanently silence many of the country mills. Imported wheat was shipped into the major ports, and there transhipped into coasters and railway waggons for distribution to distant milling centres. Only those mills which adopted rollers, or were well sited near a port or railway, could compete with the new city mills. The milling industry shrank geographically and became concentrated in fewer and larger mills situated in the major ports, large cities and more important market towns. The old country mills were turned to other purposes or allowed to decay and collapse; the few survivors, sometimes restored by preservation societies, remain to remind us of what was once a very common feature of the landscape.

Much of the grain, of course, was converted not into meal and flour but into drink. In England distilleries were sited mainly in large towns, and country stills were rather few and far between. However, John Booker points out in his study of Essex that a distillery was established in Colchester in 1812, and by 1825 was making use of steam power. At the height of its prosperity it produced 300,000 gallons of spirits a year. The business came to an abrupt end in mid-century, but the road leading to the site is still called Distillery Lane. Generally, country malthouses and breweries were much more common than distilleries. In 1853 England and Wales had as many as 2470 brewers consuming 21m. bushels of malt annually; and there were another 31,000 brewing victuallers and beersellers, who disposed of another 11m. bushels of malt.

Maltings proliferated in barley districts, and particularly in places near to canals, ports and navigable rivers. Hertfordshire was a great barley county, and the Stort navigation a great transporter of malt; Bishop's Stortford boasted as many as a hundred malt warehouses. The navigation drew malt also from west and mid-Essex: Saffron Walden had some twenty malt kilns in 1848, while a further eleven were sited at Sawbridgeworth and ten at Harlow. A good deal of the malt was sold in the capital to the great London brewers, but at one time there were large numbers of small breweries in country towns, and many village inns and beer houses brewed for themselves. But as brewing tended to concentrate in the larger centres of consumption and the breweries bought up inns to become tied houses, malting, like milling, moved to the towns and gathered in the ports and by the railways. In his day the independent maltster was a man of some importance. He was often among the wealthiest members of the country community, and frequently combined farming with malting; indeed, maltsters sometimes began as farmers, erected a malthouse to malt their own produce, and expanded the malting side of the business to cater for the needs of other farmers. Some of the malt went back to the farms to be used in brewing beer for the farmer and his men. On a large farm the expenditure on malt was considerable – especially so if it were in Dorset, for example, for there the men were allowed a gallon a day: a quart for breakfast at ten o'clock, a pint at half-past eleven for luncheon, a quart during dinner between one and two o'clock, a pint at four, with something to eat at five, and the rest when work was finished for the day. On a large Dorset farm some £70 or £80 was spent a year on malt.

The concentration of brewing and growth of tied houses were not innovations of the nineteenth century. By 1800 the great London and Burton brewers were already long-established, and the small country breweries were acquiring outlets in the market towns and neighbouring villages. The Bests, brewers of eighteenth-century Chatham, made a sufficient fortune from the thirsty sailors and citizens of that naval port to enable the family to retire to a country mansion and assume the life-style of Kentish gentry. A large number of the hostelries in the Medway towns were theirs, and the Bests are still remembered in Chatham by a street named after them. In Essex in the early years of the nineteenth century, George Williams, brewer of Ongar, bought up the *Marquis of Granby* at Harlow, the *Crown* at Ingatestone, *White Horse* at Brentwood, *King's Head* at Ongar, *White Lion* at Epping, and the *Ship* at South Hanningfield. This was a process which became characteristic of the industry, and brewers' acquisitions of inns spread widely over county borders. When a Saffron Walden concern was leased in 1838 over 70 licensed houses in Essex, Cambridgeshire, Suffolk and Hertfordshire were involved in the transaction. Where the inns had their own brewhouses, the old equipment was disused or might be transferred to the main brewery of the company. Inns' brewhouses could be substantial – that of the *Swan* at Stanway in 1830 measured 31 feet by 17 feet, and held a malt mill, pumps, wort troughs, copper, and much other equipment.

By the later decades of the nineteenth century amalgamations of country breweries were frequent, though a few had occurred earlier. In due course, especially after the First World War, the enlarged country firms were themselves taken over by the great national companies. The object was not so much the acquisition of the local brewing plants, which were generally demolished or converted to other purposes, as the control of more outlets. The value of the business was measured by the number of tied houses which it possessed. So the country breweries declined to the remnant who survive today. The village innkeepers, however, remained, although they, too, became much reduced in numbers in the course of the years. The great coaching inns situated at strategic points on the main roads decayed after the collapse of the coaching business in the 1830s and 1840s. But the village inns continued, because local horse-drawn traffic was for long little affected, and might even be increased by the railways.

The village inn was once an important centre of commerce, where farmers and graziers, dealers and middlemen, drovers, carters, and boatmen met to transact business over their pipes and punch. All those wanting news of local trade would drop in to see who might be in the inn-parlour. Drovers called there to collect beasts intended for sale at a distant market, and many inns had extensive paddocks where stock could be kept overnight. Commercial travellers, too, put up there, as did pedlars, packmen, and travelling showmen with their performing bears and dogs or Punch and Judy. Most of the farm horses were so accustomed to stop at wayside inns that they drew up there of their own accord.

There were really two classes of country alehouses. The principal village inns were the resort of farmers, dealers, carters, local tradesmen and skilled craftsmen. The hedge alehouses or beer shops catered for a much lower class of customer. They were often mere converted cottages, houses of dubious reputation, which attracted the labourers who wanted to drink and talk out of the sight and hearing of their superiors. The home brew of the "low public", a heady liquid, nauseous to those not acquainted with it, was what the labourers liked. As Richard Jefferies said:

> He prefers something that he can feel; something that, if
> sufficiently indulged in, will make even his thick head spin
> and his temples ache next morning. Then he has had the value
> of his money. So that really good ale would require a very
> large bush indeed before it attracted his custom.

The low public became the club, almost the home, of the labourer. Richard Jefferies reminds us of what it would have been like to enter one in the 1880s:

> Beware that you do not knock your head against the smoke-
> blackened beams of the low ceiling, and do not put your elbow
> carelessly on the deal table, stained with spilled ale, left
> uncleaned from last night, together with little heaps of ashes,
> tapped out from pipes, and spots of grease from the tallow

candles. The old-fashioned settles which gave so cosy an air in the olden time to the inn room, and which still linger in some of the houses, are not here – merely forms and cheap chairs. A great pot hangs over the fire, for the family cooking is done in the public apartment; but do not ask to join in the meal, for though the food may be more savoury than is dreamed of in your philosophy, the two-grained forks have not been cleaned these many a day.

The landlord of the low public lived well, for food and fuel seemed there to gravitate by some mysterious means. The carters, for instance,

> halt at the public, and are noticed to enjoy good living there, nor are they asked for their score. A few trusses of hay, or bundles of straw, a bushel of corn, or some such trifle is left behind merely out of good fellowship. Waggons come up laden with tons of coal for the farms miles above, far from a railway station; three or four teams, perhaps, one after the other. Just a knob or two can scarcely be missed, and a little of the small in a sack-bag. The bundles of wood thrown down at the door by the labourers as they enter are rarely picked up again; they disappear, and the hearth at home is cold. The foxes are blamed for the geese and the chickens, and the hunt execrated for not killing enough cubs, but Reynard is not always guilty. Eggs and poultry vanish. The shepherds have ample opportunity for disposing of a few spare lambs to a general dealer whose trap is handy . . . Perhaps the man is genial, his manners enticing, his stories amusing, his jokes witty. Not at all. He is a silent fellow, scarce opening his mouth except to curse the poor scrub of a maid servant, or to abuse a man who has not paid his score. He slinks in and lights his pipe, smokes it silently, and slinks out again. He is the octopus of the hamlet, fastening on the cottage homes and sucking the life-blood from them. He misses nothing, and nothing comes amiss to him.

Eventually the spread of the railways reduced the prosperity of the inns and helped kill off the low public. The labourers, somewhat better off and no longer so much in need of credit, preferred to go off into town on a Saturday, the wife to shop and he to sample the wide variety of public houses. Village innkeepers found their customers shrinking, and those who remained were mainly the less credit-worthy. Landlords began to insist on cash, and found their taprooms even emptier. The custom of the carters and roadmen fell off as traffic on the country roads dwindled, while the drovers disappeared almost completely. Farmers transacted their business more in the towns. Even the commercial traveller popped into the village by one train and popped out again by another. There was a change of fashion: pubs and shops in the town were better, cheaper, more up-to-date, more sophisticated; country ones were rustic, old-fashioned, boring.

Few shops existed in villages in the early years of the nineteenth century. Supplies of groceries, cloth and household necessities were bought from travelling packmen or on occasional visits to neighbouring towns. Everyday foodstuffs were produced and prepared at home. The gentry households had their own home farms and dairies, and were largely self-sufficient in corn, meat, milk, butter, cheese, poultry, eggs and vegetables. The farmers, too, lived pretty much off their own produce, while the labourers, who in any case had a very simple diet, often got their milk, bacon, corn and cheese from the farms. Cottagers with large gardens or allotments sold or exchanged their surplus fruit and vegetables; their wives kept chickens and often had eggs to spare, while some women baked pies or made sweets for the custom of their neighbours. Cloth purchased from a travelling dealer or in a nearby town was made up by the village tailors and dressmakers, and the numerous village shoemakers produced footwear. Cottagers made their own rush lights by dipping dried rushes, collected and peeled in summer, in mutton fat. The lighted rushes were fixed in iron holders, or laid on the edge of tables or boxes when the light was needed. Pedlars brought round fancy goods, crockery and pots, or advertised their 'original prophetic almanac'; there were menders of chairs and umbrellas, and tinkers who called to repair pans and sharpen knives and scissors on their foot-driven grindstones. Goods not available in the village, and luxury items, such as books, newspapers, writing paper, soap, medicines, tea and coffee, were ordered from the nearest large town and delivered by the regular weekly, twice-weekly, or daily services of carriers' waggons. The London evening newspapers, for example, were printed in time to catch the carriers' deliveries to numerous villages in the home counties. But these were things of interest only to a limited number of well-to-do families. Most country people lived a remarkably simple and self-sufficient existence. This was the more marked in remote areas or in districts of poor roads, which were virtually cut off for weeks at a time during bad weather in winter.

Turnpike roads, canals, and eventually the railways broke down country isolation – not completely by any means, but to a very considerable extent. By mid-century grocers' shops had appeared in the larger villages, and in southern counties, vans delivered town-made bread. The appearance of the village store was associated with the spread into general consumption of such former luxuries as tea, coffee and sugar, but it also stocked a wide range of non-perishable foodstuffs and household goods, and the business was sometimes combined with a village craft or profession. Easier access to towns meant that the gentle families' housekeepers preferred to go further afield in search of better-quality, and perhaps cheaper, goods. On Saturday nights the labourers' wives tramped back up the lanes laden with shopping bags filled at the markets and shops of a nearby town. The Saturday shopping excursion, laborious though it was, formed a welcome break in the dull monotony of cottage existence. By 1880, as Richard Jefferies noted, the cottager bought almost everything and produced nothing for himself except vegetables – not even a home-made loaf. He bought his clothes and boots at the town outfitters, and the village tailor, seamstress and cobbler found it increasingly difficult to compete with the new, cheap, factory-made goods. They kept going by giving credit when the town emporium demanded cash. Pack-drapers still came round the villages on foot, calling at every cottage, but frequently they were now the representative of some urban wholesaler. The Cotswolds, it is said, were regularly perambulated, not by 'bagmen', but by the merchants themselves, who in some cases combined preaching and lecturing with the solicitations of orders. Town grocers, similarly, sent out men to take weekly orders from the more wealthy households, and the orders were delivered by van or bicycle a few days later. In consequence, the once large numbers of tradesmen and craftsmen in small country towns and large villages diminished sharply after mid-century. In Cerne Abbas, a small Dorset town not served by the railway, the 57 tradesmen of 1851 had shrunk to a mere eleven by the end of the century.

The village still saw a few independent travelling dealers:

> The village butcher has his round, his cart tail being counter and chopping block, sometimes taking back eggs and farm produce to sell at his shop; the grocer whose cart is covered with advertisements and hung with household requisites; the oilman who has a carefully mapped route for every day in the week; the leather seller who supplies the cobbler and those

who mend their own boots; and the tin and china-ware trader and travelling ironmonger who keep to the villages and larger hamlets, seldom turning off their direct route to visit scattered groups of houses.

There was often a man bringing round weekly supplies of fish and fruit, and occasionally a cheapjack called with a cartload of crockery and tinware set out on the grass by the roadside, 'before a back-cloth painted with icebergs and penguins and polar bears. Soon he had his naptha lamps flaring and was clashing his basins together like bells and calling: "Come buy! Come buy!"' The once familiar packman or pedlar, was seldom seen in Flora Thompson's Candleford district in the eighties. Only one last survivor of the once numerous clan still visited the hamlet:

He would turn aside from the turnpike and come plodding down the narrow hamlet road, an old white-headed, white-bearded man, still hale and rosy, although almost bent double under the heavy, black canvas-covered pack he carried strapped on his shoulders. 'Anything out of the pack to-day?' he would ask at each house, and, at the least encouragement, fling down his load and open it on the doorstep. He carried a tempting variety of goods; dress-lengths and shirt-lengths and remnants to make up for the children; aprons and pinafores, plain and fancy; corduroys for the men, and coloured scarves and ribbons for Sunday wear.

Some country businesses, however, expanded with the changing times. Enterprising blacksmiths and carpenters sometimes developed into specialized manufacturers of agricultural implements. Thomas Smail, blacksmith of Lanton, produced in 1852 his own design of swing plough, widely used on the farms of the border country. The craft was carried on at the village smithy by succeeding generations of the family until as late as 1910, and Scottish farmers who emigrated took it with them to distant parts of the world. At Maisemore, near Gloucester, a Benjamin Heatheridge made for many years a wooden swing plough of traditional design, with a cast-iron share and turn-furrow produced by a Gloucester foundry. He continued to make his plough without change for the 1870s down to the 1930s, when its price was £7. Jobbing ironfounders, too, who began by making a variety of equipment for farmers' barns, wheelwrights' work, and householders' wells, became manufacturers of cheap patent ploughs, casting them from moulds in quantity, and assembling the complete ploughs on a production line system. Ironmongers were invaluable as agents for the large companies' machines and as stockists of small metal goods such as tools, nails, screws, and household ironware.

Blacksmiths survived, of course, because they were so much in demand for repairs and wrought-iron work, and for their hand-made tools. But like the saddler, their mainstay was the horse, and it must be remembered that the horse remained a vital source of power until relatively recent times. It was the late nineteenth century before steam engines finally eclipsed the horse-driven gins and threshing machines on farms. Long after that the horse remained essential for drawing farm implements and for local transport. Indeed, the total number of horses was still rising in the 1880s and 1890s and reached its peak only in the early years of the present century. The decline of the blacksmith was coupled with the coming of the tractor and the motor-car. Fewer carriages and traps, the decline in carriers' wagons, in vans and horse-drawn farm implements, meant a loss of custom to the village smithy. In Kent, for instance, the number of farm horses alone fell by a quarter from 23,000 in 1898 to 17,000 in 1924, and many village forges had to be abandoned.

The smithy, with its spare chains, iron wheels, and the shoes marked with the names of the horses for whom they were intended, was a lively feature of the old village. There were always many people calling about repairs or waiting for their horses to be shod. Children peeped in, fascinated by the brightness of the fire and the sparks flying from the anvil. Another important establishment was the wheelwright's shop. The old farm waggons had huge and stout wheels, the rear ones commonly five feet high, and the front ones four. The nave or hub was shaped from seasoned elm, the spokes from cleft heart of oak to give strength, and the felloes or rim sections from ash, elm or beech. Many years of training and experience went into the making of a perfect wheel which would see out a great many years. The wheel had to be dished, or made slightly concave, in order to resist the sideways thrust of a load swinging from side to side on an uneven road. Iron tyres were fitted by the blacksmith, red hot, and then were rapidly cooled by dowsing with buckets of water. As the tyre contracted the whole wheel was strained together, and the degree of dish required was obtained. Though great skill was needed, and careful attention to design and detail was the hallmark of the proficient wheelwright, a waggon or cart was not expensive. In 1860 they cost about £40 and £20 respectively. Wheelwrights, together with millwrights, were sometimes called in to repair farm machinery and sometimes, like the blacksmith, they branched out into designing their own implements. James Smyth, wheelwright of Peasenhall, Suffolk, perfected with his brother a new type of seed drill, fitted with coulters which could be raised and lowered for different widths of work.

Another village craftsman much in demand was the carpenter. Householders required new doors and window frames, farmers wanted gates, sheep troughs, cribs and ladders. The carpenter was called in to repair barn floors, put new cogs on wheels and replace defective spouts, bins and hoppers. With his basket of tools on his shoulders, the carpenter making his way through the lanes to some distant house or farm was once a common sight. Among the tools in his canvas-lined basket were an axe and saw, a clawed hammer, mallet and gouge, gimlets and bradawl, smoothing plane, chisels, iron square, rule and chalk line. In an inner pocket of the basket were a nail punch, a pot of grease for the saw and a file for sharpening it. The basket was carried on the shoulders by an axe helve passed through the webbing-bound handles, its blade just behind the man's neck. Among the items made in the shop itself was the travelling clothes box, a stout chest fitted with lock and key and iron handles at each end. No maid leaving home for domestic service could go away without her box. Typically the shop also held a selection of wheelbarrows and rat traps, and a newly-made coffin rested on trestles in one corner, for the carpenter served as the village undertaker. Coffins were made to size from selected pieces of wood, and the sides were curved by making partial saw-cuts on the inside against the grain and applying boiling water. The carpenter's wife often assisted in making the lining for the coffin.

It was quite common for village craftsmen to have a little land of their own, especially when it might be convenient to have their own team for fetching timber, coal or other raw materials and for delivering finished products to the farms. Sometimes a craftsman branched out into farming and ran a carter's business on the side. George Sturt, who wrote under the pen-name of George Bourne, once told of how his grandfather, William Smith of Farnborough, came to combine his pottery business with farming. The farm waggons came in very useful for fetching the clay and for carrying the finished pots to market.

For us, accustomed to villages containing little more than a couple of inns, a small general store and post office, and perhaps a butcher's shop and tea-shop, it is difficult to realize how numerous and varied were the occupations in the more important villages of the last century. There were tailors, dressmakers and shoemakers, and in the north clog-makers; fellmongers and tanners, leather dressers and saddlers; blacksmiths, wheel-wrights and millwrights; bricklayers and carpenters; maltsters and millers; butchers, bakers and barbers. Whittawers or dressers of white leather were sometimes found, and saddlers who prepared their own leather. Some craftsmen took up other jobs when work was slack, and tradesmen often combined several businesses, as when carters were coal merchants and higglers, and innkeepers were farmers or general dealers. At Cropwell Butler in Nottinghamshire the local saddler was also the dentist.

A large Nottinghamshire village like Tuxford, long a posting station of the Great North Road, had saddlers, a tinker, an umbrella repairer, a ropemaker, coal merchants, a pikelet and muffinbaker, and home-made sweet shops – in addition to a chemist, two veterinary surgeons and a lawyer. Even in the remote wolds of Lindsey the large village of Binbrook boasted as many as 109 craftsmen in 1851 who lived alongside 31 tradesmen and 11 professional people. The village had a total population at that time of 1269, of whom 23 were farmers and 251 farmworkers. The professions included two doctors, a solicitor, architect, and a surveyor who also kept the post office. There were as many as seven millers and five butchers, but no brewer or maltster. The three leading drapers and grocers each kept a shop assistant and a female servant. Ten people described themselves as builders and bricklayers, but manufacturing was confined to a single rope-maker, a tinplate worker, a machine maker, and a maker of agricultural implements. The crafts were very strongly repre-sented with as many as 14 wheelwrights, 13 blacksmiths, 13 tailors, 18 dressmakers and 15 shoemakers. Several carriers provided the village with regular services to Louth, Market Rasen, Grimsby and Caistor. Clearly Binbrook was, in its locality, an important centre for the trades and crafts, and it performed the numerous and valuable functions of a processing and service centre for a wide neighbourhood.

Binbrook, though off the beaten track, was in its district exceptionally populous and important. Smaller villages and hamlets had little beyond a few scattered farms and cottages, perhaps a clergyman and a schoolteacher, a single shop – quite likely not so much. In some ways the small country places were quieter and less frequented than nowadays, but the changes in them have been small. What has really been transformed is the busy activity of the large village which once had its professions, its numerous tradesmen and its small army of craftsmen. The centralizing influence of the railways, the competition of cheap, factory-made goods, and the supplanting of ancient crafts by new techniques, gradually stripped such villages of their old importance and their old vitality. With the old craftsmen went eventually the women's trades, such as pillow-lace and straw-plaiting.

The change began slowly in the early eighteen-hundreds and gathered pace after mid-century. Villages became either more purely agricultural or more largely industrial, dominated on the one hand by farmers and their men, or on the other by some large new factory or works. The independence and self-sufficiency of the past, never complete but very real, declined. Country communities became mere satellites of the towns, increasingly reliant on urban sources for their goods and services. The change was already far advanced when Jefferies wrote about *Hodge and his Masters* in 1880, or Anderson Graham discussed *The Rural Exodus* a dozen years later. Country tailors used to visit the farmhouses and sit in the kitchen at so much a day, repairing old clothes and making new from materials provided by the farmer's wife. But they disappeared, their living destroyed by the competition of the cheap outfitters in the towns. The old craftsmen who made wicker baskets, cutting their own willows by the streams of Somerset's Athelney marshes, lingered on, but were increasingly thinned out by rival foreign goods. Much the same happened to the women who made baskets and mats from rushes grown in the Norfolk Broads. Some craftsmen managed to survive: the horse-hair workers of Castle Cary, for instance, who made stuffing for mattresses and furniture, and produced wigs, whips, sieves and fishing lines; and the women of County Durham and Monmouthshire, who specialized in making quilts. Some crafts have been revived by the modern cult of the antique and hand-made, and by the restoration of old cottages as weekend residences – the potters, and the manufacturers of hand-made bricks and tiles, and, especially, the thatchers.

By the end of the century, however, the changing character of country life was apparent in a variety of different ways, as Flora Thompson remembered:

After the Jubilee nothing ever seemed quite the same. The old Rector died and the farmer, who had seemed immovable excepting by death, had to retire to make way for the heir of the landowning nobleman who intended to farm the family estates himself. He brought with him the new self-binding reaping machine and women were no longer required in the harvest field. At the hamlet several new brides took possession of houses previously occupied by elderly people and brought new ideas into the place. The last of the bustles disappeared and leg-o'-mutton sleeves were 'all the go'. The new Rector's wife took her Mothers' Meeting women for a trip to London. Babies were christened new names; Wanda was one, Gwendolin another. The innkeeper's wife got in cases of tinned salmon and Australian rabbit. The Sanitary Inspector appeared for the first time at the hamlet and shook his head over the pigsties and privies. Wages rose, prices soared, and new needs multiplied. People began to speak of 'before the Jubilee' much as we in the nineteen-twenties spoke of 'before the war', either as a golden time or as one of exploded ideas, according to the age of the speaker.

The new ease of communication between country and town, the new products and the means of making them, drove the country tradesman into a town business and the village craftsman into a factory. Some left for a new career in the colonies, where their skills were still valued. A few, who had saved money and had perhaps some experience of farming, took up land when it was going cheap in the agricultural depression of the eighties and nineties. Rider Haggard noted that some of the landholders in Norfolk and elsewhere were not legitimate farmers of the old sort but new men who combined farming with a trade; they often brought a more strictly commercial, more economical, attitude to agriculture. The decline in village trades and crafts was perhaps less remarked upon by contemporaries because it was gradual, spread over the better part of a century, and because at its height it was overshadowed by the great depression in farming itself. But it was much more than a spin-off of the farmers' decline. It was, in fact, one of the long-term consequences which flowed from the transformation of Britain into an industrialized and urbanized society. As such, it has not attracted much attention from historians. But it was, nevertheless, highly significant in the rural context, for the going of the miller and the maltster, the dying out of the packman and pedlar, and the eventual disappearance of the saddler, wheelwright and blacksmith made their own conspicuous contribution to the decay of the old country life.

9   The End of the Old Order

The nineteenth century witnessed the closing phase of a rural society which, through gradually adapting itself to the times, had shown a remarkable degree of stability over a period of some four or five hundred years. By the later seventeenth century it had developed its classical tripartite form of a landed aristocracy and gentry, who owned the greater part of the land, a tenantry who farmed it, and a numerous proletariat who laboured on it. With these three basic groups in the countryside have to be coupled the parsons and the craftsmen, the five together represented, as H.J.Massingham said, by the manor, the rectory, the farmstead, workshop and cottage. And to these should be added also the other professional people, the tradesmen, and the workers in cottage industries such as gloves, lace and straw.

The enterprise of the farmers and the labour of the workfolk (as the labourers referred to themselves) supported a *rentier* or leisured class of landlords. In reality the landlords were neither so leisured nor so superfluous as is often thought. Landowners frequently managed home farms, and sometimes industrial concerns as well; they supported agricultural societies, and not infrequently experimented with crops, breeds, manures and implements; they played an invaluable role in governing both the country and the county; their younger sons staffed the professions, the army and navy, the civil service and the colonial service; the landowners, moreover, acted as the mouthpiece of the landed interest and took up the grievances of the farmers; they set social standards and, though their paternal role was in decline, assumed a degree of responsibility for the security, education and general welfare of the community. In the nineteenth century their tradition of social responsibility, casual and haphazard as it was, yet continued. One or two examples must suffice: at Spelsbury in Oxfordshire Viscount Dillon practised a common form of regular charity when he helped villagers through the winter months with gifts of blankets, soup and rabbits; in Essex Colonel Bourchier gave £10 each year to the poor of Bures, where he had land, and £15 in especially bad seasons. C.G.Round of Birch in the same county was influenced by aesthetic considerations: he was concerned that his tenant should not enclose a small piece of waste land lying between the Rectory and the Church, for when the Rector and his family went to church their walk was 'made pleasant and pretty to them by the unenclosed little piece'.

But it must be admitted that much of the time of the aristocracy was taken up by their own pleasures and sport, and that much of their attention was given to the pursuit of measures designed to perpetuate their families and estates. Carefully-devised trusts were established to ensure that the property passed intact to the next generation, and land was set aside to produce the dowries without which their daughters could hardly expect to find partners of suitable wealth and rank. The two operations were to some extent incompatible, for there was a tendency to be over-generous in specifying dowries, jointures for widows, and portions for younger sons – to such an extent as to threaten the financial stability of the estate. In consequence, heirs who succeeded to great estates inherited with them enormous debts, and were put to much care and even frugality in maintaining ancestral homes and acres. It was thus that Lord Stanley wrote in 1863:

> I cannot exactly make out what my sisters are to have, but it will be near £1400 which I think quite ample and a very large sum to be taken out of the estate. My father used to abuse his father for having left his sisters an income very little larger . . . In short he was full of complaints about his father but burthened the estate without remorse – with but little consideration for his successor.

Some landed proprietors had so ardent a passion for sport that hunting, horses and gaming ruined their fortunes and distorted their judgment. Sir Richard Sutton, a Lincolnshire owner, left, most unusually, the greater part of his wealth – £40,000 – to his second son, 'who hunts', while his eldest son, 'who plays the organ', received a mere £14,000.

There was also a good deal of snobbery, though it must be said that country people expected the squire of an old family to adopt a certain *hauteur*. Polite and kind, as he often was, the squire usually thought it below his dignity to go into the villagers' homes and try to get to know them individually. Nor, as W.H.Hudson noted, did the villagers expect it. 'He was the squire, a gentleman – any one might understand that he could not come among them like that!'

That is what a parson can do because he is, so to speak, paid to keep an eye on them, and besides it's religion there and a different thing. But the squire! – *their* squire, that dignified old gentleman, so upright in his saddle, so considerate and courteous to everyone – but he never forgot his position – never in *that* way!

Maria Josepha, Lady Stanley, told of an incident which involved one of her family in 1873. Her daughter wrote to say

There was a family on board the steamer, a lady and 6 children, at first we took no notice of them, they looked so shabby in their dress we did not think they were ladies, but by degrees we were showed they were *above* their dress – their manners & all their ways so pretty & ladylike & their faces so lovely. Luciebella kept looking at them, saying how like Aunt Stanley, & I saw the Dillon resemblance & said, quite in a joke, perhaps it is Mrs Constantine Dillon, & so it was. I then introduced myself & we talked till they got out at Lausanne. She must have enough to do, 6 children & only one maid among them all.

In 1909, when Hudson was writing about the dignified, unbending kind of squire, he found in the countryside an increasingly rigid caste feeling which, he said, created a gulf or barrier between the different classes. Much more recently H.J.Massingham noted that the 'structural equilibrium' of village society had been thrown out of gear – 'the craftsman has become a museum piece, the squire and the parson little more than figure-heads'. The heightening of class divisions, the breakdown of the old ordered village community based on acceptance of rank and respect for position, went back far beyond the time of Hudson and Massingham. The changes on which they remarked were rooted in the fundamental movements which gradually transformed the whole of English society from the later eighteenth century onwards – the growth of population, the rise of modern industry and the appearance of great urban agglomerations. From these developments flowed many of the stresses and strains which changed the nature of rural life. Landowners found their pre-eminence challenged by new industrial wealth and urban aspirations, and the gradual deterioration in the status of land led ultimately to the selling up of estates. The fall in rents after 1879 initiated the process, though the seeds of the decline had been sown long before, in the political and economic reforms of 1832 and 1846. In only a few short years between about 1910 and 1921, great accumulations of land which had been patiently put together over many generations were parcelled up and sold, mansions closed, and the old families dispersed for ever. The squire whose ancestors had dominated a village for many long years was known no more. No longer useful in the old agricultural community, and governmental ways, the landowners became, as Massingham said, an irrelevance, a feudal survival, a mere figure-head.

Farming was itself deeply affected by the growth of an industrial Britain. The cultivation of the soil became more commercial, more technical, more capital-intensive. Free trade, the logical policy of a triumphant industrialism, eventually brought disaster to farmers in the shape of unchecked imports of cheap produce. The old-style farmer could hardly survive. He had not been too closely watchful of his costs, and he took a pride in the neatness of his land as well as in his support of progressive techniques, and he had continued to maintain a large labour force, believing that his responsibility extended to both land and men. His kind gave way to more harshly realistic cultivators, men who knew that only new uses for land and the strictest economy could make farming pay when they were faced with Argentine beef, Australian mutton, Danish cheese and bacon, and American wheat down to 26s 2d the quarter. Often the new kind of farmer was literally a newcomer. His origins were in another part of the country, or in a trade or other kind of business. He could not, therefore, feel much sense of loyalty to an estate or a particular family, and when he saw that the landowners had no real power to alter things he broke away from aristocratic leadership. Hence the rise of the farmers' movements, and the appearance in due course of the entirely independent farmer, whose banner was that of the National Farmers Union.

The labourers, by far the most numerous body of countryfolk, could not help but be affected too by the growth of industry and the intrusion of cheap food. But they were affected in a different way, for they were wage-earners and had no capital in the land. Before mid-century the increase in non-agricultural employment had merely had the effect of creaming off some of the growing labour force, leaving the numbers on the land still greater than before. Wages stagnated, under-employment was commonplace and poverty rife, particularly in southern counties. A change came with the railway mania of the 1840s and the mid-Victorian boom which followed. Now conditions began to alter in a significant way. Industrialized villages and great conurbations offered country people a wider variety of work and better conditions. For those who remained on the land – the great majority – cheap food after 1875 helped eke out the low but rising wages, and enabled them slowly to lift their living standards. The more enterprising and more imaginative were influenced by the propaganda of emigration agents and urging of railway and shipping companies to leave the country altogether. The flight from the land was at its height when the agricultural depression was most severe. Hence the farmers' search for economies, their shift to cheaper modes of cultivation, had little impact on the labourers. The men's wages continued to rise as their numbers continued to fall. A growing scarcity of good men made also for some small signs of independence. Now it was the masters who sought the hands, who enquired anxiously at the end of the season: 'I hope you do not mean to leave us this year.' Little wonder that labourers evinced scant interest in the farmers' plight. For them cheap bread made sense, and unlike the farmers they had no wish to see free trade replaced by 'fair' trade.

It was often the women who felt most keenly the attraction of a new life in the towns. It was they who first rejected the old country ways and urged their cautious, conservative, but complaisant partners into making the move. Women who could not be bothered to keep a two-roomed cottage clean and neat found pleasure in looking after much more capacious homes in a town.

> Country women look upon town as a kind of Eden for them. It is not only that feminine vanity and curiosity will be gratified by gadding about and seeing the smart things in the shop windows, but how much easier a life their will be! No more pigs to be fed and tended, no more toil in the garden or on the allotment, hardly any baking to be done; why, it is a lady's life complete. The very water is brought into the house, whereas in the village it had to be carried from a distant well in a pitcher or with two pails and a girdle. The laborious peasant woman is not at all unwilling to undertake the care of several additional rooms when she is relieved of the burden of work that in the village bowed and aged her mother and her kindred before their time.

As women began to go into towns for their shopping on a Saturday so they became more aware of the different, more exciting existence that awaited them there. Moreover, many of the old country occupations which once kept them busy and provided additional money had gone, or were long sunk in decline. By the end of the century the cottage glove-making, straw-plaiting and bone lace had almost died out. There was still work in the fields, but not as much as formerly, and it was mainly part-time help picking fruit, lifting potatoes or chopping turnips – work which was arduous, dirty, and much exposed to the elements. With the influx of middle-class residents into villages had grown a great increase in the demand for maids, charwomen and washerwomen. George Bourne thought this had some effect in encouraging the country women to be more tidy in their persons and in their homes. Their doubtful standards of cleanliness and hygiene were immeasurably raised by contact with middle-class households.

> The state of the cottages is betrayed naively by the young girls who go from them into domestic service. 'You don't seem to like things sticky,' one of those girls observed to a mistress distressed by sticky door-handles one day and sticky table-knives the next day. That remark which Richard Jefferies heard a mother address to her daughter, 'Gawd help the poor missus as gets hold o' *you*!' might very well be applied to many and many a child of fourteen in this valley, going out, all untrained, to her first 'place' . . .

But charring and washing could be done in the towns perhaps more easily than in the country. The work might be nearer to hand, or if not there were trams or buses. Grocers' shops were to be found at almost every corner, and coal and milk brought round regularly to the houses. Those long tramps through muddy lanes after hours spent in picking potatoes or trimming swedes, burdened perhaps with bundles of dead wood or a sack of cones picked up in the fir woods, were not needed in towns. Women who had seen something of town dwellings or country villas were the less likely to remain satisfied with their little antiquated cottages. In the older cottages there were no conveniences:

> Everything had to be done practically in one room – which was sometimes a sleeping-room too, or say in one room and a wash house. The preparation and serving of meals, the airing of clothes and the ironing of them, the washing of the children, the mending and making – how could a woman do any of it with comfort in the cramped apartment, into which, moreover, a tired and dirty man came home in the evening to eat and wash and rest, or if not to rest, then to potter in and out from garden or pigstye, 'treading in dirt' as he came?

A Herefordshire poacher in about 1890.

Then, too, many cottages had not so much as a sink where work with water could be done; many had no water save in wet weather; there was not one cottage in which it could be drawn from a tap, but it all had to be fetched from well or tank. And in the husband's absence at work, it was the woman's duty – one more added to so many others – to bring water indoors. In times of drought water had often to be carried long distances in pails, and it may be imagined how the housework would go in such circumstances.

Towards the end of the century the labourers' 'flight from the land' became a public issue which attracted a good deal of attention from writers and politicians. A variety of investigators enquired into wages, working conditions, housing, and allotments. Legislation was passed in an effort to make smallholdings more readily available, but few labourers took them up or were capable of benefitting from them. In fact, the legislation, so far as the labourers were concerned, was not only ineffective but superfluous. Numerous smallholdings were created privately without legislative encouragement, but the difficulty was how to make the occupiers prosperous. The right kinds of soils and markets were not always at hand, and smallholders often attempted to operate on too small a margin of profit and with inadequate capital. Where men had the means of buying a holding they found themselves paying more in interest than would be charged in rent. As a result they skimped on everything possible – on seed, manure, livestock, and the house itself. 'If a landlord owned the place how he would have been dunned to make repairs!'

At all events, the vast majority of labourers who stayed on the land remained labourers. *The Land*, the report of an unofficial Liberal Land Enquiry Committee, appeared on the eve of the First World War as a severe indictment of landowners and farmers. It surveyed with a highly critical eye the lowness of wages, the bad working conditions, and the defective nature and scarcity of the housing. In their reply, *Facts about Land*, the Land Agents' Society warned against acceptance of sweeping and over-simple generalizations, pointing out that many labourers liked to have part of their wages in kind, and that many were well-housed and preferred, too, the security of a tied cottage that went with the job. In 1913 Seebohm Rowntree, the celebrated investigator of urban poverty whose book on York had appeared in 1901, turned his attention to farmworkers' wages and living standards. Except for only five counties, Seebohm Rowntree found the agricultural labourers' average earnings fell below the minimum weekly expenditure required to maintain 'physical efficiency' (which he calculated at 20s 6d in 1913 for a family consisting of two adults and three children). There is no doubt that rural poverty was widespread, but Rowntree certainly exaggerated the problem by ignoring in his calculations such considerations as additional earnings which could be gained by piece-work, the subsidiary earnings of the wife and children, and the produce of the labourer's garden or allotment. Furthermore, Rowntree's figures compared the prices of 1913 with the earnings of 1907 – but in 1913 farm labourers' earnings were higher than in 1907 by as much as 2s 4d, or 13.3 per cent.

Average figures were in any case misleading. There were considerable regional variations in both earnings and prices, while working conditions varied with the nature of the farming; it has to be remembered also that some two-fifths or so of the agricultural labour force consisted of bailiffs, foremen, woodmen and men in charge of animals who were paid at higher rates. But although it is difficult to establish the precise facts about farm labourers' incomes, it is undoubtedly true that by contemporary English standards many families were poor. It is also true, however, that in the opening decades of the twentieth century they were not as poor as they had been earlier. Average money wages rose in the years between 1850 and 1907 by some 5s 4d, or nearly 56 per cent, and the increase in family incomes was still greater. For a large part of that period the prices of common foodstuffs were falling, and information concerning the labourers' diet and general living standards shows unmistake-able evidence of substantial improvement.

Other important changes were the coming of compulsory education in the village after 1870 and the extension of the franchise in 1884. Now the farmworker was being wooed by trade unionists and politicians both. Just what was the nature of his politics, however, remained something of a mystery. The position was more evident with the better-educated, more inde-pendent, and more communicative tradesmen and craftsmen. The well-to-do butcher who served the 'quality' leaned, as might be expected, to the aristocratic view of things, as did the publican, whose prime conviction was that when Liberal prejudice put beer out of fashion the glory of the realm would be in decay. The sturdy, taciturn blacksmith seemed generally to be as Tory as that other stalwart, the gamekeeper. These, together with the school-teacher, assumed a certain air of superiority, and looked patronis-ingly on their poorer neighbours. Liberal ideas were to be found among the carpenters and mechanics, as well as the independent tradesmen, who tended to be 'decidedly Radical' in their opinions. The cobbler, remarked Anderson Graham, was 'the most revolutionary spark in the village . . . who sits on his stool all day meditating irefully on the wrongs of the working classes.'

> His face flushes as he tugs at the lingles, for it is hard work pulling the stout waxed ends through the heavy soles of a field labourer's boots, and he often attributes to the sufferings of humanity irritation really due to the irksomeness of his task, but indignation frames for him many a deadly phrase to be fired off at the more plethoric blacksmith, when the two foregather at night for the 'drop o'rum' which is their sleeping cup. He detests the landlord, and would forswear the 'Dragon' were he not afflicted with a craving for drink, that ever and anon carries him into the accursed presence. With both the parsons he is at feud, for lying beside his awls, his broad knives, his files, and his paste-pot, is a copy of *The Rights of Man*, which is his Bible. He is the Bradlaugh of his native place, and neighbours whisper that he fears neither God, man, nor devil.

But the labourer, only barely literate, massively ignorant, and profoundly distrustful of those armed with book-learning, liked to keep his opinions to himself – assuming he had any. Long days, months, and years of monotonous physical labour, beginning perhaps when he was as young as nine and continued ever since, dulled and stunted his mental powers. His experience and knowledge of the world was limited in the extreme. 'A ten-mile journey was an event that kept him in talk for a life-time', wrote Anderson Graham in 1892.

Even at this day I know rustics who live within that distance of the sea and yet have never beheld it. A man who had broken bread in two counties was reckoned to have seen a bit of the world. 'My son is a far cleverer man as me,' said old George Richardson, the village thatcher, to me once; 'he knows three languages – Yorkshire, Scotch and Irish.'

With most of his kind political education began with the rise and fall of Joseph Arch's union in the years after 1872. The grand design of a national organization collapsed, but the movement was kept alive by the devotion of men like Arch himself, workers turned agitators, who continued to stump the countryside, addressing their audiences from a cart drawn up before the village inn. They were practised speakers, fluid in language and persuasive in tone, stirring and uplifting, for many of them were, or had been, lay-preachers. Arch's very first meeting, at Wellesbourne in his native Warwickshire on a chill February evening in 1872, attracted many hundreds, a crowd gathered from miles around entirely by word of mouth. The night, he wrote later,

had fallen pitch dark; but the men had got bean poles and hung lanterns on them, and we could see well enough. It was an extraordinary sight, and I shall never forget it, not to my dying day. I mounted an old pig-stool, and in the flickering light of the lanterns I saw the earnest upturned faces of these poor brothers of mine – faces gaunt with hunger and pinched with want – all looking toward me and ready to listen to the words that would fall from my lips.

Typically a union orator began by referring to the lowness of farm wages, insinuating that the sons of toil were half-starved in order that the farmer might ride in his gig and the landlord in his carriage. Access to the land itself was often a main theme of what followed: in the early days it was the crying need for allotments; later, Jesse Collings's idea of three acres and a cow. Later still the speaker might enthuse over the prospect that the newly-formed Parish Councils would let land to labourers on reasonable terms, or he might argue that Henry George's solution of land nationalization was the only answer – particularly after the Parish

Councils had proved to be mere extensions of middle-class influence.

Land was an issue which could be counted on to arouse the labourers. In private, in the petty alehouse which few but labourers ever entered, they would enlarge on the evil of land that had been allowed to fall out of cultivation or for years had been locked up uselessly in landowners' parks. They had some vague notion, some folk legend, or perhaps an idea instilled by an itinerant orator, that the land once belonged to all, and had been appropriated by the wealthy classes to the labourers' loss. 'What was the land sent for, if it wasn't for the poor to live off?' they asked. And hence arose the stories of a better life in years past, of former comfort and independence – whose loss, perhaps, was associated with some major event, like the sale of the estate or the enclosure of the commons, which had made an indelible impact on the village memory.

The agitators, for the most part, were realistic men who understood that the clock could not be put back and that no simple or rapid solution could be applied to the labourers' situation. They spoke in favour of gradual improvement, the achievement of strictly limited objectives, in terms of better wages, cottage improvement, access to land. Thomas Hardy once wrote of an occasion when he heard Arch himself address the Dorsetshire labourers:

> there was a remarkable moderation in his tone, and an exhortation to contentment with a reasonable amelioration, which, to an impartial auditor, went a long way in the argument. His views showed him to be rather the social evolutionist – what M. Émile de Laveleye would call a 'Possibilist' – than the anarchic irreconcilable. The picture he drew of a comfortable cottage life as it should be, was so cosy, so well within the grasp of his listeners' imagination, that an old labourer in the crowd held up a coin between his finger and thumb exclaiming, 'Here's zixpence towards that, please God!' 'Towards what?' said a bystander. 'Faith, I don't know that I can spak the name o't, but I know 'tis a good thing,' he replied.

If the labourers were slow to organize and reluctant to use their newly-gained power, the fault lay in part in their own limited education and understanding. Village schools had failed, in large measure, to make the younger country people truly literate. As George Bourne commented in 1912, after visiting a village

May Day in the village of Humley, New Forest. From the *Illustrated London News* of 8 May 1852.

evening class of sixteen- to nineteen-year-olds, 'They had not the rudimentary accomplishment: that was the plain truth. They could not understand printed English.' As a result labourers were shut out from full participation in even the most ordinary of village organizations, the benefit society, slate-club, Institute, or formal meetings of the cricket club. Hence 'the greater number of Englishmen in the village have to stand aside and see their own affairs controlled for them by outsiders . . . And this customary attitude of waiting for what the "educated" may do for them renders them apathetic where they might be, and where it is highly important that they should be, reliant upon their own initiative – I mean, in political action.'

Some of the responsibility for the schools' lack of success must be laid, no doubt, at the door of the teachers, often town-bred and deficient in imagination, and also at that of the inspectors, who issued their fiats with a lofty conviction in the superiority of their own classical education. But not all of the blame should be laid there. School conditions were often unpromising. Children of all ages were crowded into one or two rooms. There was a great deal of absenteeism, when pupils were engaged in field work and cottage industry; and in those districts where labourers made it a common practice to change masters every year, their children perforce changed schools. Regular annual flitting was a feature of Dorset in Hardy's time, and as he noted,

It is the remark of village schoolteachers of experience, that the children of the vagrant workfolk form the mass of those who fail to reach the ordinary standard of knowledge expected of their age. The rural schoolmaster or mistress enters the schoolroom on the morning of the sixth of April, and finds that a whole flock of the brightest young people has suddenly flown away.

Even where the family stayed put, the parents, who often had little education themselves, thought it wasted on their children; parents valued more their children's earnings, and able young-sters were given little encouragement to pursue their school-work; facilities for study at home were poor or non-existent. Many of the children were overworked, undernourished and ill-clothed. Sometimes lack of shoes or winter coats kept them at home, or they came to school already tired from some early morning employment, and hungry to boot. The cottage environ-ment was not one which encouraged curiosity or intelligent enquiry. School visitors commented on the blank, vacant looks on many of the faces, the slowness in comprehension, the inability to grasp underlying general principles or abstract ideas. The schools at least enabled them to read the newspapers, and this line of communication with the wider world had its advantages. But what did they read? Anderson Graham found that a London paper called the *Weekly Budget* was far and away the most popular with country workfolk. It seemed to be

concocted largely of hotly-spiced divorce cases, sensational stories by authors one has not heard of, and answers to correspondents. Politics do not seem to occupy a very prominent position in it. Without desiring in any way to praise or censure the paper, it may be said that the aim of those who direct it does not seem to be the 'elevation of the masses'. There is a Sheffield publication somewhat similar in character that in some districts is its rival, and in Northumberland the *Newcastle Weekly Chronicle*, a journal of distinctly higher tone, is the most widely read.

The country labourer, towards the end of the nineteenth century, was poised between two civilizations. He had moved out of his old rural isolation and away from his position of tutelage under farmer and landowner. He was no longer a member of the lower orders but of the lower classes, and a world of difference is reflected in that slight change in terminology. But having emerged from a state of complete dependence he had not yet achieved complete independence. He was still too poorly educated, too ignorant, too apathetic and too lacking in initiative for that. The old style of rural life had broken down, but the farm labourer had not yet fully entered, or was equipped to enter, the new, semi-urbanized existence which had taken its place. His culture had become town-oriented, revolving round town goods, town amusements, town newspapers, town ideas, but his life and work were still rooted in the country.

Perhaps the insecurity of his transitional situation helps to account for the restlessness and dissatisfaction that observers detected at this time. Hardy noticed it in his native Dorset, where many farmworkers changed masters and cottages annually. The men were better off than formerly, much more independent, and were treated with more respect by the employers. But

> while their pecuniary condition in the prime of life is bettered, and their freedom enlarged, they have lost touch with their environment, and that sense of long local participancy which is one of the pleasures of age. The old *casus conscientiae* of those in power – whether the weak tillage of an enfeebled hand ought not to be put up with in fields which have had the benefit of that hand's strength – arises less frequently now that the strength has often been expended elsewhere. The sojourning existence of the town masses is more and more the existence of the rural masses, with its corresponding benefits and disadvantages. With uncertainty of residence often comes a laxer morality, and more cynical views of the duties of life. Domestic stability is a factor in conduct which nothing else can equal.

With the ending of the old way of life many things were lost. The old provincialism diminished, local habits and amusements, local dishes, local peculiarities of speech, all tended to die out. North-country terms like 'ettle' for yeast and 'darn' for dough were disappearing. 'It's the schoolmaister does it', said an aged Borderer. His granddaughter had told him not to say 'yebble' for 'able' as the teacher had told her it was not a word. At one time the countryside was rich in local terms, some of which went back to Saxon times. Some Sussex folk said 'twitten' for a narrow alleyway, 'bleat' for cold, and 'drythe' for drought. People in Essex had 'clunchy' for fat, 'craker' for a braggart, 'clanjanderer' for someone who was talkative, and 'slud' for mud. In Berkshire a young man was always a 'boy-chap' and an elderly one 'arky', and a grave was a 'pity hole'. A few shepherds by the lakes of Cumberland and Westmorland called their sheep by ancient numbers which ran 'ena, tena, tethera, pethera, pimps, saffra, laffra, ofra, dofra, dix'.

The speech which replaced the old unwritten tongue was sometimes 'a sad hash', as Hardy called it, infected by a variety of absurdly inappropriate words, picked up, remembered and repeated because they sounded learned and impressive. Thus Anderson Graham once heard a yokel describe a badly-built haystack as 'a most egregious blunder', and a teamster refer to 'my colleague the cattleman'. Nothing, perhaps, was more significant of the fading of interest in rural affairs than the decay of weather-lore and knowledge of plants and birds – marked by Jefferies as early as the 1870s. Thirty years later some time-honoured institutions, such as the annual dance round the Maypole, had altogether passed away in many places. Local feasts, wakes and fairs were gradually disappearing, though in Lincolnshire the men on Plough Monday – the beginning of a new farming year – still carried round a coulter decorated with ribbons and begged money for a supper. George Bourne found some few boys still going round his Surrey village mumming at Christmastime. But the old pieces had degenerated lamentably, the players hardly understanding the words they gabbled, as witness the transformation of the Turkish Knight into the Turkish Snipe. Here and there some traditions lingered on till recent years. In the north of England ill luck was believed to dog the household whose threshold was not crossed first on New Year's Day by a dark-haired man, preferably a stranger. But many of the ancient rural festivals have become quite forgotten – Candlemas, marked by candle processions in Church and rum drunk by candlelight for as long as the candle lasted; and Shrove Tuesday, traditionally a holiday for labourers, and for schoolchildren too, who got to school early and barred the teacher out until he gave in to their demand for a respite from slates and books.

With the decay of the old village life went a change in its appearance. Rider Haggard was one observer who commented on the ruinous cottages whose inhabitants had gone, and which it paid no-one to repair. Abandoned homes were accompanied by deserted mills, their sails rotting and falling off, by silent smithies, and the shut-up workshops of former carpenters and wheelwrights. When new industrial establishments appeared in the countryside they were designed as smaller versions of urban models, with great brick walls and staring windows, out of place, and out of scale with the environment. Discordant rows of red-brick cottages were planked down without regard to situation, appearance, convenience or access to open country. D.H. Lawrence could remember when his family lived in a colliery company's house by the edge of fields at Eastwood in Nottinghamshire:

> A field-path came down under a great hawthorn hedge. On the other side was the brook, with the old sheep-bridges going over into the meadows. The hawthorn hedge by the brook had grown tall as tall trees, and we used to bathe from there in the dipping-hole where the sheep were dipped, just near the fell from the old mill-dam, where the water rushed. The mill only ceased grinding when I was a child. And my father, who always worked in Brinsley pit, and who always got up at five o'clock, if not at four, would set off in the dawn across the fields at Coney Grey, and hunt for mushrooms in the long grass, or perhaps pick up a skulking rabbit, which he would bring home at evening inside the lining of his pit-coat.

The great crime, Lawrence said, was the condemning of the Victorian worker to ugliness: 'meanness and formless and ugly surroundings, ugly ideals, ugly religion, ugly hope, ugly love, ugly clothes, ugly furniture, ugly houses, ugly relationship between workers and employers.' If the farming village was less blighted than its industrial fellow, it was only a matter of degree. But amidst a certain destruction of surroundings, a loss of vitality and of a sense of completeness in the community, there were some offsetting gains. The harshest poverty diminished, there was a greater degree of independence, and much more opportunity for the able and enterprising. Life was easier, more comfortable, if duller and in some sense less satisfying. There is much that is misleading in looking back to a mythical golden age 'before the factory' or 'before enclosure'. For with the loss of the old country ways was destroyed too a great mass of misery and hardship. Progress worked both ways, destroying both good and bad. The character of the village, and of rural society itself, was changed permanently as land became more and more enveloped in an industrial environment and was permeated by urban influences. The smart middle-class villa invaded the countryside, to be followed in turn by the new industrial development and the housing estate. What happened to the countryside and its inhabitants in the old century was only a prelude to what was to follow.

REFERENCES AND SELECT BIBLIOGRAPHY

1 Introduction

Barnes, D.G. *A History of the English Corn Laws*. Routledge, London 1930.
Bourne [Sturt], George. *Change in the Village*. Duckworth, London 1912.
Caird, James. *English Agriculture in 1850–51*. Cass, London 1852, new ed. 1968.
Chambers, J.D. & G.E.Mingay. *The Agricultural Revolution 1750–1880*. Batsford, London 1966.
Dodd, A.H. *The Industrial Revolution in North Wales*. University of Wales Press, Cardiff 1933.
Jobson, Allan. *Victorian Suffolk*. Robert Hale, London 1972.
McCord, N. *The Anti-Corn Law League 1838–46*. Allen & Unwin, London 1958.
Mee, Graham. *Aristocratic Enterprise : the Fitzwilliam Industrial Undertakings 1795–1857*. Blackie, Glasgow 1975.
Oxley Parker, J. *The Oxley Parker Papers*. Benham, Colchester 1964.

2 The Landowners

Blake, Robert. *Disraeli*. Eyre & Spottiswoode, London 1967.
Buxton, Charles. *Memoirs of Sir Thomas Fowell Buxton Bart*. John Murray, London 1885.
Haggard, H. Rider. *Rural England*. 2nd ed., Longman, London 1906.
Havinden, M.L. *Estate Villages : A Study of the Berkshire Villages of Ardington and Lockinge*. Lund Humphries, London 1966.
Jefferies, Richard. *Hodge and his Masters*. Smith, Elder, London 1880.
Mee, Graham. *Aristocratic Enterprise : the Fitzwilliam Industrial Undertakings 1795–1857*. Blackie, Glasgow 1975.
O'Brien, D.P. *The Correspondence of Lord Overstone*, 1. Cambridge University Press, Cambridge 1971.
Oman, Carola. *The Gascoyne Heiress : the Life and Diaries of Frances Mary Gascoyne-Cecil, 1802–39*. Hodder & Stoughton, London 1967.
Peel, George (ed.). *The Private Letters of Sir Robert Peel*. John Murray, London 1920.
Raybould, T.J. *The Emergence of the Black Country : a Study of the Dudley Estate*. David & Charles, Newton Abbot 1973.
Richards, Eric. *The Leviathan of Wealth : the Sutherland Fortune in the Industrial Revolution*. Routledge, London 1973.
Thompson, F.M.L. *English Landed Society in the Nineteenth Century*. Routledge, London 1963.

3 The Farmers

Board of Agriculture. *The Agricultural State of the Kingdom, 1816*. New ed., Adams & Dart, Bath 1970.
Caird, James. *English Agriculture in 1850–51*. Cass, London 1852, new ed. 1968.
Carter, Clive. *The Blizzard of '91*. David & Charles, Newton Abbot 1971.
Chambers, J.D. & G.E.Mingay. *The Agricultural Revolution, 1750–1880*. Batsford, London 1966.
Fisher, J.R. 'The Farmers' Alliance: an Agricultural Protest Movement of the 1880s', *Agricultural History Review* (forthcoming).

Haggard, H. Rider. *Rural England*. 2nd ed., Longman, London 1906.
Harvey, Nigel. *Old Farm Buildings*. Shire Publications, Princes Risborough 1975.
Hennell, T. *Change in the Farm*. Cambridge University Press, Cambridge 1934.
Hyams, E. (ed.). *Taine's Notes on England*. Thames & Hudson, London 1957.
Jefferies, Richard. *Hodge and his Masters*. Smith, Elder, London 1880.
Kendall, S.G. *Farming Memoirs of a West Country Yeoman*. Faber & Faber,
London 1944.
McConnell, Primrose. 'Experiences of a Scotsman on the Essex Clays',
Journal Royal Agricultural Society of England, 3rd ser., II (1891).
Olney, R.J. *Lincolnshire Politics 1832–1885* Oxford University Press, Oxford
Orwin C.S. & E.H.Whetham. *History of British Agriculture 1846–1914*.
Longman, London 1964.
Oxley Parker, J. *The Oxley Parker Papers*. Benham, Colchester 1964.
Perkins, J.A. 'The Prosperity of Farming in the Lindsey Uplands,
1813–1837', *Agricultural History Review*, XXIV, 2 (1976).
Street, A.G. *Farmer's Glory*. Faber & Faber, London 1932.
Thirsk, Joan & Jean Imray (eds.). *Suffolk Farming in the Nineteenth Century*.
Suffolk Record Society, Ipswich 1958.
Scott Watson, J.A. & May Elliot Hobbs. *Great Farmers*. Selwyn & Blount 1937.

4 The Farmworkers

Barker, T.C., J.C.McKenzie & John Yudkin (eds.). *Our Changing Fare : Two
Hundred Years of British Food Habits*. MacGibbon & Kee, London 1966.
Barnett, D.C. 'Allotments and the Problem of Rural Poverty, 1780–1840', in
E.L.Jones & G.E.Mingay (eds.), *Land, Labour and Population in the
Industrial Revolution*. Edward Arnold, London 1967.
Burnett, John. *Plenty and Want : a Social History of Diet in England from 1815
to the present day*. Nelson, London 1966.
Chadwick, Edwin. *The Sanitary Condition of the Labouring Population of Great
Britain*. 1842, new edition Edinburgh University Press, Edinburgh 1965.
Clapham, J.H. *Economic History of Modern Britain*, I. Cambridge University
Press, Cambridge 1926.
Darley, Gillian. *Villages of Vision*. Architectural Press, London 1975.
Dunbabin, J.P.D. *Rural Discontent in Nineteenth Century Britain*. Faber &
Faber, London 1974.
Lord Ernle. *English Farming Past and Present*. 6th ed., Longman, London 1961.
Fearn, Hugh. 'Chartism in Suffolk', in Asa Briggs (ed.), *Chartist Studies*.
Macmillan, London 1959.
Gauldie, Enid. *Cruel Habitations : a History of Working-Class Housing
1780–1918*. Allen & Unwin, London 1974.
Haggard, H. Rider. *Rural England*. 2nd ed., Longman, London 1906.
Hardy, Thomas. *Far from the Madding Crowd*. Macmillan, London 1874.
Hobsbawm, E.J. & G. Rudé. *Captain Swing*. Lawrence & Wishart, London 1969.
Mingay, G.E. 'The Transformation of Agriculture' in A. Selden (ed.), *The
Long Debate on Poverty*. Institute of Economic Affairs, London 1972.
Olmstead, Frederick Law. *Walks and Talks of an American Farmer in England*.
Michigan University Press, Ann Arbor 1969.
Peacock, A.J. *Bread or Blood*. Gollancz, London 1965.
Peacock, A.J. 'Village Radicalism in East Anglia 1800–50', in J.P.D. Dunbabin,
Rural Discontent in Nineteenth Century Britain. Faber & Faber, London 1974.
Samuel, Raphael. *Village Life and Labour*. Routledge, London 1975.

5 Industrial Workers in the Countryside

Cossons, Arthur. 'The Villagers Remember', *Thoroton Society Transactions*, LXVI (1962).

Green, J.L. *The Rural Industries of England*, E.Marlborough, London 1895.

Harris, Alan. 'Colliery Settlements in East Cumberland', *Cumberland & Westmorland Antiquarian and Archaeological Society Transactions*, LXXIV (1974).

Heath, F.G. *British Rural Life and Labour*. P.S.King, London 1911.

Hill, Sir Francis. *Victorian Lincoln*. Cambridge University Press, London 1975.

Horn, Pamela. *The Victorian Country Child*. Roundwood Press, Kineton 1974.

Hudson, Kenneth. *The History of English China Clays*. David & Charles, Newton Abbot 1969.

Hudson, Kenneth. *Towards Precision Shoemaking : C. & J. Clark Ltd., and the Development of the British Shoe Industry*. David & Charles, Newton Abbot 1968.

Kerr, Barbara. *Bound to the Soil : A Social History of Dorset 1750–1918*. J.Baker, London 1968.

Leyland, N.L. & J.E.Troughton, *Glovemaking in West Oxfordshire*. Oxford City and County Museum, Oxford 1974.

Mee, Graham. *Aristocratic Enterprise : the Fitzwilliam Industrial Undertakings, 1795–1857*. Blackie, Glasgow 1975.

Pulbrook, Ernest C. *English Country Life and Work*. E.P. Publishing, Wakefield 1922, reprinted 1976.

Samuel, Raphael. *Village Life and Labour*. Routledge, London 1975.

Savage, W.G. *Rural Housing*. T.Fisher Unwin, London 1915.

Strong, H.W. *Industries of North Devon*. Barnstaple, 1889; new ed. David & Charles, Newton Abbot 1971.

6 The Land Agents

Beastall, T.W. *A North Country Estate : The Lumleys and Saundersons as Landowners 1600–1900*. Phillimore, London 1975.

Donnelly, James R. Jr. *The Land and People of Nineteenth-Century Cork : The Rural Economy and the Land Question*. Routledge, London 1975.

Lord Ernle, *Whippingham to Westminster : the Reminiscences of Lord Ernle*. John Murray, London 1938.

Haggard, H.Rider. *Rural England*. 2nd ed. Longman, London 1906.

Jobson, Allan. *Victorian Suffolk*. Robert Hale, London 1972.

Kerr, Barbara. *Bound to the Soil*. J.Baker, London 1968.

Mee, Graham. *Aristocratic Enterprise : the Fitzwilliam Industrial Undertakings 1795–1857*. Blackie, Glasgow 1975.

Mingay, G.E. 'The Eighteenth-Century Land Steward', in E.L.Jones & G.E.Mingay (eds.), *Land, Labour and Population in the Industrial Revolution*. Edward Arnold, London 1967.

Olney, R.J. *Lincolnshire Politics 1832–1885*. Oxford University Press, Oxford 1973.

Parker, J.Oxley. *The Oxley Parker Papers*. Benham, Colchester 1964.

Parker, R.A.C. *Coke of Norfolk : a Financial and Agricultural Study 1707–1842*. Oxford University Press, Oxford 1975.

Raybould, T.J. *The Emergence of the Black Country : a Study of the Dudley Estate*. David & Charles, Newton Abbot 1973.

Richards, Eric. *The Leviathan of Wealth : the Sutherland Fortune in the Industrial Revolution*. Routledge, London 1973.

Spring, David. *The English Landed Estate in the Nineteenth Century : its Administration*. Johns Hopkins Press, Baltimore 1963.

7 Professional People

Ashby, M.K. *Joseph Ashby of Tysoe 1859–1919 : a Study of English Village Life*. Cambridge University Press, Cambridge 1961.

Barnett, D.C. 'Allotments and the Problems of Rural Poverty 1780–1840', in E.L.Jones & G.E.Mingay (eds.), *Land, Labour and Population in the Industrial Revolution*. Edward Arnold, London 1967.

Clark, G.Kitson. *Churchmen and the Condition of England 1832–1855*. Methuen, London 1973.

Dunbabin, J.P.D. *Rural Discontent in Nineteenth Century Britain*. Faber & Faber, London 1974.

Graham, P.Anderson. *The Rural Exodus : the Problem of the Village and the Town*. Methuen, London 1892.

Harnsberger, John L. & Robert P.Wilkins, 'New Yeovil, Minnesota : a Northern Pacific Colony in 1873', *Arizona and the West* XII, 1 (1970).

Holdenby, Christopher. *Folk of the Furrow*. Nelson, London 1913.

Horn, Pamela. *The Victorian Country Child*. Roundwood Press, Kineton 1974.

Hurt, J.S. 'Landowners, Farmers and Clergy and the Financing of Rural Education before 1870', *Journal of Education Administration & History*, I, 1 (1968).

Jefferies, Richard. *Hodge and his Masters*. Smith, Elder, London 1880.

Kerr, Barbara. *Bound to the Soil*. J.Baker, London 1968.

Martin, E.W. *Country Life in England*. Macdonald, London 1966.

Martin, E.W. *The Secret People : English Village Life after 1750*. Phoenix House, London 1954.

Martin, E.W. *Where London ends ; English Provincial Life after 1750*. Phoenix House, London 1958.

Mitford, Nancy (ed.). *The Stanleys of Alderley : their Letters between the Years 1851–1865*. Chapman & Hall, London 1939.

Olney, R.J. (ed.). *Labouring Life in the Lincolnshire Wolds : a Study of Binbrook in the Mid-Nineteenth Century*. Society for Lincolnshire History and Archaeology, Humberston 1975.

Parker, J. Oxley. *The Oxley Parker Papers*. Benham, Colchester 1964.

Thompson, Flora. *Lark Rise*. Oxford University Press, London 1939.

Turner, E.S. *Call the Doctor : a Social History of Medical Men*. Michael Joseph, London 1958.

Watson, J.A.Scott & May Elliot Hobbs. *Great Farmers*. Selwyn & Blount, London 1937.

8 Tradesmen and Craftsmen

Bailey, Jocelyn. *The Village Wheelwright and Carpenter*. Shire Publications, Princes Risborough 1975.

Booker, John. *Essex and the Industrial Revolution*. Essex County Council, Chelmsford 1974.

Bourne [Sturt], George. *William Smith : Potter and Farmer, 1790–1858*. Chatto & Windus, London 1919.

Bourne [Sturt], George. *The Wheelwright's Shop*. Cambridge University Press, Cambridge 1923.

Cossons, Arthur. 'The Villagers Remember', *Transactions of the Thoroton Society* LXVI (1962).

Graham, P.Anderson. *The Rural Exodus : the Problem of the Village and the Town*. Methuen, London 1892.

Hennell, T. *Change in the Farm*. Cambridge University Press, Cambridge 1934.

Jefferies, Richard. *Hodge and his Masters*. Smith, Elder, London 1880.

Jekyll, Gertrude. *Old West Surrey : some Notes and Memoirs*. Longman, London 1904.

Jobson, Allan. *Victorian Suffolk*. Robert Hale, London 1972.

Olney, R.J. (ed.). *Labouring Life on the Lincolnshire Wolds : a Study of Binbrook in the Mid-Nineteenth Century*. Society for Lincolnshire History and Archaeology, Humberston 1975.

Pulbrook, Ernest C. *English Country Life and Work*. E.P. Publications, Wakefield 1922, reprinted 1976.

Rose, W. *The Village Carpenter*. Cambridge University Press, Cambridge 1937.

Stowe, E.J. *Crafts of the Countryside*. Longmans Green, London 1948.

Thompson, Flora. *Lark Rise*. Oxford University Press, London 1939.

Wymer, Norman. *Village Life*. Harrap, London 1951.

9   The End of the Old Order

Arch, Joseph. *Joseph Arch : the Story of his Life, Told by Himself*. Ed. Countess of Warwick, Hutchinson, London 1898.

Bourne [Sturt], George. *Change in the Village*. Duckworth, London 1912.

Graham, P.Anderson. *The Rural Exodus : the Problem of the Village and the Town*. Methuen, London 1892.

Hardy, Thomas. 'The Dorsetshire Labourer', *Longman's Magazine*. July 1883.

Horn, Pamela. 'Aspects of Labouring Life: the Model Farm at Ditchley, 1856–73', *Cake & Cockhorse* VI, 1 (1974).

The Land : the Report of the Land Enquiry Committee. Hodder & Stoughton, London 1913.

Land Agents' Society. *Facts about Land : a Reply to 'The Land', the Report of the Unofficial Land Enquiry Committee*. John Murray, London 1916.

Lawrence, D.H. 'Nottingham and the Mining Country' (1930), in *Selected Essays*. Penguin, Harmondsworth 1950.

Martin, E.W. *Country Life in England*. Macdonald, London 1966.

Mitford, Nancy (ed.). *The Stanleys of Alderley : their Letters between the Years 1851–1865*. Chapman & Hall, London 1939.

Parker, J.Oxley. *The Oxley Parker Papers*. Benham, Colchester 1964.

Rowntree, B.Seebohm & May Kendall. *How the Labourer Lives : a Study of the Rural Labour Problem*. Nelson, London 1913.

Wymer, Norman. *Village Life*, Harrap, London 1951.

INDEX

208

USA *see* America

ACKNOWLEDGEMENTS
The publishers thank the following for permission to use extracts from the works listed:
Blackie & Son Ltd: *Aristocratic Enterprise : the Fitzwilliam Industrial Undertakings
1795–1857* by G.Mee. John Burnett (and the Royal Economic Society): *Plenty and
Want.* Cambridge University Press: *The Correspondence of Lord Overstone* by
D.P.O'Brien. Chapman & Hall Ltd (and A.D.Peters & Co. pp Estate of Nancy Mitford):
The Stanleys of Alderley : their Letters between 1851–1865 by Nancy Mitford. Duckworth
& Co. Ltd: *Change in the Village* by G. Bourne. E.P.Publishing: *English Country Life
and Work* by E.C.Pulbrook. Robert Hale & Co.: *Victorian Suffolk* by A.Jobson. William
Heinemann Ltd/Penguin Books (and Laurence Pollinger Ltd pp Estate of Mrs Frieda
Lawrence): *Phoenix/Selected Essays* by D.H.Lawrence. The Johns Hopkins University
Press: *The English Landed Estate in the Nineteenth Century : its administration* by D.
Spring. Longman Group Ltd (and A.P.Watt & Son) *Rural England* by H.Rider
Haggard. Methuen & Co.Ltd: *The Rural Exodus : the Problem of the Village and the
Town* by P.Anderson Graham. Michigan State University Press: *Walks and Talks of an
American Farmer in England* by F.Law Olmstead. John Murray Ltd: *Whippingham to
Westminster : the Reminiscences of Lord Ernle* by Lord Ernle and *The Private Letters of
Sir Robert Peel* edited by G.Peel. Colonel J.Oxley Parker: *The Oxley Parker Papers.*
Oxford University Press: *Lark Rise* by Flora Thompson. Phillimore & Co.Ltd: *A North
Country Estate : The Lumleys and Saundersons as Landowners 1600–1900* by
T.W.Beastall. Suffolk Records Society: *Suffolk Farming in the Nineteenth Century,*
edited by J.Thirsk and J.Imray. Thames & Hudson Ltd: *Taine's Notes on England,*
edited by E.Hyams.
The publishers also thank the following for permission to reproduce the illustrations on
the pages listed: City of Manchester Art Galleries: 8. Hereford and Worcester County
Libraries: 6, 190. Museum of English Rural Life, University of Reading: 23, 25, 37, 59,
76, 101(2), 115, 141, 168. Radio Times Hulton Picture Library: frontispiece, 15, 19, 41,
48, 68, 69, 83, 91, 151, 157, 161, 171, 195. Taskers Trailers Limited: 122.